BEATRICE

BEATRICE

From Buildup through Breakup

NEIL R. GAZEL

Published for the University of Illinois
Bureau of Economic and Business Research
by the
UNIVERSITY OF ILLINOIS PRESS
Urbana and Chicago

© 1990 by the Board of Trustees of the University of Illinois
Manufactured in the United States of America
C   5   4   3   2   1

This book is printed on acid-free paper.

Library of Congress Cataloging-in-Publication Data

Gazel, Neil R., 1921–
   Beatrice : from buildup through breakup / Neil R. Gazel.
      p.   cm.
   "Published for the University of Illinois Bureau of Economic
Research."
   ISBN 0-252-01729-3 (alk. paper)
   1. Beatrice Foods Company—History.   2. Food industry and trade–
United States—History.   3. Consolidation and merger of
corporations—United States—Case studies.   I. Title.
HD9009.B38G38   1990
338.7′664′00973—dc20   69-20673
                                                                CIP

This book is dedicated to the thousands and thousands of members of the Beatrice "family" who contributed to the building of the company as the leader in the food business in the United States.

Contents

Illustrations follow pages 4 and 136.

Foreword

The Preface to this book promises a description of the history and the philosophies, policies, and practices that enabled Beatrice to become one of the world's leading companies. The book does that and much more.

All written history tends to reflect the biases of the author, and *Beatrice: From Buildup through Breakup* reflects the undisguised pride of the architect of a venture that experienced unusual and profitable growth for many years. Neil R. Gazel has captured the viewpoint of the obviously strong-willed William G. Karnes, who believes that his success formula for building Beatrice would have continued its considerable momentum. Readers should bear in mind that no successful CEO is a shrinking violet, and that no CEO can describe events that he or she directed in the analytical and objective manner of a nonparticipating historian. However, the subjective nature of the book provides managers and students with personal and insightful observations that might otherwise be lost. For example, consider how the acquisition guidelines from chapter 3 mesh with Beatrice objectives. Beatrice sought to acquire only profitable companies with high growth potential and that brought qualified present and back-up managers, avoiding commodity-type products. Other guidelines would fit other companies, but these fit Beatrice.

The management policy of hands-off at the top, hands-on at the plant level also uniquely fit Beatrice, at least in its early years. Hands-on at the plant helped meet sanitation and quality levels demanded. Hands-off at the top, with minimal financial controls but enough capital to expand from regional to national markets, allowed entrepreneurial managers to fulfill personal as well as corporate objectives.

Dannon and La Choy are examples. Their entrepreneurial managers observed and accelerated the changing food habits of consumers, which were starting to emphasize health and convenience. Strict control was maintained over ingredients, consistent with Beatrice standards. Distribution methods and advertising messages were adapted to expand markets from regional to national. Market leadership was quickly established, a position which is apparently maintained to this day.

Chapter 12 on negotiating friendly mergers may provide the best insight of all. Karnes's advice for the two parties to get to know each other, to understand each others' philosophies, to discuss how they intend to operate after merger, and to find out whether they are compatible—all before discussing price—is sound advice indeed. How many unwise combinations would have been avoided if all mergers had proceeded in that manner?

The concluding chapters reflect opinions that are obviously personal and deeply felt by Karnes. Readers should respect their genuineness, but should also feel free to experience dissenting views.

The following total return (growth in value plus dividends) on Beatrice common stock as tabulated by *Fortune* and compared to the S & P Index helps one understand the Gazel/Karnes narrative.

Year Ended Feb. 28/29	Beatrice (%)	S & P 500 (%)
1985	70.44	38.28
1984	−6.90	6.27
1983	42.34	22.51
1982	38.77	21.41
1981	0.66	−4.91
1980	0.12	32.42
1979	−4.74	18.44
1978	−4.32	6.56
1977	−9.06	−7.18
1976	70.04	23.84
1975	−30.21	37.20
1974	−20.74	−26.47
1973	31.77	−14.66
Average	13.71	11.35

For this total period of time, Beatrice stockholders' returns compared favorably with that of the market. The 1984–85 management turbulence described by Karnes is plainly reflected in the market for Beatrice stock.

Persons interested in the Beatrice history will want to read these pages. Students who are interested in an insider view of the rise and fall of a modern corporate giant will also find it worthwhile.

—Ivan O. Bull

Preface

After I had retired for the second time in April of 1986 from active service with Beatrice Foods Co., I was urged by many friends, associates, and members of the business and academic communities to set down the story of the company on paper. At first, I was reluctant because it might appear to some to be self-serving to do so.

However, I was persuaded to become involved in this study of Beatrice for several reasons. It is a story that needs to be told because it mirrors almost a century of evolution of the dairy industry, an industry that was a major factor in the development of the Plains States from the 1890s to the present. It also is a history of the crafting of Beatrice into one of the world's leading companies in the food and food-related businesses.

But the strongest argument of all was the conviction that the philosophies, policies, and practices that had enabled Beatrice to become one of the world's leading but least-known companies were of significant importance to both the business and academic worlds; and further, that there should be recognition of the many dedicated people who contributed to the company's growth. Another reason for producing this book is that no other publication consolidates the entire Beatrice story.

Neil Gazel was the logical person to prepare the book. A writer by profession, he was associated with Beatrice from 1956 to mid-1978. In that time he prepared hundreds of announcements of acquisitions and other company activities, wrote more than two hundred speeches for various executives, and was responsible for the preparation of annual and interim reports. He visited many of the company's operations around the world and scripted motion pictures about several of them. He helped in the preparation of programs for the company's major management, sales, and annual shareholder meetings. He knew the company and most of the men and women in management positions.

What made the preparation and documentation of this study more challenging was that by 1986 many of the records had either been lost or trashed, and a number of key people had either retired or died. Neil fortunately was able to salvage some important documents and publications from dumpsters in warehouses. We contacted scores of Beatrice employees past and present during the information-gathering process that involved almost four years.

Ultimately, the objective was achieved, a narrative about Beatrice and the people who built the company. The stories they tell collectively provide insiders' explanations of how this pioneer company was assembled and managed.

And if this study enables one person in some small way to become a better manager, it all has been worthwhile.

—William G. Karnes

Acknowledgments

This story of Beatrice Foods Co. was prepared after numerous consultations with William G. Karnes over a period of four years. In the twenty-five years he served as chief executive officer of Beatrice, he earned a worldwide reputation as a master in negotiating mergers and acquisitions. The company completed more than four hundred friendly mergers, joint ventures, and purchases in those years from 1952 to fiscal 1977.

Karnes retired from the Beatrice board of directors in 1980 but was called back to serve as a director and chairman of the executive committee when the Beatrice board replaced James L. Dutt as chairman and chief executive officer in August of 1985. Karnes was directly involved in the negotiations that led to the leveraged buyout of Beatrice in April of 1986. Among the many honors he has received are the Horatio Alger Award, the B'nai B'rith Great American Award, the University of Illinois Alumni Achievement Award, election to the University of Illinois board of trustees, the Distinguished Service Medallion Award, the Alumni Award of Merit from Northwestern University, and honorary degrees from Knox College and DePaul University.

Sincerest appreciation is expressed also to the following people for their contributions to this book: Harry Berns, Robert Cooper, Louis Degen, Robert W. France, Leo Floros, John P. Fox, Jr., William W. Granger, Jr., Don L. Grantham, John F. Hazelton, Sr., André J. Job, James A. Johnson, Warren Johnson, Charles Long, Samuel R. Marotta, Juan E. Metzger, John J. McRobbie, William S. Mowry, Jr., Carl F. Obenauf, Fred K. Schomer, Robert I. Seger, Leo Singer, Robert L. Skummer, Douglas J. Stanard, John A. Stevens, Gordon E. Swaney, Carl T.E. Sutherland, Richard A. Voell, H. Jack Warner, Harry C. Wechsler, James Weiss, and H. Robert Winton.

I also appreciate the contributions of Frank H. Cassell, professor emeritus, J. L. Kellogg Graduate School of Management, Northwestern University, and Josef Lakonishok, William G. Karnes Professor of Finance, University of Illinois at Urbana-Champaign, as well as Sally Gregosanc, who patiently typed and retyped these chapters. In addition, the contributions of Virginia K. Karnes and Betty K. Gazel were invaluable.

Introduction:
Beatrice, the Unheralded Leader

As recently as 1985, Beatrice Companies was the leading food corporation in the United States, with sales of $12.6 billion and net income of $479 million for the fiscal year ended February 28.

• Following the acquisition of Esmark, Inc. for $2.7 billion in June 1984, it ranked twenty-sixth in the list of the five hundred largest United States corporations published in the April 28, 1986, issue of *Fortune.*

• It marketed more than nine thousand products in the United States and a hundred countries around the world. Although few of them were aware of it, almost every resident of the United States used or was served by a product of Beatrice every day.

• It employed more than 120,000 people.

• Its common stock was held by more than fifty thousand investors.

• It led the nation in sales of the brands in the following categories (according to research by Beatrice and Salomon Brothers, a New York City investment firm): yogurt: Dannon, Meadow Gold, Viva, Johnston, and Mountain High; butter: Meadow Gold, Blue Valley, Sugar Creek, Holland, Hotel Bar, and Keller's; fresh frozen orange juice: Tropicana, with 26.4 percent of the market; pickles: Bond, Ma Brown, L & S, American, Delta, and Rainbo; canned and frozen Chinese foods under the LaChoy label; bottled water: a 12.2 percent market share nationally; water treatment equipment: Culligan, with 30 percent of the household market; public cold storage warehouses: a national capacity of 191 million cubic feet, accounting for 24 percent of the national market; and luggage: Samsonite, with 20 percent of the U.S. market.

• It was the largest manufacturer in the world of soft ice cream freezers (Taylor Freezer).

• It ranked with Kraft and Borden as one of the country's top three dairy companies, with annual sales of $955 million.

• It was the world's largest manufacturer of chemicals for tanning leather, with plants in eight countries.

• Its Avis Division was the nation's second largest car rental operation, with a 26 percent market share.

• It was one of the nation's leaders in sales of specialty meats: Eckrich, Kneip, Swift, Berliner & Marx, and Lowrey's.

• It was the country's second largest processor of nut products (Fisher and Tom Scott).

• It was the leading manufacturer of candy and snacks in Venezuela and in ice cream in Puerto Rico, Mexico, Jamaica, Belgium, Denmark and Singapore.

Over ninety-one years, Beatrice had been developed conservatively into an international presence with people, products, and policies in place to continue furthering its profitable growth. Yet, in just two years, the company was almost completely dismantled following the most famous and flamboyant leveraged buyout until the $25 billion RJR–Nabisco deal in 1989 by a group of investors led by Kohlberg Kravis Roberts & Co. (KKR). The Beatrice buyout price of $6.2 billion, nineteen times earnings, by KKR was equal to two and one-half times its net worth.

Not measurable in dollars, however, was the cost in terms of loss of people. A visitor wandering the corridors of the palatial headquarters of the Beatrice Co. at 2 North LaSalle Street in Chicago in the spring of 1988 would have seen office after office, each elegantly appointed, each abandoned. The luxurious offices of Beatrice's U.S. Foods Division at 55 East Monroe Street, also in Chicago, were closed. The former general offices of, first, the entire company and later, the Dairy and Warehouse divisions atop the ten-story Chicago Cold Storage Warehouse at 1526 South State Street in Chicago also were vacant.

These days, there are no friendly discussions around the watercoolers; few if any of the remaining officers go out for coffee and doughnuts with other staff members. Only a handful of the more than eight hundred members of the three offices are still in place. And many of them approach each working day as if it will be their last with the company. All divisions except a few food companies have been sold.

This book is not merely a chronological narration of the building—and ultimate demise—of an internationally successful company from a tiny butter-and-egg business started in 1894 by George E. Haskell and William W. Bosworth. Nor is it a glorification of the members of management who directed it through its greatest period of growth. It is, instead, a study of the philosophies, policies, and practices that were the bases for Beatrice's growth, including its most productive period during the quarter of a century it was guided by the "management by a feather" skills of William G. Karnes, its president, and officers such as John F. Hazelton, Sr., and Don L. Grantham.

During the twenty-five-year period from 1952 through 1977, Beatrice averaged an annual growth rate in sales of 13 percent, an average annual growth rate in profits of 15 percent, and an average annual rate of growth in earnings per common share of 7 percent (table 1).

Sales and earnings climbed by twenty-four and fifty times, respectively, in that period. Sales rose from $229 million to $5.6 billion, and net earnings went up from $3.9 million to $196 million (fig. 1). Beatrice increased its profits every quarter over the comparable quarter of the preceding year from March 1952 to February 28, 1983 (fig. 2). There is no record of any other major company that has been able to match that performance.

During that time, Beatrice was the virtually unnoticed pacesetter in making friendly acquisitions. It effected more than four hundred of them, diversifying into specialty foods, next expanding into the international market, and then into manufactured products and specialty chemicals. As Linda Grant Martin wrote in *Fortune* (April 1976), "While nobody was looking, these Midwestern dairymen built one of the nation's fastest growing companies. And they did it without taking risks.

"The textbook rule about this kind of growth is that it must reflect a monopoly position or a remarkable amount of risk taking. In the case of Beatrice, it doesn't reflect either. The acquisition program has been almost fanatically cautious. The companies that were picked up tended to be solid, on-going operations—yet they were acquired at bargain prices.

"Perhaps the most extraordinary stunt of all has been the management's ability to maintain a posture of near invisibility during all of that growth. The company is sneaking up on a $5 billion sales rate (sales for the fiscal year ending February 29, 1976 are $4.6 billion), and now it earns more money than any other food processor in the United States with profits in that fiscal year of $150 million, but nobody paid much attention to it."

Contrary to the belief by many that Beatrice achieved its primary growth through acquisitions during this period, internal growth was a dominant factor contributing to its progress. Other keys to Beatrice's success were its philosophies of decentralized management and its concept that people were its greatest asset.

When these philosophies and policies were abandoned by the successors to the Karnes-led management team, the company drifted down from preeminence in the marketplace, leading to the leveraged buyout of what *Dun's Review* once described as one of America's best-managed companies.

Was it hubris—the egos of the management that took command in mid-1977 and those that followed? Was it vaulting ambition on the part of a few that led to a bitter series of divisive battles in the boardroom? Did the members of the new teams forget the precepts that made the company a great one for which to work?

Table 1. Beatrice Foods Company,
Twenty-five-year Financial Summary on Reported Basis

| Year Ended February 28/29 | Net Sales (Millions) | Pre-Tax Income (Millions) | Percent of Sales | | Net Income (Millions) | Return on Invested Capital(a) | Per Common Share (b) | | | | Range Price-Earnings Ratio |
			Depreciation	Pre-Tax income			Cash Flow(c)	Earnings	Dividend	Price Range(d)	
1977	$5.289	$362.8	1.2%	6.9%	$182.6	16%	$2.88	$2.13	$ .82	28–22	13–10
1976	4.691	298.3	1.2	6.4	153.1	16	2.57	1.86	.74	25–14	13–8
1975	4.192	260.8	1.2	6.2	134.8	16	2.38	1.71	.69	23–12	14–7
1974	3.541	223.4	1.3	6.3	117.0	15	2.19	1.55	.63	30–17	19–11
1973	2.787	176.3	1.4	6.3	90.4	16	1.95	1.36	.59	30–21	22–15
1972	2.384	151.0	1.5	6.3	77.7	16	1.81	1.23	.58	22–17	18–14
1971	1.827	119.1	1.5	6.5	61.8	16	1.61	1.10	.50	20–12	18–11
1970	1.576	105.9	1.5	6.7	52.5	15	1.47	1.00	.50	21–16	21–16
1969	1.350	89.7	1.4	6.6	44.9	15	1.41	.96	.45	21–14	22–15
1968	1.093	75.3	1.4	6.9	39.1	17	1.37	.94	.40	16–11	17–12
1967	933	58.8	1.5	6.3	30.7	14	1.25	.82	.38	15–10	18–12
1966	796	47.9	1.5	6.0	24.6	14	1.12	.73	.34	14–12	19–16
1965	681	36.5	1.5	5.4	18.0	12	.98	.62	.29	13–10	21–16
1964	606	30.2	1.6	5.0	14.7	10	.90	.53	.26	10–8	19–15
1963	569	26.1	1.5	4.6	13.0	10	.80	.48	.22	10–6	21–13

Year Ended February 28/29	Net Sales (Millions)	Pre-Tax Income (Millions)	Percent of Sales Depreciation	Percent of Sales Pre-Tax income	Net Income (Millions)	Return on Invested Capital(a)	Per Common Share (b) Cash Flow(c)	Per Common Share (b) Earnings	Per Common Share (b) Dividend	Price Range(d)	Range Price-Earnings Ratio
1962	539	23.2	1.5	4.3	11.8	10	.78	.46	.22	12–7	26–15
1961	478	21.1	1.5	4.4	10.8	10	.74	.44	.22	8–5	18–11
1960	443	20.5	1.5	4.6	10.3	10	.71	.43	.20	6–5	14–12
1959	385	17.9	1.5	4.7	8.9	10	.69	.41	.20	6–5	15–12
1958	354	15.3	1.5	4.3	7.6	10	.68	.40	.20	6–4	15–10
1957	342	15.1	1.4	4.4	7.3	10	.66	.39	.18	4–3	10–8
1956	325	13.3	1.3	4.1	6.4	9	.58	.34	.18	4–3	12–9
1955	287	11.9	1.3	4.1	5.6	9	.56	.32	.17	4–3	13–9
1954	275	10.4	1.1	3.8	4.8	9	.49	.30	.17	4–3	13–10
1953	235	8.3	.9	3.5	4.0	9	.43	.27	.17	3–2	11–7

a. Relating net income plus debt charges to year-end capitalization after deducting intangible assets.

b. Adjusted for 3-for-2 stock split in March 1957, 5-for-4 stock split in March 1960, 4-for-3 stock splits in March 1963 and March 1965, 2-for-1 stock splits in March 1969 and December 1972.

c. Depreciation plus earnings.

d. For calendar year preceding Beatrice fiscal year.

SOURCE: Beatrice Foods

Figure 1. Diversified Food Companies
Historical Trends in Sales

BILLIONS OF DOLLARS

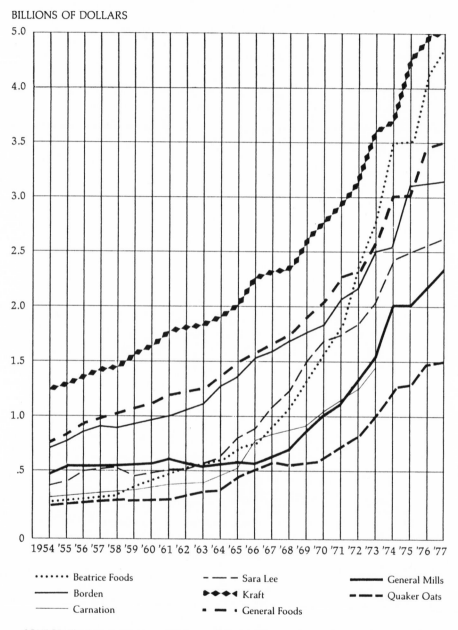

1954 '55 '56 '57 '58 '59 '60 '61 '62 '63 '64 '65 '66 '67 '68 '69 '70 '71 '72 '73 '74 '75 '76 '77

•••••• Beatrice Foods   – –– – Sara Lee   ▬▬▬ General Mills

———— Borden   ◆◆◆◆ Kraft   ▬ ▬ ▬ Quaker Oats

———— Carnation   ■ ▬ ■ General Foods

SOURCE: The Fortune Directory, 500 Largest Industrial Corporations and company annual reports.

Figure 2. Diversified Food Companies
Historical Trends in Net Income

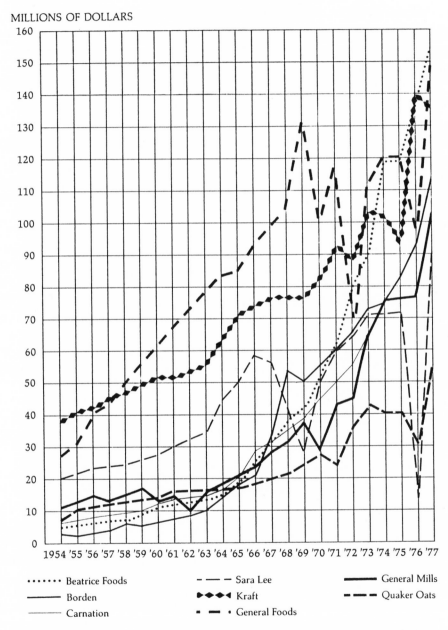

MILLIONS OF DOLLARS

SOURCE: The Fortune Directory, 500 Largest Industrial Corporations and company annual reports.

The Beatrice story is considered a classroom case history of the building and breaking up of a major company. All of the events from the beginning in 1894 to the reckoning in 1986 and subsequent actions are detailed herein in an attempt to explain what happened and why.

CHAPTER ONE

Pioneer Ideas

Great ideas—and great men—often come from humble beginnings. The word *idea* stems from the Greek word meaning *to see*. And it was the vision of George Everett Haskell and his successors, principally Clinton H. Haskell and William G. Karnes, that guided them in building Beatrice Foods Co. into one of the world's leading companies. George Haskell's progressive ideas of pioneering the system of financing cream separators on farms in the Prairie States, organizing cream collection, using transcontinental rail transportation, and centralizing quality controlled churning formed the foundation for Beatrice Foods.

Haskell's early years offered little hint of the leadership qualities that earned him recognition as a pioneer in the dairy industry. Born in 1864 in Osage, Iowa, he was one of five children and was left fatherless at age four, when Josiah Haskell died from an illness contracted during his service in the Civil War. Haskell, his older brother, John Franklin, who subsequently joined him in expanding Beatrice Foods, his sister, Nellie, and half-brother, Edward, were placed in the Soldiers Orphans Home in Cedar Falls, where they received their secondary education.

Subsequently, Gilbert Rice, owner of a mill in Cedar Falls, took an interest in Haskell and sent him to Cedar Valley Seminary, a combination high school and junior college that also numbers Hamlin Garland as an alumnus. After graduating in 1884, he worked for two years as a clerk before going "west" from Osage to Fremont, one of the first creamery towns in Nebraska, to take a position as bookkeeper for the Fremont Butter and Egg Company.

In 1889, Haskell, by then secretary of the Fremont firm, opened a branch for the company in Beatrice, Nebraska, where a predecessor, the Beatrice Creamery Company, launched in 1882, had failed. The Fremont Butter and Egg Company also went under during the Silver Panic of 1893, and Haskell found himself jobless at the age of twenty-nine. But not only did he have the perseverance of a pioneer, he also had several ideas. Undaunted by the depressed economic times, he invested his small savings to found the partnership of Haskell & Bosworth with William W. Bosworth, an employee of the Beatrice branch in 1894. They set up business in the Beatrice branch plant to deal in poultry, eggs, butter, and produce.

Dairying was a sideline to farming then, for this part of Nebraska was grain country. The average was one cow for each sixty-one acres. A large number of small local creameries—possibly more than six hundred—were founded in the area, but most failed in the face of seemingly insurmountable obstacles, particularly poor transportation facilities. Even the better roads were primitive in most areas—muddy bogs when wet, almost impassable in winter. Further, it was virtually impossible to have cream pick-ups made at the height of wheat season. Harvesting required every man and horse. Compounding these limitations of transportation and supply was the extreme seasonal variation in production; 50 percent of the butter was made in the three flush months of the spring, and the rest in the other nine. Each farmer's wife was her own butter expert, and the product varied accordingly. It was churned by hand, primarily by farmers' wives, who exchanged it in grocery stores for other food products. Butter sold for 7 to 10 cents a pound, and eggs netted as little as 5 cents a dozen at the farm.

When the first transcontinental railroad spanned the Missouri River in 1869, it opened up a vast new food processing area in the Midwest to world markets. Haskell quickly sensed these opportunities, and Haskell & Bosworth began buying farm butter, eggs, and poultry. The better butter was graded, sorted, and packed for sale in ladles. The lower grades were packed in butter stands, barrels, and boxes and shipped to processors to be reworked. The partners also purchased butter from small creameries and shipped it with eggs and dressed poultry.

Late in 1894, they began churning butter at Beatrice and using their own delivery wagons to distribute creamery butter in the special protective packages that they had devised to grocery stores, restaurants, and hotels. Subsequently, skimming stations were established to which farmers delivered their milk daily to have the cream separated from the whole milk. Because the milk was heated to separate the cream, by the time it was returned to the farm the skim milk often was too sour to use to slop the hogs.

Haskell's innovative solution to the problem was to provide farmers with hand-operated DeLaval cream separators. Thus, they could separate the milk on the farm, thereby saving the daily trips to town and having the fresh skim milk immediately available as feed. The proceeds from the cream checks paid for Haskell & Bosworth's financing of the separators. The program worked so well that the company financed the purchase of more than fifty thousand cream separators by farmers in Nebraska and Kansas from 1895 to 1905. However, the partners, who had incorporated as the Beatrice Creamery Company in Lincoln in 1898 with a capital of a $100,000, were acutely aware of the need for more efficient and sanitary methods. The next major step then was to consolidate churning operations in one central creamery in Lincoln, where railroad facilities were more extensive.

Convenience of rail facilities dictated the locations for the eleven branches of the company established by 1898. The procurement territory was widened to increase the supply of cream, most of which was shipped by rail. However, the Lincoln plant burned down a month after it was opened, delaying operations there by almost a year while it was being rebuilt. The only thing salvaged from the fire was a brass cow.

As was to be the pattern for Beatrice from the day it was formed until 1985, steady growth in sales, earnings, and product lines was the result of a strategic combination of internal expansion and acquisitions. Branches were established in Cuba, Kansas, in 1893 and Herington, Kansas, in 1895. Herington was the Kansas headquarters for Haskell & Bosworth, with branches in Wichita, Salina, and Hutchinson under the direction of George Haskell's older brother, John Franklin. In 1899, Bosworth left to form his own produce company in Beatrice—and became only a footnote in company history. In 1902, another plant was opened in Topeka as the headquarters for the Kansas and Oklahoma market. Earnings that year rose to $158,706. In 1904, the company churned 10,061,032 pounds of butter, compared to 940,000 in 1898.

George Haskell had traveled east at the turn of the century to study milk and butter operations. Following his tour, he commissioned the construction of the Littleton Creamery Company in Denver. Completed in 1902, it was considered a model for the entire industry. The company also acquired the Continental Creamery Company in Topeka in 1905. Continental had held a contest among its employees to select a brand name for its butter. The winner, "Meadow Gold," was patented in 1901 and became the primary brand for Beatrice Creamery Company as one of the first trademarks for butter. In 1905, the company was incorporated as the Beatrice Creamery Company of Iowa, with a capital of $3,000,000. Pioneering was not only a way of life, but it was also a way to prosperity for the company, which changed its name to Beatrice Foods Co. in 1946 and to Beatrice Companies, Inc. in 1984.

Meadow Gold was one of the first to package butter in cartons, first to sell butter in a sealed package, and one of the first to pasteurize churning cream on a large-scale operation. Meadow Gold was the first to advertise butter in a national magazine and the first to establish a nationally advertised brand of ice cream.

A cold-storage business was a natural early development because refrigeration plants are necessary for the storage of all dairy products. These plants also were the sites of large public storage businesses for other perishable products. The first Beatrice ice cream plant began operation in Topeka in 1907, and the first fluid milk plant was opened in Denver in 1923.

By 1913, when the company transferred its headquarters to Chicago and reincorporated in Delaware, it had created a firm national market for cream produced by farmers in the Prairie States. As a result of this new source of steady income during a period in the country's history when farmers' finances were at a critically low ebb from time to time, the milk cow was referred to as "the mortgage lifter of the West." Further, the creamery industry is credited with helping to develop many communities west of the Missouri River.

George Haskell's great service to the dairy industry and his country ended in 1919, when he died at age fifty-four. His contributions included positions as administrator of the Dairy Division in the U.S. Food Administration under Herbert Hoover during World War I and as president of the National Creamery Buttermakers Association. The career of one pioneer in the creamery industry was ended, but George Haskell had built the foundation for another to begin. He was succeeded by W. H. Ferguson as president of the company in September of 1919. A. E. Wilkenson, who had retired in 1917, was called back to take over the post of general manager in 1921, when H. S. Johnson, who had been named to that position in 1919, resigned. Building upon the strong foundation George Haskell had established, the company continued to prosper under the leadership of Wilkenson and Ferguson, who was an absentee president for most of his term.

Reviewing the ranks for a successor, Wilkenson selected a young man who had grown up with Beatrice to join the general office in Chicago as assistant general manager in 1923. He was Clinton H. Haskell, the eldest son of John Franklin Haskell, and George Haskell's nephew. At age thirty-four, C. H. was in a position to introduce a management style that was to accelerate the growth and diversification of Beatrice.

George E. Haskell and William W. Bosworth formed a partnership to distribute poultry, eggs, and produce in 1894, with offices in this small facility.

Original plant of Beatrice Foods Co.

Cream collection station near Muncie, Indiana, ca. 1900.

Meadow Gold was the first butter advertised nationally; this advertisement appeared in the February 17, 1912, *Saturday Evening Post*.

George Haskell introduced the innovative idea of financing the sale of cream separators to farmers between 1895 and 1905.

Around the time of World War I, a Meadow Gold distribution branch was located on Pennsylvania Avenue, within sight of the White House.

Beatrice Creamery operated the most modern distribution system in Nebraska during the 1920s from its plant in Lincoln.

CHAPTER TWO

C. H.: Another Haskell
for the Times

Soothsayers studying the formative years of Clinton H. Haskell certainly would not have predicted that he was destined to become president of Beatrice and one of the nation's outstanding leaders in the dairy industry.

Born in Lynxville, Wisconsin, on July 7, 1888, he nearly died of diphtheria in 1891, a disease that claimed his eldest sister, Gladys. He had another close brush with death in 1904, when he fell through the ice on a pond near Herington, Kansas, trying to save another boy who had broken through. Using a chain of broom handles and hockey sticks, several companions pulled them both out of the water. The incident nearly caused Haskell to succumb to pneumonia. In yet another close call, he was severely stricken but survived the flu epidemic in 1918, when more than twenty million died worldwide.

He quit high school in Topeka because of a threat to expel him if he didn't quit smoking. Instead, he attended a business school for a term. Reluctantly, he then enrolled in 1907 at Western Military Academy in Upper Alton, Illinois, at the request of his father and his Uncle George, but withdrew after a short time because the institution's confinement made him uncomfortable.

Haskell's first job for Beatrice was during the summer of 1898, when he made three thousand egg cases for 1 cent each for the plant at Herington managed by his father. His earnings totaled $30. Beginning at age sixteen, he roved the country as an itinerant worker from 1904–6. He joined a harvesting crew in Kansas, did farm chores, rode fences on a farm near Pueblo, Colorado, worked in an unemployment office, loaded coal, and toiled as a carpenter and mechanic. Before Haskell was twenty, he had roamed through Kansas, Missouri, Arkansas, the Indian Territory, Oklahoma, Texas, Nevada, Colorado, and California. That experience was an important part of his education. He returned to Topeka in 1906 to reenter business school, where he studied penmanship, banking, book-keeping, shorthand, and typing, then began work in the produce department of the Topeka plant, handling payments of shipments of butter and eggs from country stores in Kansas and Oklahoma. At the same time,

Haskell attended business school two nights a week, taking such courses as cost accounting, traffic law, corporation financing, and bank accounting.

Once again, he was afflicted by wanderlust and headed back to California, where he worked in Los Angeles for several months as an egg candler for $60 a month. En route to California, he had another brush with death when the engine of the train blew up at Cathan, Colorado and killed the engineer. Fourteen miles out of Leadville, Colorado, the brakes of another train failed while the train was rolling down the Tennessee Pass. The uncontrolled train jumped the tracks, killing three people aboard.

As he approached twenty-one, Haskell was ready to settle down. He returned to Topeka to work in the plant's office for $40 a month beginning on January 1, 1908. In December of that year, he married Ethel Miller and, as he recalled, "I threw myself into business with great eagerness. My office hours were nine hours daily, six days a week. I also continued to study accounting and business administration at night." Within a year, his salary had increased to $85 a month.

Until 1909, every Beatrice plant had its own bookkeeping system. However, that year the Topeka plant was chosen for a test of a uniform accounting system and periodic auditing developed by J. H. Greenhalgh, an accountant from England. C. H. Haskell played a major part in introducing the system, which later was expanded to all plants. Thus, Beatrice became the first large dairy company to put in an up-to-date system of accounting. Haskell was viewed as ready for greater responsibilities and was promoted to office manager of the Denver plant in 1910. While there, he tried to persuade the company to buy a milk plant in Colorado Springs and open an ice cream plant in Salt Lake City. Both times the answer was no.

By 1917, Haskell was back at the Topeka plant as assistant manager. There he continued to press for expansion into the ice cream business. Topeka had been the site of a small ice cream plant since 1907, but it had been sadly neglected. Haskell learned of a new ice cream bar called the Eskimo Pie and negotiated a deal with the company's representative for the exclusive rights in Topeka. Early in January, he had two men dressed as Eskimos parade the main streets of Topeka. "The Eskimo Pies sold like hot cakes and we made $3,000 in January," he related. "That really established us as being in the ice cream business and gave us some needed prestige."

On January 1, 1923, at age thirty-four, he was called to the company's corporate offices to be assistant general manager under A. E. Wilkenson. The company continued to prosper, with sales increasing to $52.7 million and net earnings to $1,143,701 in 1928, the year before the Beatrice Creamery Co. was listed on the New York Stock Exchange.

The circumstances could be viewed in retrospect by some industry analysts to harbinger what transpired in 1986, for Beatrice came close to disappearing from the marketplace in 1927. Thomas McInnery was assembling National Dairy (now Kraft, owned by Philip Morris) as a giant holding company for milk, butter, eggs, and ice cream processors and distributors across the country in the 1920s. Because Beatrice's annual sales at that time were flat at about $53 million, and earnings were stalled at a plateau of about $1 million, W. H. Ferguson and Wilkinson decided that the advisable action to take on behalf of their shareholders was to sell out to National Dairy. Other major shareholders agreed, and a committee was sent to New York City to sell the company.

During the same meeting at which the directors elected to sell, they also appointed Haskell as general manager. The committee was in New York when Haskell returned to his office from a business trip and learned of his promotion. He was extremely apprehensive; if the merger went through, his new title would be of no value to him. However, the committee had pegged the market price for Beatrice at $60 per common share, about what it was selling for across the counter in Chicago. Prince and Whitely, the brokers in National Dairy stock, thought a share was worth no more than $45. The committee, in a huff, returned to Chicago, and Haskell got his chance.

Haskell and Vice President John T. McGreer then decided to play turnabout and put through their own mergers. They were outbid a number of times before acquiring Pioneer Creamery of Galesburg, Illinois, in 1928 for $1,500,000 in stock. The acquisition added the Holland brand to the Beatrice butter line, as well as the services of Louis Nielson, Pioneer president, who became a vice president of Beatrice and promptly recommended that Haskell be president. The directors concurred. In that same year, when he was only thirty-nine, Haskell was president of a company that consisted of butter manufacturing and the operation of cold-storage warehouses. He developed it into a leading corporation in the food industry that handled a wide diversity of products with national distribution.

His first actions as Beatrice's chief executive were to expand into the milk and ice cream businesses in the Midwest and the East. With the assistance of Nielson, the Illinois district manager, Beatrice purchased a number of dairies in Illinois. Next, they acquired the White Mountain Creamery in Lima, Ohio, and the Carry Ice Cream Company in Washington, D.C. More additions followed: an ice cream company in Brooklyn and the giant Liberty Dairy in Pittsburgh.

Going west, the company acquired the successful Hutchinson Ice

Cream Company in Des Moines, and Charles H. Hutchinson joined the management team. Then Haskell purchased the Windsor Farm Dairy in Denver from an old friend, H. Brown Cannon. Both Cannons, H. Brown and his son, Brown W., played important roles in the growth of Beatrice over a fifty-year period. Haskell also expanded the poultry and egg business with the purchase of the A. F. Thibideau Company of Detroit, which made Beatrice the largest egg processor in the United States.

Beatrice made thirteen more dairy acquisitions in less than a year, and by 1930, had 159 plants in operation. Then came the depression, and the company sat on its acquisition hands. In 1919, the company operated only four milk plants. By 1932, it had milk plants in thirty-two cities and had become the nation's third largest dairy. Only National Dairy and Borden were larger. In 1927, the company had sold fewer than one million gallons of milk. By 1932, volume had grown to twenty-seven million gallons. Sales of ice cream also rose from fewer than one-half million gallons in 1927 to 9.5 million gallons in 1931, and Beatrice was the leading processor of butter and eggs.

The fact that Beatrice made money even during the worst times of the depression was attributable primarily to Haskell's tight rein on cash, inventory, and expenses. For example, the company omitted dividend payments on its common stock in 1934 and 1935 — an action not taken for lack of cash. Rather, the directors did not believe that the net earnings of $753,067 and $738,325, respectively, in those two fiscal years justified dividend payments.

Haskell also established a district manager form of operations, surrounding himself with people of similar beliefs. Among these experienced, capable district managers were Arthur McClintock in Denver, Louis Nielson in Illinois, Clifford Huenke in Ohio, Charles Hutchinson in Des Moines, George Gardella in Detroit, and John T. McGreer in Nebraska. McGreer, a tough, seasoned operations executive, was appointed general manager in 1931 and moved to Chicago. He had come up through the creamery business and was a demanding but fair manager and a tireless worker. He and Haskell worked as a team for more than twenty years to keep the company growing and solvent through their strict compliance with the established Beatrice management philosophies.

Although Haskell, who remembered the panic of 1907, was extremely conservative, in his efforts to expand the company's product line into ice cream and milk he was an innovator, as well as a strong believer in the values of marketing and advertising. For example, for years, ice cream had been made in machines called batch freezers. When a continuous ice cream freezer was perfected, Beatrice equipped all of its plants with these freezers and introduced "Smooth Freeze Meadow Gold Ice Cream." Milk bottles had been capped with a cardboard plug seated in the recessed rim of the bottle. Beatrice perfected a machine in conjunction with Reynolds Metals that placed an aluminum seal—advertised extensively as the "Silver Seal Cap"—on all bottled products, thus protecting the pouring surface from contamination. As far back as the 1890s, butter had been wrapped in parchment. Again working with Reynolds, Beatrice developed an aluminum foil wrap that was introduced in the late 1940s. Such innovations provided Beatrice with an edge in the marketplace and were promoted heavily. Extensive magazine advertising was employed for all Meadow Gold products, and one of the first TV series for any food product was Beatrice's Chicago-area sponsorship of the "Lone Ranger" on Sunday nights in the early 1950s.

Another major diversification program Haskell initiated was expansion into grocery specialties. Four major branches to distribute frozen foods were established in 1945 in Chicago, Pittsburgh, Cleveland, and St. Louis, in addition to frozen food distribution in the western states. By 1950, Beatrice was one of the largest distributors of frozen foods in the U.S. Haskell also diversified the company into an entirely new field that was the precedent for future expansion. On the recommendation of George Gardella, in 1943 Beatrice purchased a small company in the Detroit area that produced canned Chinese foods and sold fresh Chinese foods such as mung bean sprouts: LaChoy Food Products. LaChoy also packaged a vegetable juice product called Vegemato when it moved to a new plant in Archbold, Ohio.

C. H. Haskell constantly promoted quality, sanitation, productivity, and safety and regularly sent "Dear Manager" letters to all plants on these subjects. Following World War II, Beatrice adopted a unique sanitation program called "Sanitary Sam," which also became the name of a coveted company award. Food scientists from leading universities were engaged to make monthly inspection at all plants. Copies of their reports were sent to the manager, the district manager, and to Haskell. Plants falling below a required standard were immediately put on notice of a future inspection. In extreme instances, clean-up crews were sent in from surrounding plants to sanitize the offending plant. Productivity reports were sent to the general office monthly, and the results were distributed to all plants to show where they ranked. As part of the constant quest for quality, Beatrice began an intensive program to convert all of its milk to Grade A. By 1950, before most health departments required it, all bottled milk sold by the company met Grade A standards.

Perhaps the most important action Haskell took in providing for the future progress of Beatrice was in 1948 when McGreer elected to take semiretirement. Haskell appointed William G. Karnes as executive vice president. Beatrice had never had an executive vice president, and Haskell's announcement was a two-sentence letter to the plants: "I hereby appoint William G. Karnes executive vice president. I am sure you will give him your complete support." Karnes's responsibilities were never defined.

In 1950, Haskell learned that he had cancer. He was in and out of hospitals for the next two years and, therefore, far less active in the management of the company. He died on March 23, 1952. During his twenty-four years of leadership as president and chief executive officer, the distinguished executive had guided the company to a position of preeminence in the business community. Beatrice sales were increased from $52.7 million in fiscal year 1928 to $228.7 million in 1952. Net earnings rose from $1,143,701 in 1928 to $3,908,234. The company had diversified extensively and no longer relied on butter as its primary source of sales and profits. In 1952, fluid milk and cream accounted for 32 percent of sales, ice cream for 16 percent, and butter for 22 percent. Poultry and eggs were down to 6 percent.

Haskell earned respect throughout the industry as one of the true pioneers in the modern dairy business in the United States. He served the dairy industry in many capacities. He was a moving spirit in the American Butter Institute and was a director of the National Dairy Council at the time of his death. He also had been a director of the U.S. Chamber of Commerce and a member of the National Association of Manufacturers. During World War II, he served on the Milk Conservation Committee of the War Foods Administration. His legacy to his successor was a well-organized, decentralized company with experienced, capable management people, no debt, and a strong foundation upon which to continue the company's growth.

The Karnes Years Begin

At a special meeting of the board of directors held two days after Haskell's death, Karnes was elected president and chief executive officer, one day after his forty-first birthday. Karnes's background differed sharply from those of George Haskell and C. H. Haskell. His great-grandmother, grandfather, and father were all born in Illinois and had all been engaged in the real estate business. His father's business was located first in Chicago and later in the suburb of Flossmoor. His mother was also born in Chicago but died when Karnes was only five years old. During his early years he was raised by his father's two sisters in Chicago and educated in the Chicago public schools. He then attended the University of Illinois, from which he was graduated with honors in 1933 with a Bachelor of Science degree from the School of Commerce. He borrowed money to attend Northwestern University Law School, earning a J.D. degree in two-and-a-half years.

Karnes knew virtually nothing about the food business when he joined Beatrice as a $110-a-month law clerk in April 1936 upon his graduation from law school. In fact, he did not attend his graduation from Northwestern. He was already working for Beatrice, and on that particular day was in Washington, D.C., filing documents with the Securities and Exchange Commission. Karnes was hired by Walter L. Dilger, general counsel of Beatrice and a native of Chicago. His father, Robert Dilger, had been manager of the Holland Butter plant in Chicago and was a close friend of Nielson's. After finishing law school, Walter Dilger had practiced with a law firm in Quincy, Illinois, before coming to Beatrice in 1929.

Dilger was a hard-worker, conservative, conscientious, and thorough with any task assigned to him. C. H. Haskell and the Beatrice board had complete confidence in his loyalty, trustworthiness, and ability. The Beatrice Law Department at that time consisted of Dilger and Karnes, and Dilger was a fine teacher and helped Karnes learn the dairy and food business. Karnes had high respect for his boss; he and Dilger thought alike and became close friends.

In 1939, Karnes was named director of the company's new Employee Relations Department, which was set up to help plant managers deal with wage and hour problems, Social Security, and labor issues. The Federal Wage and Hour Act and the Wagner Act, which set up regulations for labor relations, had just been passed, and Social Security had become effective in 1936. All three federal statutes had immediate effects on dairy and food plants across the country.

John F. Hazelton, who was to become Beatrice's chief operating officer as executive vice president in 1954, recalled the first time he met Karnes. Hazelton was the manager at the Beatrice ice cream and butter plant at Muncie, Indiana. "We were having union negotiations," he related. "I never had much experience with unions. I had a superintendent who didn't like unions. He got us into trouble, and the union called a strike. He almost ran over one of the union officers with his car. So I called the general manager in Chicago, and he sent Bill Karnes down to help me negotiate a contract. I met Karnes's train at the depot. He had a paper suitcase with a leather handle. It was raining and all that was left was the handle. I was so surprised, I said to him, 'I thought I was going to get a Philadelphia lawyer, and they sent me a Boy Scout.' With Karnes's help, we settled the contract. Karnes was twenty-five years old then. When I retired in 1966, Karnes came to my retirement party dressed as a Boy Scout."

Karnes applied his skills at union negotiations at other locations and in the process set in motion a major change at Beatrice Foods. As Hazelton put it: "I give Karnes a lot of credit. He changed the thinking of Beatrice. Their policy used to be to fight the unions, but Karnes was smart enough to see what was coming and sold the superiors on the idea we had to deal with labor. That permeated all through the company, and after that we didn't have much trouble with unions."

Unions were active in the dairy business, and it became Karnes's almost fulltime job to negotiate contracts throughout the United States. He quickly adopted some practices that would guide him in his negotiations. For example, when entering into meetings with union representatives, he would settle himself in the softest chair in the room with his back to the window. He always had a pocket full of cigars, and was prepared to wait the union bargainers out. He also had a standard contract form and would fill it out and have it signed by the union as well as the plant manager before he left town.

In one instance, Beatrice had a creamery plant in Cadillac, Michigan, that became unionized by Teamsters from Detroit in the late 1930s. When the union representatives walked into the room, it was obvious to Karnes that they both wore shoulder holsters, so his first order of business was to tell them "all guns on the table." They were embarrassed, but claimed that they were deputy sheriffs of Wayne County. In another memorable experience, Karnes was negotiating a contract for the company's Detroit warehouses in 1940, when one of the union business agents walked in with a short, stocky man in shirtsleeves, who sat quietly over in the corner. During a heated discussion, the company's warehouse manager made a statement, to which the man in the corner responded, "You are a liar." They both jumped up and started for each other. Karnes had to step between them to quiet the dispute. He later learned that the man's name was Jimmy Hoffa.

One of Karnes's first union negotiation assignments was at the dairy plant at Vincennes, Indiana, in 1940. Karnes got off the train, which had arrived at 5:00 A.M., and directed the cab driver to take him to the dairy. The driver said, "I don't think you want to go there, mister. They're on strike, and there are pickets all around the plant," and left Karnes off about a block away. Karnes had to walk through the picket line amid shouts and boos as the strikers threw bricks through the windows. He entered the plant and saw the manager, John Risch, standing at the top of the stairs. Risch, who was then more than seventy, chomped on a cigar, looked down at Karnes, and demanded, "Who in the hell are you?" That was Karnes's introduction to the negotiations at Vincennes, which were soon settled peacefully.

A few years later, Karnes was sent back to Vincennes to inform Risch that he had to retire. Risch met Karnes, one of the few people to whom he would talk, at the railroad station and started to drive him uptown. "I want you to see a motion picture I saw today," he said and took Karnes into a showing of *Going My Way*. All through the film, in which Bing Crosby as a young priest comes to replace an old priest played by Barry Fitzgerald, Risch kept nudging Karnes and saying, "That's what you're doing to me." After the film, Karnes finally talked with Risch about retiring. Then Risch went back to the plant, cleaned out his desk, and never returned to the plant.

The success Karnes achieved in dealing with personnel issues and the visibility that the job gave him led to a promotion to assistant to the president and vice president in 1943. His salary of $7,200 a year was the lowest paid any vice president in the history of the company, but he had an office with a window at last. He handled a variety of assignments, including the organizing of the new sanitation program in 1945 and negotiating the original Beatrice pension plan with John Hancock Insurance Company in 1946. A few years later he assisted in installing the Beatrice hospital plan underwritten by Bankers Life Insurance of Des Moines. Karnes started acquiring companies for Beatrice in 1945.

In every assignment, he demonstrated not only his skills in carrying out assignments effectively, but also his ability to get along with and motivate people. His performance was further rewarded by his election to the board of directors in 1947. Then, in 1948 when Karnes was thirty-seven, Haskell made him executive vice president—the first one at Beatrice. In the job, Karnes had the opportunity to work even more closely with Haskell. "I did whatever I thought necessary to be done unless I was otherwise advised by Haskell," Karnes said. "It was a tremendous training program for me to work closely for nine years with this man who had been so instrumental in building the company."

By 1951, it was clear that Clinton Haskell was grooming Karnes to succeed him as president. Many factors led Haskell to the choice, but persons familiar with the developments in those days cited Karnes's skills with people as a critical factor. As Wallace Rasmussen put it many years later, "Haskell was impressed by Bill's attitude towards people—Bill had the ability to get along with the many different types of people that we had in this company." F. C. "Salty" Salter, head of Beatrice's butter operations for many years, recalled that Haskell often told him, "Every time I look at Karnes [who is six feet one] I see tall timber."

During the next twenty-four years, twenty as chairman, president, and chief executive officer and four years as chairman and chief executive officer, Karnes led Beatrice to the greatest era of growth in increases in percentages of sales and net earnings in the company's history.

This discussion would not be complete without reference to Virginia Grace Kelly, whom Karnes met when he was a boy vacationing in Warsaw, Indiana. She was graduated from Purdue University, where she became a member of Mortarboard, and they were married in 1937 after a long courtship. Virginia Karnes was named the first woman chair of the President's Council at Purdue University, and after thirty years as a volunteer at Rush Presbyterian Medical Center in Chicago, she became president of the Women's Board in 1976. She is her husband's closest friend and counsel and has been a major factor in contributing to his success. As of 1989, they had been married for fifty-two years.

CHAPTER THREE

Milking the
Cash Cow: 1952–76

William Karnes inherited the leadership of a company with annual sales of $229 million, almost entirely in dairy products, several poultry and egg plants, six public cold-storage warehouses, several specialty food branches, and LaChoy Products. The net earnings were $3.9 million, down from $4.8 million in fiscal year 1951. The company had a fine balance sheet, with strong cash ratios and no debt. It was structured on a decentralized basis and had excellent, experienced district managers: John F. Hazelton, Brown W. Cannon, Alvie J. Claxton, Edward J. Comegys, Jr., Carl N. Hansen, Charles H. McConnell, Jay G. Neubauer, and George A. Gardella.

A number of trends in the food business could possibly curtail the company's growth. Home delivery (retail) milk sales were declining, and many large retail milk companies such as Bowman and Wanzer in Chicago, Peveley in St. Louis, Hood in Boston, and Knudson on the West Coast, were struggling to maintain sales. Margarine sales were rising at the expense of butter. More captive dairies—owned outright by the chains— were being formed by companies such as Kroger in Cincinnati and Safeway in California and Denver.

Beatrice had been bottling all of Safeway's milk for the Denver market— twelve thousand gallons a day. In the spring of 1952, Safeway built its own milk plant in Denver, and that business evaporated for Beatrice. California was rapidly growing into store-door milk deliveries (milk dropped off directly at the retail outlet), and many retail food chains combined to bottle their own milk in captive plants. Other concerns were the growing power of unions in the food business and the changes in the American public's eating preferences. People were becoming more diet conscious and buying fewer products containing milk fats, or any type of food with high fat content.

Karnes's predecessors, George Haskell, A. E. Wilkenson, and C. H. Haskell, had all been men familiar with the actual workings of a dairy. Karnes had never even milked a cow. The first need he saw for the company was the addition of a top operating executive in the general office, where only two department heads had ever worked in a processing plant. After a quick review, Karnes selected the district manager who had made the greatest profits for Beatrice, John F. Hazelton of Muncie, Indiana, the district manager of Ohio-Indiana and the southern plants. He also knew how to milk a cow.

Karnes was elected president on March 25, 1952, and after picking Hazelton to come to Chicago, he called him in late April and asked him to have Leo White, the Louisville manager, buy four tickets for the Kentucky Derby. He then invited Hazelton and his wife, Irene, to meet him and his wife at the French Lick Hotel in Indiana the Friday before the race. Karnes wanted to talk to the Hazeltons about coming to Chicago. "Red" Hazelton had been a top high school basketball player in Indiana. He started with the company in 1921 as a cream buyer, was promoted to salesman, and then in 1936 became manager of the Muncie ice cream and butter plant. A profit-maker who clearly understood Beatrice's decentralized managing philosophy, Hazelton had taken over some mediocre plants and led them and their managers to become some of the biggest money-makers in the company. "He had to hire me," Hazelton said later. "I was bringing in twenty-five percent of the company's entire profits."

John and Irene Hazelton had lived in and around Muncie all their lives. Their son and daughter had both received fine educations there, and the Hazeltons owned considerable real estate in the town. However, after a great deal of discussion and persuasion, they agreed to come to Chicago. For a number of months they lived in the Whitehall Hotel on the near North Side until they built a home in Wilmette. One factor that persuaded them to come to Chicago was that it would give their son, John, Jr., a chance to work in the Muncie plant after graduating from Indiana University in Bloomington.

It was an ideal choice. Karnes and Hazelton, who was elected executive vice president in 1954, worked closely together for the next fourteen years and built the company to $800 million in annual sales. Beatrice never had a down year in sales or earnings during this time. The two formed a winning team; Hazelton and Karnes thought alike, operated alike, and were able to work easily with people. As Hazelton observed later, "Karnes handled the money, bought the plants, and I ran them. We operated them like a country store."

Karnes's next step after appointing Hazelton was to marshall the best management people in the company into an operating committee for the future. Formed in 1953, it included Gardella, vice president and district manager in Detroit; Cannon, vice president and district manager in Denver; Claxton, vice president and district manager in Pittsburgh; and Hazelton and Karnes. All were directors of the company.

This committee met monthly for at least one full day. It quickly determined that Beatrice must expand in the dairy business, but that this should be in states and areas growing in population faster than the national average. They pinpointed the South, the Southwest, and the West. It was apparent that many Beatrice plants in South Dakota, Nebraska, Iowa, Kansas, and Oklahoma had little growth potential in the dairy business other than by increasing their share of market, which was a slow process. A second decision was to expand the company's specialty food lines in the larger eastern and midwestern cities, as well as its public cold-storage warehouse facilities in response to the increasing demand for warehouse space because of the growth in the popularity of frozen food.

Creameries of America and Other Acquisitions

A first major step by the new management team was a giant one toward the objective of expansion into growing states. Creameries of America, the seventh largest dairy company in the United States, was offered to Beatrice in 1952, which ranked third in size, by Walter Moffet of the investment banking firm of Kidder, Peabody in New York City. Creameries operated twenty-five milk and ice cream plants in California, Texas, New Mexico, Western Colorado, Utah, Idaho, and Hawaii. The company was available because G. Stanley MacKenzie, the chief executive officer, was seventy, and the company needed more working capital to expand in its growing markets.

Beatrice directors were concerned about Creameries' Hawaiian operation because of its distance from the Mainland and the substantial amount of military presence that was involved. Beatrice had always maintained the policy of not selling too much to the military or to any governmental agency because military and government business was generally low margin and not very stable. (Later, however, Beatrice did operate two government-owned plants in South Vietnam and five in Japan during the Vietnam War under an exclusive government contract on a fixed price formula and for a fixed period of time.) Another guideline that presented a minor problem was to avoid the liquor business; Creameries also owned the Primo Brewery in Honolulu. The brewery later was sold to the Schlitz Brewing Company, however, which built a new plant and operated it successfully in the Islands. To resolve the directors' concerns, directors McGreer, Cannon, and Claxton were assigned to the pleasant task of visiting Hawaii and returned with a glowing report.

Thomas Reynolds, Sr., of the Chicago law firm Winston & Strawn, represented Beatrice in Federal Trade Commission matters, along with a young and capable assistant, Edward Foote. They filed a petition for

Beatrice with the FTC to obtain approval of the Creameries of America merger. After several meetings, and the filing of many documents, Reynolds, Foote, Karnes, and an attorney for Creameries of America appeared before Joseph Sheehy, a long-time official of the FTC. Beatrice asked for a written approval, but Sheehy indicated that there was no violation of the Sherman Act that he could see and suggested that Beatrice proceed with the merger, which was completed in August 1954. In October 1956, however, the FTC brought a restraint of trade suit against Beatrice. Suits were filed against National Dairy and Borden, at the same time, about one month before Dwight D. Eisenhower's second election (chapter 16).

MacKenzie, the founder of Creameries of America, had started in the dairy business in California and then merged his business with various dairy plants in the western states. The first plant was Mission Creameries, with California plants in the Bay Area, at Watsonville, Santa Cruz, and Bakersfield, where there was also a large dairy farm with 1,500 acres of land. MacKenzie then bought the Peacock Dairy in Pasadena, operated by Aaron Marcus, who later managed the plant in Honolulu. Idaho Creameries of America, with plants in Pocatello, Boise, and several distributing branches in Idaho that served Yellowstone National Park and Glacier National Park, was acquired next. This group was operated by the capable Grant Dougal. A group of milk and ice cream plants in Salt Lake City, a milk plant in Provo, and branches in Ogden and Cedar City were then added and directed by D. O. Lamb and E. A. Walker, who later became a Beatrice senior vice president. Creameries also had a milk and ice cream plant on the western slopes of the Rocky Mountains in Colorado at Grand Junction.

Price's Creamery, with general offices in El Paso, Texas, was headed by Robert Price. The volume and quality leader of the area, it had a major milk and ice cream plant in El Paso and distribution branches in western Texas and southern New Mexico. The Price family also owned and operated dairy farms at El Paso and at Las Cruces and Roswell, New Mexico. They supplied a major portion of the milk processed by Price's Creamery, which also owned the major share of Valley Gold Dairy in Albuquerque. MacKenzie and Price were both named to the board of Beatrice.

MacKenzie's wife, Frances, was from Hawaii and, therefore, he spent much time there. He became interested in the dairy business in Hawaii and acquired a major plant in Honolulu. Creameries became dominant in Hawaii and had an excellent profit record; it was the leader in milk and ice cream sales and had a reputation for top quality. The Honolulu operation's dairy farm—at first on rented land on Oahu—was later moved further inland and became a model dairy farm on the Islands and the principal source of milk for the Honolulu plant. The Honolulu operations also included a plant at Hilo, with distribution plants on other islands. The Honolulu dairy also had a contract to process recombined milk (made from powder and butter) to supply the Navy and Army bases on Oahu. Products from the Creameries' ice cream plant were also shipped to various islands in the Pacific, such as Guam, where Beatrice later built a plant, and Samoa.

The merger with Creameries, effective in 1954, was extremely important to Beatrice; it gave the company a grand lift in sales and earnings and called Beatrice to the attention of stock analysts throughout the United States. It also put Beatrice into growing areas in the West and Southwest and in Honolulu. Under the capable management of Marcus, the prestige of the Honolulu plant was also a boost for Beatrice.

Creameries had operated on a decentralized basis and was quickly integrated into Beatrice's philosophy of decentralized management, with the same plant structure and internal procedures; MacKenzie reported to Brown Cannon in Denver. The Los Angeles headquarters was gradually phased out, and many of Creameries' employees were assigned to other dairy operations.

Subsequently, Beatrice added a series of dairies operating in growth areas. Among them were Tro-Fe's milk and ice cream plants in Gadsden, Alabama, a milk plant in Tuscaloosa, Alabama, Boswell Dairies in Fort Worth, Greenbriar Dairies in Beckley, West Virginia, Durham Dairies in North Carolina, an ice cream plant in Alexandria, Virginia, Westerville Dairies in Covington, Ohio, Eskay Dairy in Fort Wayne, Indiana, Russell Dairy in Brainerd, Minnesota, and Louis Sherry, a premium ice cream facility in Brooklyn. Other acquisitions were two major butter companies: Hotel Bar in Brooklyn and Keller's in Harleysville, Pennsylvania.

Beatrice continued to expand in the milk business—which has low profit margins and is highly competitive on a local basis—first because the consumption of milk, ice cream, and dairy products was increasing during the 1950s. Further, raw milk is purchased through producer cooperatives and from individual farmers. The price paid by the dairy for raw milk is based on a federally required minimum price. A basic milk price is established monthly based on the previous month's wholesale price paid for raw milk at plants in the Minnesota-Wisconsin area and is referred to in the industry as the "Minnesota-Wisconsin Price Series." To determine raw milk prices in other parts of the country, a hypothetical freight premium is added to the base formula price. Dairy cooperatives may add a further premium and notify the dairies of the monthly price.

The price paid by the processor varies, depending on how the milk is used. For example, it is higher per hundred-weight for raw milk purchased and used for bottled fluid milk (Class I price) than for butter (Class III price). Therefore, the exact amount the processor must pay for the milk it uses is not known until the end of the month. The farmer is paid a blend or uniform price for all milk, based upon the classified prices paid by all of the processors in the market. On the first day of the following month, the processor makes a partial payment based on the Class III price for milk received in the first half of the month, and final settlement is made for each month by the fifteenth of the following month. By the time the processor makes this payment, it customarily has received payment from its customers for the milk and other products processed and sold during the prior month. The dairy receives payment from its customers before settlement with its suppliers, so it can rely on customer payments to finance inventories and accounts receivable, an advantage few industries enjoy. Thus, Beatrice's dairy business was a "cash cow" that helped finance expansion of current operations and acquisitions without incurring significant long-term debt. As Jay Neubauer, a director and vice president, often commented, "You took all the money we made in the dairy division and put it into expanding the food business."

When Hazelton retired in 1966 after forty-four years of active service to Beatrice, he and Karnes had a worthy successor already in place. The logical choice, Don L. Grantham, was a veteran of thirty-two years with the Dairy Division. He was a proven money-maker with strong convictions about the importance of people and the Beatrice entreprenurial system of decentralized management. Grantham had come to the top of the corporate ladder literally from the bottom rung. A certified public accountant and an alumnus of Eastern Illinois College and the University of Illinois, he joined the company as a member of the office staff of Beatrice's dairy plant in his hometown of Mattoon, Illinois, in 1934. He advanced to manager of the Mattoon milk and ice cream plant following the death of Lawrence Fulton, the long-time manager there. Under Grantham's direction, the Mattoon plant expanded its distribution east to the Indiana state line; west to the Mississippi River, north to Decatur, and south to Olney, Illinois. It became one of the largest dairy distribution areas in the entire company.

When George Loufek, manager of the Meadow Gold-Louis Sherry ice cream plant in Brooklyn, died in 1956, Hazelton promptly named Grantham to succeed him. An aggressive competitor (he was a 135-pound quarterback in high school), Grantham turned the Brooklyn plant into one of the most profitable in the division despite the presence of such powerful rivals in the New York City market as Kraft's Breyer's brand, Borden, Swift, and several local companies. Beatrice had just acquired the Louis Sherry Company, and Grantham guided its expansion substantially to include institutional accounts such as the Waldorf Astoria Hotel and leading restaurants and clubs in Manhattan and the New York metropolitan area.

In 1957, Grantham was promoted to manager of Beatrice's Eastern District and also was assigned to supervise Dannon Milk Products after it was acquired in 1959. He was named eastern regional vice president in charge of all Beatrice plants in New England, New York, Baltimore, Maryland, and Washington, D.C. in 1961. He was then elected executive vice president of the company in 1965, moved to the general office in charge of the Dairy, Warehouse, and Agri-Products Division, and subsequently was in charge of all divisions when John Hazelton retired in 1966. Grantham was first elected as a director in 1963 and named the company's fifth president as well as chief operating officer in 1972, when Karnes was elected chairman and chief executive officer. The office of chairman had not been officially filled for forty-four years.

In the decade that Grantham and Karnes worked efficiently and closely as a team, sales of the company were increased almost seven times, from $796 million in fiscal year 1966 to $5.3 billion in fiscal year 1977 on a reported basis. Net earnings rose more than seven times, from $24.6 million to $182.6 million. This decade from 1966–76 was the most significant period of growth in Beatrice history. Grantham capably directed the plant operations, and Karnes continued to handle the money and expand the company. Among their important contributions was the realignment of Beatrice's decentralized management system to provide trained leadership at every level of operations.

Once, when Grantham was asked why the company was considered the most successful of all food companies in the nation, he replied, "That's simple. We work half days, 6 A.M. to 6 P.M." "Grantham was a hard worker," Hazelton said, "No job was too hard for him. He'd go right after it. He was a fighter." Grantham's faith in the dairy business never wavered despite increasing competition, narrowing margins, changes in eating habits, and more stringent health regulations.

Through the period from 1950 to 1977, Beatrice's Dairy Division grew in dollars and units and profits each year. Its sales of bottled milk, ice cream, and specialty units grew annually. More important, its dairy profits increased and produced the cash to allow Beatrice to expand into other more profitable fields. The only dairy product that did not grow was butter. However, Beatrice's acquisition of several butter companies supplying institutional customers like restaurants and clubs made it one of the leaders in the country in butter sales.

In its search for higher profit margins, Beatrice began concentrating more on acquiring dairy specialty companies and added Dannon yogurt in 1959, Sanna in 1967, County Line cheese in 1970, and Meinerz cheese in 1975. Subsequent additions were Longlife Dairy Products in Jacksonville, Florida, Sanitary Dairy Products in Minden, Louisiana, and Green Valley cheese, Model Dairy, and Sugar Creek butter.

Acquisition guidelines were defined carefully. (1) Only profitable companies were considered. Turn-around situations were never considered. Beatrice had losing plants of its own and didn't need to take on any more. One of Karnes's first moves as president was to close four poultry operations that were losing money. (2) The acquired plants had to be growing faster than the general company and be located in markets with excellent growth potential. (3) Present management would continue to operate the plant, and qualified back-up management was in place to carry on. (4) The products had growth potential either because of population growth or increasing demand for them. (5) Beatrice was not interested in commodities such as coffee and sugar. It was interested in products it could buy today, process tomorrow, and sell the next day without significant price fluctuations and with short storage time.

Executives Guide Beatrice Development

Many fine people helped build Beatrice over the years; most had a dairy background. For example, the Cannon family played an important part in the growth of Beatrice in the western states. Hugh Brown Cannon was born in Three Oaks, Michigan, and lived on a farm until he was about eighteen. In 1885, as a young man, he arrived in Denver with $25 and went to work with a dairy north of the city, milking cows and driving a milk truck. In later years, he formed a partnership in a dairy plant with a man named Penrose, the beginning of Windsor Farm Dairy. Clinton Haskell and his wife, Ethel, were long-time friends of Cannon and his wife, and as a result, Cannon sold the Windsor Farm Dairy to Beatrice for stock in September 1929 and joined the board of Beatrice.

The Cannons' two sons, Brown W. and his younger brother George, were both born in Denver and worked at various times at the Windsor Farm Dairy. Brown W. Cannon graduated from Stanford University and then attended Harvard University, from which he was graduated with an MBA degree in 1939. He became a traveling auditor for Beatrice and served in the Navy during 1941–44. After returning from overseas duty, he took over the retail department of the Denver milk plant. Around 1950, at the death of Vernon Hubbard, he became manager of the Denver milk plant and was made district manager of the western dairy plants and a member of the Beatrice board when he was only thirty-five.

Brown Cannon was personable, outgoing, and possessed a keen profit sense as well as the ability to motivate and lead the people who worked for him. He was extremely active, as was his father, in civic affairs in Colorado and was regarded as one of the leading businessmen of the Rocky Mountain area. He was responsible for much of the company's growth in the western states and before his death at age fifty-nine was given many responsibilities, which he performed very well.

Jay Neubauer was typical of Beatrice's fine district managers who excelled in developing people as well as generating profits. He was a native of Illinois and attended the University of Illinois, graduating around 1927 with a degree in engineering. He went to work in Beatrice's Illinois District and then became a troubleshooter for Louis Nielson, the district manager at Galesburg. Neubauer visited Illinois dairy plants, improving the manufacturing procedures and recommending machinery, before he became manager of the Jacksonville, Illinois, plant. When Beatrice needed a manager at the Nashville, Tennessee, ice cream plant, he was transferred there and developed a growing, profitable facility. He brought Wallace Rasmussen out of the General Office engineering department and made him superintendent at Nashville.

When John Hazelton was moved into Chicago in 1952, Jay Neubauer was made district manager of the southern plants. In later years, he came into the Chicago headquarters to help Hazelton with the general supervision of all Beatrice plants, but after a short time, Neubauer wanted to be put back into a field position. He was put in charge of the Wisconsin plants, particularly those in Beloit, with an office at Waukegan, Illinois. From there he helped the Beloit group of plants expand its dairy specialty business to become one of the biggest profit-makers in the Dairy Division.

Another district manager, Lewis Komminsk, was the grandson of Clifford Huenke, the founder of the White Mountain Creamery Company of New Bremen, Ohio. After earning a degree from Ohio State University in dairy technology and engineering, Komminsk immediately went to work at New Bremen where his father, Harry, was the manager. At that time, New Bremen was largely a milk bottling and ice cream manufacturing plant with some milk drying facilities. After his father's death, Lewis Komminsk became manager and began developing New Bremen into a successful and unique bulk milk distributing and milk drying plant. He developed sources of raw milk from Michigan, Indiana, and various parts of Ohio and shipped tank milk out of New Bremen to other parts of the country. During the fifties and sixties, there was a shortage of grade A milk in certain metropolitan areas, and this became a very profitable business for New Bremen.

Komminsk had great imagination and tremendous energy. He developed his own trucking system and also one of the largest milk drying opera-tions in the Midwest. For the ten years before his early death, New Bremen became one of the best profit-makers in the Beatrice Dairy Division. In later years, Komminsk also became district manager of all the Ohio milk plants. He was responsible for a number of dairy acquisi-tions in the fifties and sixties, such as Keller butter, Westerville Dairies, an ice cream company in Puerto Rico, and certain other foreign operations through his friendship and business connections with Melvin E. Frank, a dairy products broker in New York. Komminsk was another outstanding example of the ability, imagination, and fine profit sense that can be developed through the decentralization policies followed at Beatrice.

New Ventures

Dairy

Beatrice carried on extensive dairy research beginning in the early thirties—research that was constantly expanded and that led to the addition of many specialty dairy products. Through research, Beatrice created an entire Specialty Products Division, which was unique and quite profit-able (chapter 11).

Warehouse Development

Cold-storage warehouses were essential to Beatrice's operation literally from the day the company sold its first pound of butter; almost all of its products were perishable. In the late twenties and thirties, Beatrice was the largest handler and processor of storage eggs; its A. F. Thibideau Company was a leader in the field. Many of the eggs were stored in Beatrice's warehouses, but most of the egg products were stored in other warehouses throughout the United States. Accordingly, the warehouse operations grew hand in hand with the dairy, egg, and frozen food distribution business. Among the first were warehouses in Lincoln, Topeka, and Denver. Chicago Cold Storage, built during World War I, was acquired several years later to refrigerate Beatrice butter and egg products. The general office was located in this building until 1944. Terminal Refrigerating was built and operated in Los Angeles by Ernest Thompson and Beatrice as equal partners. Located in the produce market, it contin-ued to grow profitably under the able direction of Harlan Nissan, its manager for many years. Nissan hired Robert Cooper as a clerk in the office, and Cooper later became division manager of all of the warehouses. The company also had warehouses in Detroit and Scranton, as well as the Soo Terminal in Chicago.

Only a small portion of the products that Beatrice stored in its warehouses were its own items; the vast majority was tonnage of a wide range of products stored for other food companies and manufacturers. These houses, called public cold-storage warehouses, also stored substantial quantities of butter and milk powder for the U.S. government under its dairy price support program. Beatrice was one of the first companies to anticipate the accelerating demand for refrigerated warehouse space to accommodate the rapidly rising popularity of frozen food. By the end of the decade of the fifties, Beatrice was the leading distributor of frozen foods in the nation. Between 1952 and 1970, it built new warehouses in Denver and Los Angeles after buying Thompson's widow's half-interest in the Los Angeles warehouse from her estate. Next, Beatrice acquired Quincy Market Cold Storage, which had two warehouses in Boston, two in Gloucester, Massachusetts, and another in Portland, Maine. The principal owner and manager was Herbert Farnsworth. Another major acquisition was Tampa Cold Storage and Warehouse, which operated warehouses in Tampa, Bartow, Lakeland, and Plant City, Florida to service the shrimp and citrus industries in that area. William B. Haggerty, Sr., was the principal owner and a fine operator who stayed with Beatrice until his death.

The warehouses of Quincy Market and Tampa Cold Storage rented space to food processors, who processed items with their own employees. Then the warehouses froze the product and stored it until it was moved out into retail channels. Quincy Market rented space to several companies that processed fish products. The fish were brought into the plant, where the renter's employees cleaned and packaged the products and the warehouse froze and stored them.

Tampa Cold Storage in Tampa rented space to the largest shrimp processor in the world. Shrimp from all over the world were brought to Tampa to be cleaned and packaged and then frozen and stored. The other warehouses in Lakeland, Bartow, and Plant City rented space to independent food companies that processed frozen orange juice. The warehouses received rent for the space, a service charge for the refrigeration, and a charge for storage, additional services that were unique in warehouse operation at the time.

Then Beatrice went "underground." In 1965, it acquired Inland Underground Facilities, the Kansas company that operates the largest storage facility of its kind in the world. The originator and principal owner was Leonard Strauss, who ran the plant for Beatrice for many years. The company had tunneled forty acres of refrigerated space into limestone caves a hundred feet below ground level along the Kansas River in Kansas City. It has a capacity of more than fifty million cubic feet of space under the solid rock that keeps the temperature at almost a constant 58 degrees. Humidity also is easier to maintain, virtually eliminating problems of package deterioration and rust. Food retailers would purchase a substantial quantity of fruit and vegetable crops at harvest time, package them, and store them at Inland to draw the stock as needed during the year. The facility by the mid 1980s was serviced by 154 truck docks, 82 railroad loading areas, and three miles of trucking roads. It also was equipped with a duty-free foreign trade zone for storage of imported or exported products. Inland rented approximately 20 percent of its developed space to outside firms, including light manufacturing businesses and a trout farm, but foodstuffs constituted 85 percent of its storage inventory.

New warehouses were completed in Denver and in Allentown, Pennsylvania, in 1976. The latter, Lehigh Valley Refrigerated Services initially had more than two million cubic feet of refrigerated and freezer storage space to supplement the capacity of the division's Lackawanna Cold Storage facilities in Scranton. Four additions were added to Lehigh Valley to bring its capacity to ten million cubic feet.

Beatrice then effected an acquisition that made it the operator of the largest refrigerated warehouse system in the nation. It outbid another group to purchase Termicold Corporation for $115.2 million in December 1982, a price equal to $141 per share of Termicold. Headquartered in Portland, Oregon, Termicold had nineteen locations in eight states, two in Iowa and one each in Wisconsin and Tennessee, with the rest situated in the West. The addition of these facilities, the capacities of which totaled 102,933,966 cubic feet, to those of Beatrice's twenty-two warehouses raised the division's capacity to 175 million cubic feet of refrigerated space. Beatrice's warehouse revenues in fiscal year 1982 were $77 million, while those of Termicold for 1981 were $41 million.

Termicold's growth paralleled that of Beatrice's Warehouse Division. It was founded as the Terminal Ice and Cold Storage Company in 1911 in Portland, and in its early years produced block ice and provided refrigerated space for the preservation and storage of such products as eggs, cheese, butter, meat, berries, and vegetables. Its first major expansion was the purchase of a warehouse in Salem, Oregon, about forty-five miles south of Portland and central to the productive farmlands of the Willamette Valley. Subsequently, it built a new facility there which has been expanded several times. The complex is the largest above-ground refrigerated warehouse in the world, with 12,487,000 cubic feet of capacity.

In the early thirties, Hillsboro, Oregon, located amid the farmlands of the Tualatin Valley about twenty miles west of Portland, was selected for Termicold's next expansion. It was through this facility that Termicold became associated with Clarence Birdseye, who had sold his quick-freezing process for foods in 1929 to the Postum Company, which became General Foods. The Ray Malting Company in Hillsboro began processing and freezing locally grown fruits and vegetables for Birdseye and storing them at Termicold's Hillsboro warehouse.

One of the key services of the Termicold facility built in Nampa, Idaho, in 1946 was to provide ice for the rail cars that transport perishables. Later, when mechanically refrigerated rail cars were developed, the Nampa warehouse stored a wide variety of frozen products, particularly processed potatoes. In response to the phenomenal growth in the demand for processed potatoes, Termicold also built warehouses in Walla Walla, Moses Lake, and Connell, Washington, and in Ontario and Hermiston, Oregon. Other Termicold facilities were located near the processors of other types of vegetables and fruits. Among these locations are Woodburn and Brooks in Oregon; Burlington in Washington; Plover, Wisconsin, and Bettendorf in Iowa; and Turlock, which is located in the San Joaquin Valley of central California. The Wallula, Washington, facility is dedicated to the storage of meat products for Iowa Beef Processors. In 1982, Termicold acquired the Jacobson Cold Storage Company of Fort Dodge, Iowa, and completed a 2.8 million cubic foot warehouse in Murfreesboro, Tennessee.

Consistent with Beatrice's firm policy, the management of Termicold continued to operate its facilities. The team included Joseph L. Heinz, president, Robert D. Affolter, senior vice president, Roland W. Mersereau, executive vice president, Joel M. Smith, treasurer, and James A. Vahey, controller.

In 1984, Beatrice opened a $9 million facility with a capacity of more than five million cubic feet in Watsonville, California. With this addition, Beatrice controlled 24 percent of the public cold-storage warehouse volume in the United States. The Warehouse Division was one of the most profitable for Beatrice. Its goal, to bring to the bottom line at least 25 to 30 percent of the gross warehouse income, was achieved year after year.

Beatrice built several modern warehouses, but in all cases sold them on a sale-lease back on a fixed rental over fifteen to twenty years. At the end of the fixed-rate period, Beatrice could buy the warehouse on a predetermined formula or extend the lease for an additional term at nominal rent or sublease. As a consequence of inflation during the sixties and seventies, the arrangement proved advantageous to Beatrice. Other company warehouses were older and primarily depreciated, so the policy helped produce the high return on sales.

By 1970, under the leadership of Robert Cooper, Beatrice had developed an internal warehouse organization that was the best in the industry. It was the most profitable by any measurement, per cubic foot or return on investment. "In retrospect, the 1960s can be considered as the acquisition decade and the seventies as the period of internal growth and digestion of the acquisitions for the Warehouse Division," Cooper commented. "A new marketing system was initiated using volume and product density as the basis for pricing. This enabled both the customer and the warehouse to have equitable charges. This system became recognized by the national customers and now is generally accepted by other companies in the industry. It proved to be a method for increasing profits to a standard that was higher than many considered possible.

"Along with this, the 1970s was a period of improving and professionalizing the management techniques at the individual plants," Cooper added. "Management by objectives programs along with one-year and five-year plans helped to build the Warehouse Division into the largest and most profitable operations in the industry."

Agri-Products

Recognizing the world's growing needs for protein and animal by-products and feeds, Beatrice began a logical horizontal expansion into agri-products in 1964 with the acquisition of Regal Packer By-Products, which produced animal protein feed supplements in plants at Lynn Center, Illinois, and Omaha, Nebraska. Western By-Products in Omaha, Colorado By-Products in Denver, and Utah By-Products in Ogden were added in 1964 and 1965. All are engaged in processing hides, animal by-products, and edible and inedible tallows.

The meteoric growth of Vigortone in Cedar Rapids, Iowa, since its acquisition in 1966 is related in chapter 10. Vigortone rapidly expanded its range of health products and feed supplements for cattle, hogs, dogs, and horses from plants in Cedar Rapids and Fremont, Nebraska, and Marion, Ohio. In ten years, it increased its sales tenfold. The Agri-Products Division, starting in 1967, was dramatically expanded over the next ten years by the addition of a number of companies in the rendering, poultry by-products, feed, and pet food business: San Angelo By-Products in San Angelo, Texas and three associated companies—Dreiling Hide Company in San Angelo, Lubbock Rendering in Lubbock, and Lone Star Rendering in Dallas; Ross-Wells, Inc. in Thiensville, Wisconsin; and Pfister & Vogel Tanning Co. in Milwaukee.

By the end of fiscal year 1977, the division, formed in 1965, was operating more than fifty plants and branches in nineteen states. Sales had climbed to a record $224 million, compared to $10 million in 1965, and operating earnings were almost $21 million.

These three divisions of Beatrice—dairy, warehousing, and agri-products—are typical examples of how the company accelerated its expansion in the quarter of a century from 1952 to 1977. The dairy grew by acquisitions but also by internal growth with new products, improved products such as low-fat milk and cottage cheese, and specialty products developed by research. The dairy business also grew by establishing branch distribution points around the central processing plant such as those around the Tulsa milk plant; five branches around the Lima, Ohio milk plant; eight around the Vincennes, Indiana, plant; and many other milk and ice cream plants throughout the country.

Warehousing grew by acquisition, but Beatrice also built new warehouses and constantly enlarged the warehouse area of Inland Underground and Lehigh Valley. Warehouse Division income also was augmented by offering additional services such as renting space, tying in with customers' computers, and other distribution services.

Agri-Products not only diversified by acquisition, but also by the development of new products, additional services to the customer, and covering larger territories at various plants.

All of this growth was accomplished by the decentralized management system that gave capable managers the encouragement, opportunity, and tools to grow. Each of these new products, services, and plants tended to improve Beatrice's profit margin steadily and allowed it to grow in sales, earnings, and cash flow while many of its dairy competitors in the twenties and thirties disappeared.

CHAPTER FOUR

Dannon:
A Classic Case History

Before the 1950s, most Americans classified yogurt in the same category with yak's milk. It was sour-tasting stuff, popular only with a few ethnic groups, particularly as a health food. What is known today as yogurt probably dates back to the Stone Age. It is mentioned in Homer's *Iliad* and in the Bible. About two centuries ago, Turkish immigrants brought it to the United States. In the 1930s, an Armenian family began selling it in Boston and New York. However, it was Dannon Milk Products, founded in Long Island City, New York, in 1942 that made the breakthrough that popularized yogurt across the nation.

The 1959 acquisition and development of Dannon yogurt is a representative example of how Beatrice carefully planned a program of expansion into more profitable and growing specialty food products. But it is not surprising that William G. Karnes showed little enthusiasm in 1958 when a salesman for the American Seal Kap Company told him that a company called Dannon Milk Products might be for sale and that he was selling an ever-increasing number of eight-ounce cups to the company. When Karnes learned that Dannon sold eight-ounce cups of yogurt with only 1.9 percent butterfat for 35 cents throughout the New York metropolitan market, he decided it was worth investigating. By comparison, Beatrice was getting less than 35 cents for a quart of milk with 3.2 percent butterfat. Karnes and Don L. Grantham, then vice president in charge of eastern plants, met with Joe Metzger, the co-founder of the company, in 1958 to discuss a possible merger. Dannon met all of the Beatrice qualifications. It was a growing company with a profitable product in an expanding market with excellent management that would continue to operate the company as a separate profit center.

An unusual series of business circumstances together with the political turmoil in Europe in the forties led to the formation of Dannon in the United States. Born in Geneva in 1883, Metzger settled in Spain, where he became a prosperous businessman. However, political and religious pressures in Spain motivated Metzger to immigrate to the United States in 1942. There he met and joined an old friend, Daniel Carasso, who had fled Paris, also for political reasons, in 1942. Carasso was thoroughly knowledgable about the yogurt business; his father, Isaac, had started a yogurt company in Barcelona in 1917 after immigrating from Greece to Spain. He named the company Danone, after his son. In 1926, the family started another yogurt plant in Paris. When Isaac Carasso died in 1940, his son took over the management of the Paris and Barcelona operations.

Upon arriving in New York, Carasso purchased the Oxy-Gala Yogurt Company in the Bronx. It retailed only plain yogurt in ten-ounce bottles at 11 cents each plus 3 cents for a deposit on the returnable bottles. The output was about two hundred jars a day. The official starting date for Dannon in New York was October 1, 1942. At that time, Metzger and Carasso anglicized the name from Danone to Dannon. Metzger and Carasso ran the company, and Metzger's son, Juan, was in charge of sales, advertising, and promotion. In 1951, Daniel Carasso returned to Paris to repossess the Danone Yogurt plant confiscated by the Germans during the occupation of France. However, he remained the major stockholder of the U.S. company. The company operated at a loss until 1952, although its fortunes began to improve in 1947, when preserves and flavors were added to plain yogurt to make it more appealing to American tastes.

By the time Karnes and Grantham met with the Metzgers, Dannon had blanketed the New York City market. Forty delivery trucks distributed Dannon from its Long Island City plant directly to every food outlet, restaurant, hotel, and retail store of any size in the area. It had just started distribution in Washington, D.C., through distributors and was selling directly to stores from trucks in Philadelphia. Sales approximated $3 million a year. Karnes and Grantham were sold. They convinced Metzger that he and his employees would have a free hand in the manufacture, distribution, and advertising of the products. Metzger had instituted a strict policy of selecting his ingredients and bought only the highest quality. He also insisted on delivering Dannon yogurt directly off of his own trucks. The products were coded and were picked up by their route drivers when the code date on the product had expired. The yogurt consisted of homogenized and pasteurized skimmed milk with 1.9 percent butterfat with a special bacterial culture that had been developed in France and was, at that time, frequently shipped from France to Dannon. The preserves were put in the bottom of the cup, then the low-fat milk with culture was added. Under exact humidity and temperature controls, the culture developed the low-fat milk into yogurt. Leading sellers were yogurts with strawberry, raspberry, cherry, and other fruit preserves. Later, such delicate flavors as vanilla, coffee, and lemon were introduced.

The deal was just nearly closed when Karnes literally got into a "jam" when he sent Metzger a holiday gift of a selection of preserves and jam made by another Beatrice company. When next they met, Metzger was ready to call off the merger. "You're going to make me use those jams in my yogurt," he complained. After reassurances that Beatrice would not require him to use any Beatrice products or to distribute from Beatrice trucks, Dannon officially joined Beatrice on June 2, 1959. The price was $3 million in Beatrice common stock. Dannon reported to Grantham in Brooklyn, and he and the Metzgers worked very well together from the beginning.

Dannon's strict policy of delivering to stores only from its trucks often cost it customers—for a short time. Early in the sixties, Dannon's largest retail customer discontinued Dannon because it would not make warehouse deliveries instead of store-door deliveries with its own trucks. The consumer demand was so strong that the retail customer was forced to put Dannon back in its dairy cases on Dannon's terms. A major food chain in Chicago also balked at Dannon's policies. "I don't like your delivery system," the chain's dairy products buyer declared in defeat, "but our customers insist on the product."

After joining Beatrice, Dannon was urged to start distribution in Boston, where the Armenian family had met with little success in the thirties. Metzger protested. He thought New England was too provincial to accept a sophisticated product such as yogurt, and Boston was one of the most difficult areas in which to introduce a new product. However, Beatrice challenged Metzger. "If you can sell yogurt in New England, you can sell it anywhere," Karnes said to him. Sales progress in Boston was slow, but the products finally were accepted there through a combination of a superior quality, an experienced sales team, and the unique Dannon advertising campaign.

Area by area, Dannon expanded sales across the nation in the sixties. A state-of-the-art plant was built in Ridgefield, New Jersey, followed by plants in Florida, two in Minster, Ohio, one in Texas, and another in Los Angeles. Dannon stuck to its successful policies as it opened each market a step at a time. Its advertising and public relations program under the direction of Juan Metzger contributed materially to its success. A classic was the television spot created in 1973 by Peter Lubalin of the Marsteller Agency and filmed in Russia. It featured Bagrat Topagua, an eighty-nine-year-old Russian Georgian with his 114-year-old mother. Both of these long-lived people just happened to eat yogurt.

All of Dannon's advertising capitalized on the dietary qualities of yogurt—low fat, low sugar, factors that were becoming in vogue. Among the first places Dannon would approach in a new market were schools, colleges, and universities, where young people adopting new eating habits readily accepted their products. Juan Metzger continued the same Dannon policies and procedures when he became president after his father died on May 5, 1965, a few days short of his eighty-second birthday.

Under Juan Metzger's direction, Dannon increased the yogurt product line to fifteen items and introduced Danny, a frozen yogurt on a stick or in a cup, and a premixed yogurt line in six-ounce cups. A plant was opened in California, and Dannon became the first yogurt product, in fact, the first perishable food product, distributed from coast to coast that carried a twenty-five-to-thirty-day date code and was store-delivered and reclaimed at the expiration date by its own route drivers.

Many companies have challenged Dannon for the leadership in the yogurt market. There were about 150 in the nation in 1987; many had been successful, many more have failed. By the time Beatrice sold Dannon in 1982 for $84 million to BSN–Gervais Danone, a French company, annual sales were in excess of $150 million, and Dannon was the established leader; competing against a myriad of brands, it held more than 40 percent of the U.S. market. Its pretax earnings for Beatrice from 1959 to 1982 were more than $75 million. Obviously, yogurt was good for Beatrice's economic health.

Why did Beatrice management sell a proven winner such as Dannon in 1982? Several persons close to the company have suggested that there were other reasons besides the cash. There was concern that Juan Metzger, who was also a Beatrice director, was about to retire and there was no capable successor. Another cause for pessimism in the general office of Beatrice might have been the growing competition across the country. Major companies were introducing highly promoted products such as Yoplait and Whitney's, and Beatrice had not invested the money to help Dannon develop new products.

BSN had made several offers to buy Dannon while Karnes and Grantham were still active with Beatrice. Daniel Carasso had sold his company to Gervais in France, which in turn had sold Gervais Danone to BSN. Previously, Daniel Carasso had tried to purchase control of Dannon, but Beatrice had always advised him that it was not for sale. Dannon was typical of the kind of company in which Beatrice invested for the future: its growing product line fitted a trend of changing food habits of America towards diet products that were low in sugar and fat; it was profitable, more profitable in fact than any other Beatrice dairy product; and it had sound management at all levels, executive, production, and marketing. Beatrice left it alone. It furnished the money for expansion, but the Dannon management made the decisions.

Despite suggestions to the contrary, however, the primary reason for selling Dannon was financial. The offer was a high multiple, twenty-three times Dannon's earnings at the time. Beatrice believed it could make more money on the money received than Dannon was making. Beatrice management apparently had also been persuaded that yogurt was a mature product, although such a belief was unfounded in the opinion of most food industry observers and analysts. Sales of yogurt and new yogurt products continue to increase across the country.

According to an article by Alison Otto in the July 1988 issue of *Dairy Foods Magazine*, "An Unfinished Masterpiece," Dannon produces profits at a growing rate for BSN. The article states that "Dannon already sells more yogurt in the United States than its two nearest competitors combined. . . . Since 1981 when Dannon was purchased by BSN, Dannon sales have increased about 80 percent, its product line has almost tripled in size and its market share has climbed 10 percentage points." Thus, its market share has grown from 20 percent to 30 percent since 1981, and annual sales have gone from $139 million to almost $240 million.

The annual per capita consumption of yogurt in the United States has increased from .26 pounds in 1960 to 4.14 pounds in 1986, according to the U.S. Department of Agriculture, and it continues to grow. This represents an increase of almost 1,500 percent. Otto points out that the per capita consumption of yogurt in some European countries runs as high as fifty pounds per year. Surely, then, yogurt was not a mature product in 1981 and surely Beatrice should never have sold this crown jewel, but should have allowed Beatrice-Dannon management to finish their masterpiece.

The result of the sale was a bad deal for Beatrice. Rather than try to find the management for the future, develop new products, and add other methods of distribution to augment its expansion, it sold a money machine. Dannon is truly one of the greatest marketing stories of a food product in the twentieth century—it may be the greatest.

CHAPTER FIVE

Groceries
Become Beatrice Specialty

Until 1955, LaChoy Food Products was a lonely grocery specialty atoll amid a sea of Beatrice dairy products, the one and only processor of grocery products in the company. Beatrice, however, had extensive experience in the distribution of grocery specialties. It had run truck routes in Chicago, Milwaukee, St. Louis, Oklahoma City, Denver, and throughout western states such as Montana and Wyoming, selling butter, eggs, canned hams, frozen foods, cheese, and snack items. The Lambrecht Foods Division operated home delivery truck routes, selling quality convenience food items in Milwaukee and Chicago until supermarket prices and soaring labor costs forced it to discontinue the service. Beatrice also had produce branches in Richmond and Norfolk, Virginia, Rochester and Syracuse, New York, and Cleveland that sold a selection of similar items off its trucks. For a time, it owned Del Crest Stores, a small chain in New Jersey that handled specialty items akin to those which convenience stores now offer. Other than butter, eggs, and some cheese products, these items were purchased from other manufacturers.

The continuing success of LaChoy after it joined Beatrice in 1943 helped persuade the operating committee to focus its acquisition arrows on companies manufacturing specialty foods. The LaChoy success story (chapter 6) is another example of how Beatrice achieved continuing profitable growth under its decentralized management system. The operating committee was also motivated to diversify after the frozen food business began to lose margins as more and more frozen food manufacturers eliminated their distributors and sold directly to retail food chains. During the late forties and early fifties, Beatrice was one of the largest frozen food distributors in the United States and was the largest customer of Birdseye Frosted Foods, which became a division of General Foods.

The criteria were specific for the acquisition of specialty grocery products lines. The emphasis was entirely on convenience foods. "We want companies with built-in maid service," Karnes often explained to his corporate development team, shareholders, and financial analysts. "These will be foods, like dairy products, which can be served directly from the bottle, jar, can or carton or that the cook only has to heat and eat. We are not interested in commodities such as coffee, sugar and flour." The same guidelines that were applied to dairy acquisitions were mandated. An important part of the strategy was to seek out companies with at least five years of sales and profit increases and to exclude any one so large that its failure could seriously reduce the bottom line. Another rule was that a deal must not dilute Beatrice earnings per share.

George Gardella led Beatrice into specialty foods. He had joined the company in 1915 and retired in 1963 as a vice president and director of the Grocery Division. He also served as a director of the company from 1942 to 1970. He was born in Detroit in 1895. One of twelve children of an immigrant produce dealer from Genoa, Italy, he began his career in the grocery business doing odd jobs for the F. Corn grocery store in Detroit when he was in the fifth grade. Even then, he worked by the sun (and sometimes the moon), not the hour.

Gardella joined Beatrice when he was twenty as a route salesman for the Fox River Butter Company. Driving a horse-drawn wagon, he sold butter, eggs, and cheese in Detroit for $80 per month. In 1937, he was selected as one of the company's original district managers and assigned a group of unprofitable plants that he formed into the Michigan-Northern Ohio District, which he directed for twenty years. He also served as an advisor to all other district managers on issues that concerned specialty and frozen foods.

Gardella began accumulating his vast knowledge of the grocery business in 1918, when he and his wife, Rose, risked their savings to purchase a truck and shipment of dairy products and pay the rent on the front half of a small store in Detroit. They built this firm, George A. Gardella Company, into America's largest independent distributor of frozen and specialty foods to the retail and institutional trade. When he sold the company in 1961, it was operating three hundred vehicles from a network of ten warehouses and employed four hundred persons. However, Gardella never permitted this operation to interfere with the rigid obligations he imposed upon himself on behalf of Beatrice.

The Beatrice board, on April 24, 1979, cited Gardella in a memoriam that stated, "In every way, George A. Gardella truly exemplified the spirit and traditions of America throughout his illustrious career. He was a leader who developed leaders, a pioneer who inspired others, a tireless worker and a man whose integrity and code of ethics set standards." As a result of his association with Beatrice, Gardella became a close friend of C. H. Haskell, and the two spent much time together discussing their businesses.

After persuading Haskell to buy LaChoy, Gardella was able to convince him, and later the operating committee, that specialty groceries offered great opportunities for growth. How wise a decision that proved to be is indicated by the fact that by the end of fiscal year 1983, the Specialty Grocery Division had become the leading segment of operations in sales and earnings. Of course, this was even before the purchase of Esmark in fiscal year 1985, which added $4.1 billion to the company sales, including more than $1.6 billion from the Swift/Hunt-Wesson group alone.

Beatrice's extensive expansion into the field of specialty groceries was not a random acquisition campaign as some contended. The company set its sights on seven specific product lines: confections and snacks; condiments such as pickles, olives, and preserves; spices; ethnic foods; institutional food services; bakeries; and carbonated soft drinks. The program was initiated in 1955 with the addition of the D. L. Clark Co., which operated candy plants in Pittsburgh and in Evanston, Illinois. The directive in the confectionery area was to avoid box candies or hard candies. Specialty candies with well-known brand names provided higher margins and were being featured at the checkout counters of many supermarkets, as well as in their candy sections.

The Clark Bar had gained national recognition during World War I, when it was developed as a high-energy food for soldiers in the United States and Europe. Other products included Zag Nut Bars and Peanut Blossom Kisses. The Clark Company had been run by the family for two generations, and they agreed to continue to do so.

Gradually, Beatrice built what was to become the Confectionery and Snack Division. The Thomas D. Richardson Co., creator of After Dinner Mints, which it produced in its plant in Philadelphia, was added in 1957. Then came Jolly Rancher of Wheatridge, Colorado, which produced Stix bars and kisses; M. J. Holloway of Chicago (Milk Duds and Slo Poke Suckers) in 1960; and Switzer Licorice of St. Louis in 1966. Fisher Nuts of St. Paul, which invented salted-in-the-shell nuts, accepted Beatrice's offer in 1962. This group subsequently was augmented by the acquisition of Chesterton, Brenner, and Bowers candies, Dahlgren sunflower seeds, Fireside marshmallows, FPI (Jubilee) ice cream toppings, Rothchild's, Good and Plenty, Now and Later, Asher candy canes, and South Georgia brand pecans. Snack foods obtained included Adams Korn Kurls, Pik-Nik, and Kobey's shoestring potatoes, Pepi's and Rudolph's pork rinds, Treat, Lowrey's meat snacks including beef jerky, and Convenience Foods. A related acquisition was Aunt Nellie's Foods of Clyman, Wisconsin, in 1965. Aunt Nellie's specialized in glass-packed and canned vegetables and fruit drinks and later expanded into spaghetti and pizza sauces.

At the same time, Beatrice's exploration turned to condiments and spices. Consumption of pickles and pickle products in the United States is among the highest of all specialty food items. The first such company Beatrice acquired, Bond Pickle of Oconto, Wisconsin, was operated by two brothers, Howard and Don Bond, and had a modern plant from which it distributed its products throughout the Midwest.

Shortly after acquiring Bond for cash in 1957, Beatrice bought the Squire Dingee Co., a processor of pickle products, jellies, and preserves in Chicago under the Ma Brown brand. Managed by F. Olney Brown and Paul S. Brown, it also had plants in Pittsburgh (Lutz and Schramm) and in South Carolina. Along with Ma Brown came the highly profitable Brown-Miller Company, which had plants in New Orleans, Mississippi, and Texarkana, Arkansas. Its president, John A. Miller, was an expert at making a profit from pickles; Rainbo, American, Delta, and Mother's brands were the top sellers in Louisiana, Mississippi, Alabama, Arkansas, and parts of Texas. Miller promised Karnes a cash profit of $1 million a year and always made good. To supplement its pickle business, Beatrice acquired Mario's Olives of Detroit and Olive Products of Oroville, California. Mario's imported stuffed olives from Spain, packed them at a modern plant in Detroit, and distributed them throughout the Midwest. A related acquisition was Liberty Cherry and Fruit Co., a processor of maraschino cherries, glacé fruits, and fruit syrups in Covington, Kentucky.

Adopting an "if you can't beat 'em, join 'em" approach, Beatrice decided to counter the erosion of its butter volume by entering the margarine business. Although it had distributed small quantities of private-label margarine from time to time, it had no manufacturing facilities until 1957. However, George Gardella had long been acquainted with Stephen J. Bartush and his family, including his sons J. Addison and Charles, and his brother Benedict. They were the principal owners of a Detroit-based company, Shedd-Bartush Foods, then the largest manufacturer of private-label oleomargarine in the United States. Among its principal customers were Jewel Foods, A&P, Piggly-Wiggly, Kroger, Safeway, and many other chains. Shedd-Bartush had two plants in Detroit as well as manufacturing facilities in Greenville, North Carolina, Elgin, Illinois, Cincinnati, Omaha, and Dallas. After joining Beatrice, it built a plant in Sunnyvale, California. Shedd also processed grocery items such as Olde Style sauce, peanut butter, salad dressings, and pickles under the Shedd and Lady Betty brands at a plant in Louisville. Shedd expanded its distribution and product lines under the able management of Adam J. Schubel. One of its most successful products has been Shedd Spread; when the state of Wisconsin lifted the ban on colored margarine, Shedd had trucks loaded with nine hundred thousand pounds of margarine ready to cross the Illinois-Wisconsin border at midnight on the first legal day.

To supplement its successful LaChoy Oriental foods line, Beatrice extended its operations into other ethnic foods. Gebhardt Mexican Foods of San Antonio, which produced a line of canned foods and Gebhardt's chili powder, was acquired in 1959. Gebhardt had U.S. licenses to process meat distributed throughout the South and Southwest. Then Beatrice obtained Rosarita Mexican Foods of Mesa, Arizona, two years later. One of its principal items was pinto beans. The acquisition was a natural fit with Gebhardt because Gebhardt's permits to process meat enabled it to produce a number of meat products for Rosarita.

Complementing these operations were Cal-Compack Foods of Santa Ana, California, a leader in processing capsicum spices, and Knickerbocker Mills of Totowa, New Jersey, a leading importer of fine spices since 1842. G–W Foods, which later was combined with Lambrecht to become Beatrice Frozen Specialties Foods in LaChoy's hometown of Archbold, developed sales of frozen pizza throughout the Midwest. Later, Gebhardt and Rosarita added pizzas to their frozen lines; Meinerz cheese was a principal supplier to pizza bakers.

Bakery specialties were becoming more and more attractive in the sixties because a new generation of homemakers was less disposed to take the time to mix and bake breads, rolls, pies, and cakes "like mother used to make." Beatrice recognized in the early sixties that women were becoming bread-winners instead of bread-makers. It acquired Burny Brothers in 1963, a quality bakery that sold institutional items throughout the Chicago area. It also had a number of retail outlets in major chains and company-owned stores that sold a full line of breads, rolls, and sweet goods. The company had been founded by three brothers, George, Jule, and C. J. Burny, in 1910 in a basement in Chicago. All stayed with the company, as did sons Jule, Robert, and C. J., Jr. A new plant was built in Northlake, Illinois, and the company continued to expand its product lines and distribution to the East.

Murray Biscuit of Augusta, Georgia, a long-established baker of cookies and crackers, merged with Beatrice in 1965 and built a $3 million plant to provide for growing demand for its products. Then came Mother's Cookie Company, which operated its headquarters plant in Louisville, a branch plant in Watertown, Massachusetts, and Little Brownie plants in Marietta, Oklahoma, and Dallas. Among its other brands are Robert's, Golden, Mother's Golden, and Barbara Dee. Butter Krust Bakeries of Lakeland, Florida, which supplied all of the bread for the major leading chains in the state, was added in 1968. Then Palmetto Bakeries of Orangeburg, South Carolina, makers of Sunbeam bread, rolls, and other fresh-baked items, and R and T Bakeries of Birmingham, Alabama, were added in the early seventies, along with Saps' of Columbus, Indiana, a specialist in doughnuts.

Gradually, the acquisitions became larger. In 1976, Krispy Kreme Doughnut Corporation of Winston-Salem, North Carolina, with plants in Salisbury and High Point, began baking under the Beatrice aegis. The price was 1,608,683 shares of Beatrice common stock. Later that year, Martha White Foods of Nashville, Tennessee, was acquired for 1,234,858 common shares. Martha White produces a broad line of convenience package mixes, including corn meal and cake. Its national spokesman, Tennessee Ernie Ford, was a close friend of Martha White president Cohen Turner Williams, who turned over the business to Robert Dale, his son-in-law.

Institutional foods presented especially attractive opportunities for growth. The fast-food business was burgeoning as more people ate out. Beatrice developed a small volume of business, primarily dairy products, including ice cream mixes, to outlets such as McDonald's, Burger King, and Dairy Queen. LaChoy also had penetrated the market minimally.

After an intense review, Beatrice decided that the top company in quality products and reputation among all institutional distributors was John Sexton & Co. A family-owned business, it had its headquarters in Chicago and operated eighteen branches from Boston to Florida and to Los Angeles and San Francisco. It distributed more than two thousand products including a broad line of canned foods, canned and processed meats, coffee, tea, spices, and paper products, everything except frozen foods and red meat. After extensive negotiations (chapter 12), Sexton joined Beatrice in 1968, with T. Mackin Sexton, William Sexton, and William Egan continuing to manage the business. Sexton put Beatrice in the institutional foods business, and Beatrice put Sexton in the frozen food field. Subsequently, Sexton also added distribution branches across the country, including one in Hawaii. However, thirty days after the preferred stock deal was closed, the Federal Trade Commission tried to put Beatrice out of the institutional foods business. It charged that the Sexton merger created a monopoly and reduced competition. The case was tried over a four-year period before it was resolved favorably for Beatrice in 1972 (chapter 16).

Beatrice also became convinced that carbonated soft drinks was the one beverage business, besides wine, that would experience rapid growth. In a whirlwind round-up, beginning at the start of the seventies, the company added franchises spanning the country. Royal Crown bottlers were acquired in St. Paul, Minnesota, Louisville, Kentucky, Springfield, Virginia, Rockford, Illinois, Oakland and San Diego, California, and Charleston, West Virginia.

The purchase of Red Wing, a company headed by Garry Moore, the popular television star, brought in Royal Crown operations in Los Angeles and Riverside, California. The acquisition also brought Beatrice the rights to the early television shows of Carol Burnett, which Red Wing produced. The company also built a plant in Louisville. By the mid-seventies, Beatrice had become a leading bottler of Royal Crown, Canada Dry, 7-Up, Squirt, Dad's and Mug root beers, Dr. Pepper, Schweppes, and Hawaiian Punch. All of the franchises were sold for a pre-tax gain of $48 million in order to acquire the Beverages Segment of Northwest Industries for $580 million in January of 1982. The purchase included the Coca-Cola Bottling company of Los Angeles, the Buckingham Corporation, and several radio stations in the Los Angeles area and their other affiliates. Buckingham imports such brands as Cutty Sark Scotch whiskies, Finlandia vodka, and Mouton-Cadet wines. With the addition of Arrowhead, Great Bear, and Ozarka bottled water, Beatrice became the leader in that market.

With the acquisition of Coca-Cola franchises in San Diego and San Bernardino, California, plus a number of others across the country, Beatrice also became the largest bottler of Coca-Cola products in the United States. Beatrice's only other venture into alcoholic beverages (besides Primo beer in Hawaii) had been the purchase of Brookside Vineyard Company of Old Guasti, California, which had produced California wines since 1832. It operated a chain of retail wine-tasting cellars in California and Nevada. Brookside was divested in 1981, however.

Beatrice resisted the temptation to enter the fresh meat business because it was regarded as a commodity with wide price fluctuations and low margins. Conversely, it tracked the increases in the consumption of processed meats such as sausages, luncheon meat, bacon, and related products in which Oscar Mayer had become dominant in the market. These products not only had better profit margins, but also were less speculative.

Although Peter Eckrich & Sons of Fort Wayne, Indiana, resisted Karnes's advances for a number of years, the Eckrich family finally relented and joined the company in 1972, with the entire Eckrich management team continuing in charge. Both Richard Eckrich and Donald Eckrich were elected to the Beatrice board. At the time of the acquisition, Eckrich and its Kneip subsidiary in Chicago distributed its products principally in Indiana, Michigan, Ohio, and Illinois from plants in Fort Wayne, Kalamazoo, Michigan, Chicago, and Fremont, Ohio. Eckrich sold products off of its trucks in many other locations. Beatrice increased the distribution of Eckrich products to other markets in the United States, including parts of the East Coast, the Southwest, and western basin. It also augmented its product lines, particularly with specialty frankfurters and luncheon treats such as "Fun Franks," smoked sausage, sweet-smoked ham, and pickled ring bologna.

No discussion of Beatrice would be complete without relating the story of Tropicana Products of Bradenton, Florida. Why did Beatrice pay $490 million on July 11, 1978, to acquire Tropicana, the largest integrated citrus fruit juice processor in the nation? Many considered citrus juice a commodity, and a number of security analysts felt that the price was much too high, far in excess of what another suitor, Kellogg Company, had offered.

Founded in 1946 in Miami by Anthony T. Rossi as a processor of fresh fruit segments, the company moved to Bradenton that year, and after several name changes, adopted the Tropicana name in 1951. Its primary products are pure and reconstituted orange and grapefruit juice, lemonade, fruit punches, and grape juice, most of which are distributed nationally. It produces no private-label products. It occupies 214 acres on a complex in Bradenton that includes 122 refrigerated warehouses and glass, corrugated box, and plastic container plants. Its peak capacity is 240,000 boxes (90 pounds each) of oranges per day.

Tropicana operates the "Great White Train," which makes more than eighty trips per year hauling orange juice from Bradenton to its Kearny, New Jersey, distribution center. In all, it has more than 200 refrigerated tank cars, 436 trailers and tankers, and 130 tractors. Sales of $244.6 million for the fiscal year that ended August 31, 1977, earned $2.39 per share on 9,396,370 shares outstanding.

Some associated with Beatrice believed that the new senior management, headed by Wallace N. Rasmussen, chairman and chief executive officer, and Richard A. Voell, executive vice president (chapter 17), wanted to demonstrate their executive leadership by presiding over the largest transaction in the company's history until the deal for the Beverage Group of Northwest Industries was consummated in 1982. After a special Saturday night meeting of the directors, the agreement with Tropicana was effected. It was one of the swiftest that Beatrice ever negotiated.

Following its acquisition, Tropicana encountered problems, including three freezes in the next five years and three changes in leadership, as well as intensified competition from two marketing giants, Coca-Cola's Minute Maid and Procter & Gamble's Citrus Hill. The acquisition also was challenged by the FTC but was settled in Beatrice's favor in 1984.

To indicate further the problems of Tropicana, James L. Dutt, Beatrice chairman, chief executive officer, and president, announced in a February 16, 1983, letter to shareholders that Beatrice was taking a $190 million write-down of good will in the fourth quarter, largely associated with the acquisition of Tropicana.

However, despite all the problems Tropicana had with competition, crop freezes, and changes in management, its sales continued to grow. Under the management of Robert Soran, a dairyman originally with Beatrice, sales had reached $750 million in 1987. Tropicana was the leader in the ready-to-serve market, with a 29 percent market share. Coca-Cola's Minute Maid had 22 percent, and Procter & Gamble's Citrus Hill had 14 percent of the market. Minute Maid had 27 percent of the frozen market, Citrus Hill 12 percent, and Tropicana 8 percent. Tropicana controls more than 50 percent of the ready-to-serve orange juice in New York City, 40 percent in the New England market, and an equal amount in Miami. In March 1988, KKR & Co. (chapter 19) sold Tropicana to Seagrams of Canada for $1.2 billion, equal to about twenty times earnings. From the first day of its purchase in 1978, Beatrice management had kept it growing and holding its market share—in fact, Tropicana improved its share in a number of markets.

Until the acquisition of Tropicana as a subsidiary, most of the specialty food companies joining Beatrice did not have national distribution. The formula in the Grocery Division was to obtain companies with local or regional distribution, gradually take them regional, and then national where possible.

The primary sales medium for this strategy was to use food brokers, the principal marketers of LaChoy products. Beatrice adopted the LaChoy system of distribution to retailers for several reasons. First, food brokers gave them a fixed sales cost, usually 5 percent, as opposed to varying costs when the company had its own sales force. There was no expense until there was a sale. Second, Beatrice could retain brokers specializing in particular food fields. For example, certain brokers only handled pickles and condiments. Others handled confections, still others snacks, ethnic foods, or canned goods. Brokers knew the buyers of these items for retail chains and usually were more effective than the average salesperson. A third advantage was that Beatrice could expand distribution regionally, and eventually nationally, quickly by using brokers. Typical examples were LaChoy food brokers taking on the Gebhardt and Rosarita lines or candy brokers handling Richardson, Holloway, Jolly Rancher, and Switzer, among others. Further, Beatrice could increase its sales force substantially because large brokers in the major markets could have as many as forty salespersons representing its products in a concentrated area (chapter 6).

Probably the ultimate benefit in Beatrice's adherence to its policy of acquiring companies that had managements who would stay with the company and back-up personnel in place in the line of succession was expressed in a Chinese proverb Karnes often cited: "If you want a crop for a year, grow rice. If you want a crop for ten years, grow trees. If you want a crop for a hundred years, grow people."

Beatrice obtained talented and trained operations personnel who could participate in the leadership of the company and continue to record sales and earnings increases. LaChoy was one of the training schools for developing future Beatrice leaders (chapter 6). After French Jenkins, LaChoy's general manager, died suddenly of a heart attack, Edward M. Muldoon was named general manager in 1953. He then succeeded Gardella as general manager of the newly formed Grocery Division in 1957. During the decade that Muldoon headed it, the Grocery Division increased its sales to more than $350 million and its number of products to more than two thousand. Muldoon was a no-nonsense executive who frequently gave managers "grow or go" declarations in a constructive way.

Gordon E. Swaney took over LaChoy when Muldoon moved up and became a vice president and assistant general manager of the Grocery Division. J. J. McRobbie, a former food broker in Texas, succeeded Swaney and advanced to be a Beatrice senior vice president in charge of Grocery. Others who scrambled up through the ranks included Harry Niemiec, who started in sales for Mario's Olives and retired as a director, an executive vice president and director of Grocery and Confectionery Divisions and the Bakery Group. Donald Eckrich became president of Beatrice under Dutt; Charles J. Gardella, one of George Gardella's sons, became a group manager.

John Hoermann of M. J. Holloway directed the Confectionery Division and was succeeded by William J. Powers of Thomas D. Richardson. John Rudolph of Rudolph Foods served as a corporate vice president, as did Juan Metzger of Dannon and Duane Daggett from Eckrich. John Scales advanced to become head of Shedd-Bartush after Adam Schubel and went on to head Vlasic Foods. Mack Sexton became a vice president and director, as did Stephen Bartush. Harry Tidey rose to become manager of the Bakery Group and was succeeded by William Burkhardt. Kenneth McKnight and then Warren Lewis managed the Warehouse Division following the departure of Robert Cooper. Anthony Q. Sanna was named head herdsman of the Agri-Products Division.

All were able to attain senior management positions in the company as the result of the policy of obtaining top managers with trained back-up in place with each acquisition. It was the ultimate interpretation of Muldoon's mandate to "grow or go." He really was referring to people, not sales. In turn, the people grew sales. For 1976, the fiscal year in which Karnes and Grantham retired, annual sales of Grocery Specialties had risen to $2 billion and operating earnings were up to $111 million. These operations included specialty grocery and ethnic foods, specialty meats, confections and snacks, bakery products, and institutional foods. In fiscal year 1983, before the purchase of Esmark, annual sales were $2.3 billion and operating earnings were $177 million.

CHAPTER SIX

LaChoy
and the Bean Sprout

The largest processor of Oriental foods is not based in the Peoples Republic of China, but rather in Archbold, Ohio, forty miles southwest of Toledo and ten miles from the Michigan border. Once officially designated Chinatown, U.S.A., this community of 3,300 ringed by cornfields is the home of LaChoy Food Products as well as an auction center for cattle and used farm machinery. LaChoy's rise to preeminence in Oriental foods is no fairy-tale adventure, however, a few dragons and a Green Giant enter the narrative. It is a story of how a company built its sales year after year through masterful management and marketing, primarily by operating as a people-oriented company and by enjoying the skills and contacts of food brokers across the country. In doing so, it reshaped the American diet.

The beginning was truly humble. Following the ratification of Prohibition in 1920, many people used their bathtubs to mix gin. Not Charles Smith and Ilhan New; they grew bean sprouts in theirs. Smith, who operated a neighborhood grocery in Detroit, where he was known as Wally by his customers, decided there was a market for mung bean sprouts. However, he didn't know how to grow them, and neither did anybody else in Detroit. His search turned to New, a classmate at Michigan State University (then Michigan A. & M.). New wasn't of Chinese descent, he was a Korean, but he knew about bean sprouts.

They called their product LaChoy, "good vegetables" in one Chinese dialect. Initially, they packed their sprouts in little wooden boxes like those used for fresh berries and sold them at stores' produce counters. The problem was that the sprouts turned brown in a few days. At the recommendation of American Can Company, they began to use tins, and subsequently also began bottling soy sauce after moving operations to the Detroit Harbor Terminal.

Within two years, they incorporated, and the bean sprout was on its way to becoming a household staple in American kitchens as demand rose steadily. Despite prosperity during the depression, New left the company in 1930, and Smith carried on and built the first LaChoy plant in Detroit in 1937. Then a series of setbacks threatened the very existence of LaChoy. Smith was struck and killed by lightning in 1937, and the company's sales manager, French Jenkins, was named general manager by the directors. Jenkins's advertising agency in Detroit had represented LaChoy until the agency failed during the depression, and he had taken a job in sales for the Packard Motor Car Truck Division. One of his first customers was George Gardella, and they subsequently became close friends after Gardella persuaded Jenkins to join LaChoy. When the United States entered World War II in 1941, the government classified canned Chinese foods as nonessential, which meant that LaChoy could not purchase tins. To keep the business alive, the board of directors sold the plant to the government, which converted it into a munitions factory.

"Jenkins was instrumental in bringing LaChoy to Archbold," related Gordon E. Swaney, "He looked at locations in New Jersey and in Illinois, but finally decided on northwestern Ohio because it was in the center of a rich tomato farming belt." Another influencing factor was that Archbold was the hometown of Smith's widow, Miriam Stotzer Smith, and her brother, Harold V. Stotzer, who owned a hardware store there. Stotzer held a large block of LaChoy stock, as did his sister and Jenkins, and served as a Beatrice director from 1945 through 1971.

"The idea was that LaChoy could get tin cans for tomatoes," Swaney noted. "The original plant was an abandoned steel mill and the steam for cooking was produced by an engine taken from a threshing machine. The company survived by packaging tomato juice and Vegemato, a blended vegetable juice." The company tried unsuccessfully to market bean sprout juice and the juice of yellow tomatos, then returned to packaging red tomato juice and Vegemato, the product the company was marketing when Beatrice acquired it on November 1, 1943 as its first food manufacturing venture outside of the dairy industry. Beatrice's sales were $101 million that year, and LaChoy was nearing the $1.8 million level. Operating under Beatrice's decentralized system, LaChoy outbattled Chun King in this ethnic niche of the food industry.

By 1985, LaChoy was producing more than a hundred canned, bottled, and frozen items for the consumer and the food service industry. It held a 40 percent share of the market for canned entree specialty products and packaged Oriental soups. It had about 25 percent of the frozen segment, with twenty products, compared to the same percentage for Chun King, now owned by RJR–Nabisco's Del Monte Foods. Green Giant and Campbell Soup's Stouffer's held about 40 percent, with the balance spread among several other brands. LaChoy's sales for fiscal year 1985 were in excess of $135 million.

Under Jenkins's command, LaChoy began a program that led the company to become a training academy for future Beatrice officers and managers of profit centers. In 1947, he hired Swaney, who had earned a degree in marketing from Indiana University, as a member of LaChoy's sales department. He also engaged Rufus Scales, a former football coach, as sales manager. When Scales died of a heart attack, Whit Pettigrew succeeded him.

Fortunately, Jenkins was able to persuade Edward M. Muldoon to become LaChoy's sales manager. "Jenkins wanted somebody who knew the supermarket business inside and out," Swaney said. "He knew all about Ed's experiences as general manager of National Grocery Co. in Seattle and at A&P." At Jenkins's death in 1953, Muldoon became general manager.

Under Muldoon's direction, LaChoy began a number of changes that were to secure its future. His primary priority was people; one of his first moves was to retain William P. McCarthy as sales manager. Muldoon insisted on hiring men and women who knew the food industry and were willing to work hard. For example, it was—and still is—customary for many persons attending conventions to circulate and renew acquaintanships in the lobbies or reception areas of the convention hotels. Not Muldoon. He customarily was found right alongside the elevator starter in the lobby and would spend hours meeting his customers and chatting with them. He loved the personal contact and meeting with buyers and brokers in search of business.

Muldoon moved up to become the first general manager of the Grocery Division in 1957 and was succeeded by Swaney, who later became a Beatrice vice president and assistant manager of the Grocery Division. Swaney was followed by John "J. J." McRobbie, first as LaChoy general manager, then as a Beatrice executive.

"It was a whole new ball game under Ed Muldoon," Swaney said. "He wanted to expand our sales department. I had sales managers for the eastern, western and southern territories and was looking for an assistant for the southern district. One of our brokers recommended J. J. who had extensive experience as a buyer/merchandiser for a large food chain. J. J. was in my office for six or seven hours. He never sat down once, and I was worried that he'd wear out the carpet in front of my desk. The next morning he called and declined the job. Then, he called back and said he had changed his mind.

"While Chun King was one of our major competitors nationally, we had quite a bit of competition from local producers such as Chinese Maid in St. Louis and China Beauty in Chicago," Swaney said. "When LaChoy was able to get tin cans, our goal was to expand principally in the East. Jan-U–Wine and Chun King had easy pickings on the West Coast.

Nobody was selling much in the South. We used to have to give our brokers there 10 percent instead of 5 there. J. J. did a fine job there."

In 1969, eight years after he joined LaChoy, McRobbie was named manager of LaChoy. Subsequently, he was assigned additional responsibilities as a group manager and special consultant until in 1983 James Dutt appointed him as a senior corporate vice president and a director of all corporate marketing for Beatrice.

Others who honed their marketing skills at LaChoy were "Chili Bill" McCarthy, who became general manager of Gebhardt Mexican Foods, and B. Robert Kill, who eventually headed the Confectionery Division. Lyle Van Doozer advanced from LaChoy to become general manager of Beatrice Frosted Foods in New York and then Gebhardt. The LaChoy management included longtime employees such as Eugene K. Schnitkey, director of sales and marketing for canned products; Richard R. Bettison, who held the same post for frozen foods; Dale Pape, the operations manager; and Herbert A. Lantz, the comptroller. All have left LaChoy.

By the end of World War II, LaChoy was out of the vegetable juice business. "There was a sudden drop in the price of canned citrus juices in 1947, and people bought them instead of vegetable juices," Swaney recalled. "We were stuck with 250,000 cases of forty-six-ounce cans of Vegemato. Three years later we sold the whole lot to Ballard and Ballard in Louisville, Kentucky. Leo Berger, the sales manager for Meadow Gold, arranged the deal. We discontinued Vegemato in 1951 and sold it to Naas Brothers, Fort Wayne, Indiana. They sold it to College Inn and eventually, it ended up with Chun King, our major competitor."

"Ed Muldoon was a great general manager," noted McRobbie. "One of the first things he did was to change the size of the cans from No. 2 [nineteen ounce] to No. 303 [sixteen ounce]. It allowed for higher line speeds, among other things. That was the start of converting the company into a more marketing oriented organization. He introduced many other marketing improvements, and it showed at the bottom line. He hired food people who knew the industry and worked hard."

"French Jenkins was marketing oriented in his way," Swaney said. "But Muldoon brought the supermarket dimension to LaChoy. He knew the inner workings for marketing specialty food products and the best appeals to use with supermarket and wholesale buyers."

Employees, of course, were the first priority; in 1988, LaChoy employed five hundred people at the plant. "Sometimes LaChoy had trouble finding capable people because of the small town in which it was based," McRobbie recalled. "It took quite a selling job to get qualified persons, but when we did find the right ones, they stayed and were happy with what was happening. We tried to create a family environment and included the spouses in many activities as part of the company. We always kept people on the inside posted on what was happening. People want to know how we're doing and what's happening; what's making things tick and how do we stand compared to our competition. Naturally, they were interested in building LaChoy and their job security."

"We had a great tradition," Swaney said. "The annual LaChoy picnic, the Christmas party brought people together. Then, we became unionized in 1965. The meatcutter's union was strong in Archbold because the Lugbill Packing Company was there. The union appealed to the pocketbooks of the older workers with promises of high pension rights. It turned out to our benefit. It sharpened up our management techniques. We put in a short-interval scheduling system shortly after that, which did more to help control our costs than anything we had done until then. We had to examine all our standards of production and set up checks on these. If we were not meeting these standards, the system blew the whistle, and management came charging out to see what was wrong. It also assured proper crewing. After it was installed," Swaney commented, "we wondered how we ever had gotten along without it."

In the late 1970s, LaChoy began operating from a management by objective (MBO) process (as did Eckrich and many other Beatrice companies). The general manager was given objectives that he, and the corporate officers, helped set. In turn, he passed these down to those working directly for him, and they gave it to those below them. "What we tried to do," McRobbie continued, "was use the MBO process to achieve specific objectives for the company and not have our people going off the deep end and accomplishing things that had nothing to do with what the total goals were. Joe Staudt in industrial relations, trained and educated all personnel. He was the counselor for the company. To this end, we held monthly meetings with the direct staff and all key administrative people, about fifteen in all. This was consistent with Beatrice's belief in small administrative and operating staffs. The MBO system helped us accomplish several things," McRobbie said. "It gave us the direct efforts of personnel below the general manager in areas where the company could improve its performance. It also gave employees ways to improve their own performances in their realms of responsibilities. It improved communications from top to bottom. And it gave accountability and rewards for accomplishing certain objectives. We set objectives and performances that could be measured. Dale D. McConkey, a University of Wisconsin professor, was a great help in getting us started."

Muldoon didn't initiate the broker program for LaChoy, but he and his successors accelerated it over the years. The first broker, L. T. Acosta and Company, Jacksonville, New York, was signed by Smith and New in

1926. McDermott Food Brokers of Albany, New York, joined LaChoy in 1931. Muldoon had devout faith in brokers and expanded the broker network to include other profit centers such as Gebhardt, Rosarita, the candy companies, Beatrice Frozen Specialties, Beatrice Frosted Foods, Mario's olives, and the pickle and preserve firms. At one time, more than 1,400 food and confectionery brokers were retained by the Grocery Division. "We believe in brokers," Muldoon declared in an article he wrote for *Food Business* in 1961. "Anyone familiar with the Grocery Products Division of Beatrice Foods knows that the success of our products is heavily dependent on the caliber, growth and success of brokers. Our belief is built on proven sales results. For example, the House of LaChoy has been built by the efforts of our outstanding broker sales team. When you work through brokers, your sales costs are known. You have a known sales force. Any business doing less than $100 million might find it advantageous to work through broker representation. Brokers, with your aid, can provide a 'customerized' service suited to the needs of the buyers and the consumers. By using a broker organization, you multiply your sales force. For example, in a community your sales volume might justify only one and one-half men per day selling your products. In the same area, the broker will have the equivalent of twenty to sixty-five men, all of whom know the area intimately."

Brokers also were extremely valuable as a source of information about their changing needs, as well as opportunities in the markets for consumers. LaChoy formed an advisory panel of five brokers on a rotating basis; each year two of the five would be replaced by two others. "We were one of the first companies to develop this kind of a communications program with top brokers," Swaney noted. "We'd meet at the Otsego Golf Course in Northern Michigan. No telephones, no distractions. The brokers loved it and we really accomplished a great deal. It gave the brokers the chance to know us better and, in turn, we had the opportunity to find out from them what our problems were," McRobbie said. "This saved us many hundreds of thousands of dollars. Waste was a serious problem. Point-of-purchase materials would sit in the brokers' back rooms because the guys who ordered them had no idea what they were going to do with them. They also helped our inside sales force plan their sales trips to reduce waste of time. Further, they were able to advise us which contests and other incentives did not really motivate them."

Members of the LaChoy sales force held quarterly and annual reviews with all of its brokers regarding their sales quotas and what they were doing to try to achieve them. "In essence, they were an extension of our sales team," McRobbie said. "We didn't look for them to do the job while we sat back. We looked for ways in which they could help us accomplish our goals together."

LaChoy, and later other Beatrice companies, maintained a policy of avoiding changes in brokers if at all possible. Over a period of eighteen years, LaChoy changed only twelve brokers. Thus, the brokers obtained in-depth knowledge of the company, its people, and its plans. LaChoy constantly provided them with ideas and materials to help their customers' sales: Chinese food sections, suggestions for better shelf placing and facings, and point-of-purchase materials such as over-the-wire hangers, pole displays, Chinese lanterns, chopsticks, cutouts, "shelf-talkers" (signs that hang from shelves), tested premiums, tie-in sales, refunds, and special promotions. Other subjects discussed at broker meetings were co-op moneys, whereby retailers and manufacturers would share advertising costs, and contracts, competition, product quality, new items, sales trends, and Nielsen ratings.

LaChoy strongly supported the National Food Brokers Association (NFBA) and sponsored a breakfast at the annual meetings, which were attended by more than 250 brokers and food company sales and marketing executives. The annual convention afforded LaChoy and other companies opportunities to confer with their respective brokers on a one-on-one basis. "We discontinued individual meetings there after 1975 when we started to see our brokers only by exception," McRobbie said. "We didn't need to see those with whom we had no problems. We didn't want to waste their time and ours." In 1983, at the NFBA meeting in New Orleans, LaChoy held a broker appreciation night to honor fifty-four brokers who had been with the company for ten years or more as "Partners in Progress"; twenty-two of them had brokered LaChoy products for thirty-five years or more.

LaChoy was also quite active with the Grocery Manufacturers Association (GMA) particularly from the end of World War II to the late sixties. "Jenkins was a close friend of Paul Willis, former sales manager for Uncle Ben's Rice, who headed the GMA for many years. He always saw to it that LaChoy recieved special attention at GMA meetings," Swaney recalled. "LaChoy was active on the committee that wrote up recommendations that generally were followed by food brokers in their relationships with their principals. We were one of the most desirable accounts for brokers because our products were profitable. Of course, the big food companies such as Lever Brothers, Heinz, General Foods didn't use brokers. They had their own salesmen. So you didn't have to be a giant to be important to food brokers." With its extensive broker network, LaChoy did not need a large internal sales team. In all, there were twelve sales people, and offices were established in Atlanta, New York City, Dallas, and Los Angeles, with the Midwest served out of Archbold.

Every effort was pointed toward satisfying two links in the marketing chain—customers (the food stores) and consumers. "We had to be marketing-oriented because everything had to stem from marketing. We had to focus on what the consumer wanted and what he or she would do with our products. We had to look constantly for ways to serve the consumer better," McRobbie explained.

For example, LaChoy continually upgraded its products and packaging; added more meat, poultry, seafoods, and Oriental vegetables to its dinners and specialties; introduced new sizes; and developed new processes. "We upgraded one product five times over just a few years," McRobbie related. "As we got bigger and the unit costs went down, we kept adding more good things to our products. Too many companies go out of business because they don't know what their costs are. Until you know your costs, you certainly don't know how to sell it. We were always trying to give the consumer fair value."

Customers, of course, were the focus of the marketing campaign. "The company philosophy was that the customer always comes first," McRobbie asserted. "After all, we are there to serve our customers. They're the ones that are buying our products and doing the selling for us. There were a lot of times we could have taken shortcuts in many things such as deliveries. We didn't do that because the customer would have suffered. We often paid a little more, but we got the product to the customer quickly. We did not ask for things such as a two-week advance notice on orders. I think it paid off. The customers were loyal to the LaChoy brand."

The search for better quality was also a continuing endeavor for LaChoy, and it introduced many innovations to improve its products. Its growth, all from the simple bean sprout, continues to provide LaChoy with a marketing edge over its competitors. "Nobody can grow sprouts better than LaChoy," Swaney explained. "Lots of people are growing bean sprouts, but LaChoy is the best at it." LaChoy operates the world's largest hydroponic garden for growing the sprouts, and the process is a carefully guarded secret. In a long gallery in a remote corner of the plant are rows of bins, five feet wide, five feet deep, and seventy feet long. Here the mung beans lie for six days under varying pressures of water sprays and temperatures until they sprout. The daily harvest is sixty tons, totaling fifteen thousand tons a year. To assure an adequate supply, LaChoy subsidized domestic programs for growing mung beans, 75 to 80 percent of which come from Texas and Oklahoma.

Visitors roaming through the myriad of operations at LaChoy are surrounded by scores of carts, bins, conveyors, cookers, and packing equipment involved in cleaning, washing, chopping, mixing, and packaging the wide variety of products now marketed by LaChoy. Ingredients come from all over the world. For example, the company uses almost ten million pounds a year of celery from the beds in southern Michigan and Florida and a million pounds of mushrooms grown in mines in Butler, Pennsylvania. Other ingredients abound: chicken from Georgia; onions from Colorado and California; diced beef from the Midwest and Argentina; bamboo shoots and water chestnuts from Thailand, Taiwan, and Korea; peppers from New Jersey; and pineapple from Hawaii. Elsewhere are ingredients and ovens needed for preparing chow mein noodles and the vats and bottles for soy sauce.

It is appropriate to pause here to point out that chop suey, the most widely known Chinese food in the United States, did not originate in China. It's doubtful that it can be found there to this day. The legend, aprocryphal perhaps, is that it was created during the Gold Rush in California in the 1850s. One story of its origin is that tough, hungry American miners virtually commandeered a Chinese restaurant in San Francisco late one night. Although the proprietor was ready to close, he decided discretion was the better part of valor and improvised a dinner using stir-fried food scraps. Word of this new delicacy quickly spread, and other restaurants began to serve it. To explain what may be known to many, chop suey which translates into "miscellany" in one Chinese dialect, is served over rice; chow mein over noodles.

Any dissimilarities between real Chinese foods and LaChoy's products are entirely intentional. LaChoy pioneered the introduction of American-Chinese foods, not only by providing the basic ingredients such as soy sauce, water chestnuts, bean sprouts, bamboo shoots, and chow mein noodles the homemaker could use to prepare American-Chinese food, but also by providing "heat and eat" entrees, hors d'oeurves, and soups. It also developed a recipe book, *The Arts and Secrets of Chinese Cookery.*

To emphasize the nationality of its products, one of LaChoy's major advertising slogans was "LaChoy makes Chinese foods swing American." "One problem LaChoy had back in the forties was that its products were too authentic," McRobbie recalled. "So, in the fifties and sixties, LaChoy added more spice and zip to them. If LaChoy made food taste as bland as some real Chinese foods, Americans wouldn't buy them." In short, LaChoy products are as genuinely American as, well, chop suey.

The ingenuity of the LaChoy production team was tested time and again in the search for quality. In addition to its unique process for growing bean sprouts, the company developed equipment to clean and sanitize the sprouts, peel onions, clean and dice celery, wrap and cut egg rolls, and fill cans, bottles, and packages.

Its engineering staff, headed by Ed Neel, designed a tunnel fryer for chow mein noodles, which are a blend of soft and hard wheats, vegetable shortening, salt, water, and yeast. LaChoy added a secret step that produces the desired taste, texture, and aroma for its noodles, which are fried for two minutes at the rate of three thousand pounds per hour.

A major break-through for LaChoy came in 1965. Two years earlier, Pape's quality control crew began testing a new ingredient-way that slashed heat-process time in canning foods that contained sauce or gravy. This process enabled LaChoy to cut its cooking time from sixty minutes to eleven minutes for chow mein products. The benefits included superior product quality, greater process flexibility, easier initial preparation, shorter blanching time for vegetables, and reduced fuel and labor costs.

As woks became popular, most Americans became aware that the Chinese quick-cook vegetables to retain crispness and flavor. Such a system permitted LaChoy to switch to agitating continuous cookers for induced convection heating. Thus, all vegetables, especially the heat-sensitive bean sprouts, remain firm and crisp, and the LaChoy chow meins had the flavor, color, and texture of freshly homemade products. "It was upmanship for LaChoy in the market, and we had a year's exclusivity on this," McRobbie noted. "To this day [more than twenty years later], no other Chinese food company uses this process simply because none of them seem to know how to control it. Since the introduction of this process, other companies have discontinued the one-pound size product with starch because they can't compete with LaChoy's quality."

A steady procession of new and improved products came from LaChoy's research laboratory and test kitchen from the 1950s onward. The company also has two laboratories supervised by the U.S. Department of Agriculture to ensure superior quality and sanitation standards. "We always tried to introduce one or two products that made some sense every year," McRobbie explained. "A company must grow with new products. But at the same time, it must review what it currently has in order to eliminate those that are not doing well. Too many companies drag on with items that are doing poorly in the hope of squeezing the last dollar out of them. All they're doing is taking up space in the buyer's warehouses."

It is a testimonial to LaChoy's creativity that 25 percent of the items it marketed were not made by its major competitors. Among the most successful new products were almond, chicken, and shrimp chow mein dinners, which came to America's tables in 1962 along with yatka mein, a Chinese noodle dinner, and Mandarin sauce. In 1963, LaChoy introduced chicken, beef, and shrimp bi-packs, two-can packages with the vegetables in one and the meat, poultry, or seafood in the other. The cans' contents are heated separately then mixed, thus assuring greater freshness.

As Swaney noted, "They did not cut into our sales of other products, and our profits went up."

Other products included pepper oriental in bi-packs and skillet packs, beef chow mein dinner, fried rice and shrimp, canned sweet and sour pork, won ton soup and later frozen won ton soup, egg rolls, Oriental vegetable sauce mix, canned, sliced, and whole water chestnuts, brown gravy sauce, and fortune cookies. A special formula for quality soy sauce was concocted for LaChoy by Beatrice's Special Products Division in Beloit.

LaChoy was a late entry in the frozen Chinese food market because of a false start in the late forties. "Actually, we got into frozen foods at the instigation of the Beatrice frozen food department in Chicago," recalled Swaney. "The first item was a frozen meatless chow mein packed in a can like those used for frozen strawberries. It was hard to open. In those days, the frozen food cabinets in stores were so small that our packages were covered up by similar packages of frozen strawberries and orange juice. We tried new labels and introduced a chow mein with meat. We bombed out in the frozen line, and Karnes remembered this and advised LaChoy to stick with cans whenever we requested permission to produce frozen products. Finally, he agreed under the condition that we acquire Temple Frosted Foods in New York City and get some experience. This we did, and we then were able to sell the Beatrice board of directors on making an extensive investment in a frozen facility in Archbold in 1970." By the late 1980s, LaChoy offered thirty frozen products, including bite-size and dinner-size egg rolls filled with shrimp, lobster, chicken, or a meat and shrimp combination; shrimp and chow mein entrees and dinners; beef pepper Oriental entrees and dinners; fancy Chinese-style vegetables and pea pods; frozen soups; and the "Fresh & Lite" frozen line.

Then, in a radical departure from a sixty-five-year tradition, LaChoy began developing a new frozen line, Rolls International, for the food service business: Mexican and pizza-flavored egg rolls in three-ounce dinner sizes in four flavors: burrito, taco, sausage and cheese, and pepperoni and cheese.

When LaChoy ventured into the freezer cases of food stores, Chun King had 75 percent of that market in frozen Oriental foods. By 1987, each had about 25 percent, with Green Giant, Stouffer's, and several other companies dividing the rest. "It took a lot of time and money to roll out our frozen line," McRobbie related. "We didn't try to go national all at once. We tried to grow market by market. I think many manufacturers try to expand too quickly. They don't have the funds to support what they're trying to do and, as a result, everything dies."

LaChoy's task force constantly studied the consumer market to determine trends in tastes and desires. It retained Yankelovich for brand awareness and corporate image benchmark reviews and McKinsey for consumer and product profiles. It used marketing data from Nielsen and the Sales and Marketing Institute. Its employees also attended marketing management seminars conducted by Philip Kotler at Northwestern University, which detailed strategies for companies with high shares of market such as LaChoy and low-share ones such as Beatrice Frosted Foods, Gebhardt, and Rosarita. "The operational-type companies—and we had several in Beatrice—focus on what they make and want to sell, *not* what the consumer wants to buy," McRobbie noted. "Their whole thinking is backward and somehow they never get on target. What we did was look at where our niches were in the food world and where they had a place in the supermarkets and on the pantry and freezer shelves. It is essential to focus long-term on where a company or brand is going to go. We used a lot of Kotler's do's and don't's strategies to try to keep LaChoy growing."

Studies showed that Oriental food is a category that easily lends itself to contemporary life-styles. It is perceived as nutritional, good-tasting, convenient, and a pleasant eating experience. In the mid-seventies, LaChoy began down-sizing many of its products in recognition of a trend toward rising consumer concerns about health, fitness, and nutrition. It also began eliminating monosodium glutamate from all products. Along with the twenty-six-ounce family sizes, both LaChoy and its competitors began marketing products in containers that ranged from twelve to six ounces. "People don't need big quantities," McRobbie pointed out. "Better quality is in demand, food that tastes good. People will pay more for value than they did ten years ago. Those old three-for-a-dollar TV dinners no longer are on the shelves. Instead of belly-fillers, people want foods that are low in sodium and made from natural products."

"Convenience is in demand," he stressed. "Over 50 percent of the households in the U.S. are composed of two people, and they want convenience. Convenience is what every major food company is looking at today, as Beatrice began doing in the early 1950s in dairy. Such innovations as microwave cooking have dramatically changed their approach. That will be a $1 billion business soon."

McRobbie cites three markets with great growth potential in the future—convenience stores, vending, and fast-food outlets—and concedes that LaChoy almost missed out on all three. "Convenience stores such as the 7–11s and White Hens have become major outlets for food manufacturers," he said. "Some companies have done fabulous jobs with convenience stores, a high-flying segment today. What we did wrong was not to put a specialized person on this market. We did not focus full attention on these stores. We do some business, but not enough as yet."

LaChoy also was a late entry in the food service business, which accounts for more than 40 percent of the total dollars spent by consumers on food. "Other companies such as Kraft, H. J. Heinz, and Nabisco did a fine job," McRobbie said. "To us, it was a sideline. We tried to do something with a salesman who handled that along with other segments. He did not know the ropes. It's a specialized field, and I think it's a big sleeper for those who do not specialize in it."

Ultimately, LaChoy made its move in 1980. It was one of the first companies to install an orbitort that cooks No. 10 (institutional size) cans of a product. It also packed for other companies. By 1979, LaChoy was competitive in food service products. One of its first customers was the independently owned Charlie Chan restaurant chain in Ohio, for which LaChoy supplied three-ounce egg rolls and fried rice and plum sauce. It provided more than one million egg rolls to the chain that year. LaChoy did not regard the military market and export as major areas for growth because the military commissary market is relatively flat. The military market was considered as necessary but not one requiring great emphasis.

LaChoy began exporting to other countries in the 1950s and ships products to fifty other countries. "Export became a problem when the dollar was so high," McRobbie explained. "When it came down, it offered a bit more opportunity. You have to have a full program and regard export as a long-term goal. I think we exported to too many countries. In each case, you have to label the product in that country's language and there's no real margin on small orders."

LaChoy's pricing policies also gave it a competitive edge. Prices were increased only when necessary to recover the increased costs of ingredients and labor when productivity improvements could not offset the higher costs. "I remember at least three occasions when our chief competitor upped his prices in an effort to get us to go up," McRobbie said. "When I reviewed this with our cost clerk, he said, 'You don't need an increase, you're doing fine. The materials are there and our productivity is fine.' We did not move, and our competitor had to back down. We really took a leadership role in pricing in our particular category. That's something few companies obtain. Campbell has it with its soup line."

Advertising and public relations played increasingly important roles in LaChoy's marketing program. In 1952, the advertising budget was modest; it included a few radio spots supplemented by small-space newspaper advertisements and full-color ads in September in seven magazines for women. In the early sixties, the budget rose to $80,000, which wasn't enough to keep the sales team, including brokers, happy. The total was elevated in proportion to sales growth and rose to the $400,000 level in the seventies. "In later years, LaChoy was spending well over $4 million a year, and things started to happen," McRobbie said. "We started using spot TV, then went to national TV as a blanket over everything. We were a sponsor on the 'Today' and 'Tonight' shows and prime-time newscasts. Before we had the big budgets, we used radio, newspapers and magazines, particularly *Woman's Day* and *Family Circle*."

LaChoy engaged a succession of agencies, beginning with Foote, Cone and Belding in the fifties. Then, it switched to the Lou Maxon agency in Detroit, and James MacPherson, who was to be involved in many LaChoy campaigns as account executive for several subsequent agencies, entered the picture. LaChoy next hired Campbell-Mithun of Minneapolis after Maxon's death. Later, Geyer's New York office handled the account and developed the "LaChoy makes Chinese food swing American" theme. The next change was to Post, Keyes and Gardner in Chicago, where MacPherson hired the talented Alan Bloomfield to work on the LaChoy account. "One of the main ad themes was that the best chop suey was made at home," Swaney remarked. "We put receipes on our labels. Ours were the best ingredients."

McRobbie was not particularly enamored of coupons. "We used them when there was a need such as a new product introduction, market penetration, or when there was a problem in a specific market," McRobbie allowed. "I think you have to be careful how you use them because of the large redemptions you may have. They might run one and one-half percent of circulation, and that is a lot of money. Sometimes you have those coupons coming in for months, and you don't account for that. Agencies love them because they do not know what else to put into an ad. I think we need to use better creativity in advertising, not just use coupons as something to put in there. And, of course, a lot of agencies like to go for major media, particularly network TV." LaChoy's policy was to straddle the advertising debate. As McRobbie explained, "Customers want the heavy deals which give them the big bucks, but you've also got to advertise to the consumer to get her to buy your products. We just tried to run in the middle of the road."

Swaney was not enthusiastic about coupons, either. During his managerial reign at LaChoy, the company tried to introduce a system that guaranteed that the coupon would be redeemed only for a LaChoy product. "We were never sure that our coupons were being honestly redeemed," he related. "The store might take a LaChoy coupon and give the customer at the check-out counter 10 cents off on a can of coffee."

One major advertising campaign featured "Delbert," the friendly, fire-snorting LaChoy dragon, to introduce the new system for processing

LaChoy products. The introduction was made at the annual LaChoy breakfast at the NFBA convention in New York City in 1965. The star of the event was Delbert's creator, Jim Henson, who later created the Muppets, attired in a Delbert the Dragon costume and wearing a LaChoy chef's hat. Television commercials showed Delbert roaming the aisles of super-markets, knocking cans from shelves with his tail and advising customers that LaChoy chow mein was "Quick-cooked in dragon fire . . . crisp and good as the take-out kind." LaChoy placed thousand-line ads—complete with coupons—in newspapers in leading markets, starting in January 1966, for dragon-fire-cooked dinners for two. Sales jumped, but there was one surprising response. The Georgia Department of Agriculture complained that advertising the chow mein as cooked in dragon fire was "very misleading to the consumer."

In 1956, Beatrice retained the Selz Organization (later Selz, Seabolt and Associates) in Chicago as its first public relations agency at an annual fee of $36,000. The principal assignment was to assist in promot-ing the company to the financial community, but the agency also was responsible for product publicity, including newspaper clipsheets containing food hints and recipes, radio spots in the same vein, new product releases, and announcements of awards.

In the product publicity area, all the agency had to promote were dairy products, Clark candies, and LaChoy. In effect, LaChoy now had a public relations agency. In 1956, the New York Central made a special stop at Archbold to let the Selz account team—Rosemary Fox, the home economist, Larry Crail, assistant account executive, and myself, the account executive—off in what appeared to be the middle of nowhere. The next day, plans were initiated to put LaChoy on the consumer map. One of the most popular TV shows at the time was "What's My Line?" with John Daly as moderator and Arlene Francis, Bennett Cerf, Dorothy Kilgallen, and Martin Gabel as panelists. The show's objective was to determine the business or profession of the guest through a series of questions. LaChoy was invited, and Muldoon, Thomas McDonough, and McCarthy went to New York to appear on the show as three Irishmen who made Chinese food. The panel didn't come any closer than that their line involved corned beef and cabbage. Subsequently, the agency set up arrangements for LaChoy to participate on a number of game shows as a contributor rather than as a sponsor through the Ed Finch agency in New York City.

Another program that thrust LaChoy into prominence through Mul-doon's efforts came in September of 1958, when the company completed a major addition to its facilities. Food editors from around the country were invited, the majority from the Midwest and as far south as St. Louis;

Governor C. William O'Neill of Ohio proclaimed Archbold as "Chinatown, U.S.A." for the day; and the signs for the city were changed accordingly. More than a score of editors as well as the Beatrice directors were welcomed by Karnes and Muldoon, toured the plant, and then lunched on LaChoy specialties. The event led to a series of articles on LaChoy in leading publications.

"Gung Hoy Fet Toy," "Happy New Year" in one Chinese dialect, was a holiday that LaChoy and Selz developed into a national marketing event that continued after the KKR takeover in 1986.

Of all the Chinese holidays, the New Year's festival is the most important and the merriest. The traditional Chinese have no Sabbath day, and the New Year, which arrives with the first day of the First Moon (usually in early February) constitutes all of the Sabbaths rolled into one. It is also everybody's birthday because every Chinese is considered one year older on New Year's Day, regardless of the date on which he or she was born. Homes are thoroughly cleaned and decorated with the five lucky signs of happiness. The lanterns are made ready, and a feast is prepared. All debts must be settled, and gifts are given to the children.

The New Year celebrations continue until the fifteenth day of the full moon and conclude with an event called the Feast of Lanterns. A feature of this festival is a parade headed by a huge dragon borne by men and boys. The fearsome dragon, often a hundred feet long, is the Chinese symbol of strength and goodness. Both events became public relations holidays for LaChoy. New Year's cards were sent out in advance of the day to all brokers and customers. Special promotions were developed, including newspaper advertisements in major markets, particularly those with ethnic Chinatowns such as New York, Chicago, San Francisco, and Los Angeles, as well as Detroit and Boston, heralding which sign in the twelve-year cycle of the Chinese zodiac was the animal for that specific year. Feature articles were also prepared relating the ancient lore surrounding each animal. An arsenal of point-of-purchase materials was distributed, including signs, hangers, bins, chopsticks, lanterns, and hats. LaChoy hosted dinners and dances in conjunction with its brokers around the country, and Chinese beauty queens were elected and led the parades in various cities. The program grew in size and popularity year by year, and a similar program was developed for the fall, the Harvest Moon Festival. Later, Selz developed similar ethnic programs celebrating Mexico's Cinco de Mayo for Gebhardt and Rosarita.

Jeno Palucci, the father of Chun King, countered LaChoy's promotional efforts by sponsoring an hour-long TV special in Sunday night prime time to celebrate the Chinese New Year. The program was written and hosted by Stan Freeberg, whom Beatrice had engaged previously to prepare and record radio spots for Meadow Gold ice cream. Subsequently, Palucci sold Chun King to R. J. Reynolds for $63 million and used the proceeds to start another company, Jeno's Pizza. In December of 1985, he sold that to Pillsbury for $147 million in cash and assumed debt, but he remains in the food business in Minnesota and Florida.

As Beatrice grew, it became impossible for Selz/Seabolt to serve more than three hundred profit centers individually in the United States. In 1967, the company hired Selz/Seabolt's account supervisor to establish its first internal public relations department. LaChoy was set up as a special Selz/Seabolt account under the direction of Leo Floros for a separate annual fee.

The ultimate evaluation of any profit center obviously is the bottom line. LaChoy was one of the brightest stars in the Beatrice food universe. From 1965 through 1980, sales and earnings doubled every five years. To keep pace with demand and maintain quality and value, LaChoy expanded and updated its facilities fourteen times since 1958. "LaChoy financed all of its internal growth and, in addition, threw out cash for the mother company that helped other corporate entities and helped pay dividends to the Beatrice shareholders," McRobbie stated with justifiable pride. "LaChoy paid for all of the capital it needed to grow and still ended up well in the black. There never was any money invested in LaChoy other than from its internal profit structure. That was a lot. It took a tremendous amount of updating in equipment to keep up with the innovations and improvements to maintain our growth of sales." One important update was the computerization of LaChoy's entire operation. "We were not trying to build a big computerized company," McRobbie explained. "I think you can get lost in that. What we were trying to do was get all of our systems in place to enable us to obtain information we needed quickly and accurately." "We started the IBM operation when I was general manager," Swaney added. "We had the old punch card system. We've come a long way since then."

Approximately 27 percent of LaChoy earnings were turned over to Beatrice in cash as the return on investment soared to more than 50 percent in the eighties. McRobbie summarized the key factors involved in LaChoy's success: (1) planned sales growth; (2) annual increase in earnings for Beatrice; (3) strict cash management; (4) tight controls on inventories and receivables; (5) quality, well-trained people; and (6) administrative cost controls.

The LaChoy operation was a model of Beatrice's "hands-off-hands-on" management style that rewarded winners: hands-off at the top, hands-on at the plant manager and group manager levels.

At its peak in the early 1980s, LaChoy had eighty-two retail brokers, several of whom also handled food service and frozen. It also had twenty handling food service and fifteen marketing frozen. After James Dutt began centralizing marketing following the acquisition of Esmark, almost all of the brokers were eliminated except for a few for frozen. Marketing was assigned to the five-hundred-person retail sales staff of Hunt-Wesson in Fullerton, California. Chinatown, U.S.A. now is the site of only a production facility supervised by Larry Holland, a seventeen-year veteran with LaChoy. "It was a great company, still is," declares McRobbie. "I'm proud of what all of us did there."

CHAPTER SEVEN

Worldwide Expansion, the Beatrice Way

Joe and Juan Metzger of Dannon yogurt were instrumental in persuading Beatrice to venture into the international market. Immediately after they joined Dannon to Beatrice in 1959, the Metzgers began urging the Beatrice operating committee to explore opportunities in Western Europe. "You're too provincial," Joe Metzger admonished Karnes.

A number of major American food companies had entered the European market in the late 1950s, among them Kraft, Borden, General Foods, and Campbell Soup. In many instances, they built American-type plants, introduced American products and packaging, and sent Americans across the Atlantic to operate the businesses. Acceptance by European consumers was underwhelming at first because of continental differences in tastes, packaging, and marketing.

A few Beatrice companies such as LaChoy and Rosarita Mexican Foods exported to Canada, Europe, and Africa, but Beatrice did not have a plant or company outside of the United States until February 7, 1961, when it opened a new facility in Petaling Jaya, a suburb of Kuala Lumpur, Malaysia, to produce canned, sweetened condensed milk.

Aaron Marcus, the general manager of the Meadow Gold plants in Hawaii, had urged Beatrice to expand on the other side of the world, specifically Asia. His plants had been shipping ice cream and other dairy products to Guam and several other islands in the Pacific with U.S. military installations. He also was a friend of the owner of the renowned Raffles Hotel in Singapore who also headed an English-Malaysian importing company. The hotel owner advised Marcus that Malaysians were importing canned, sweetened condensed milk from Holland and Australia, but were seeking ways to have it manufactured locally.

Coincidentally, Dr. George W. Shadwick, the director of Beatrice's Quality Control Department, and Dr. Peter P. Noznick, the director of research, had developed a process for combining butter with skimmed milk powder, then reconstituting it with water into condensed milk in 1960. They perfected the product in the research laboratory in Chicago, designed the equipment to process it, and then brought a team of

Malaysians to Chicago to train them to operate it. All of the machinery was then shipped from Calumet Harbor in Chicago to Petaling Jaya and reassembled. This milk product, the first of its kind in the world, became extremely popular in Malaysia's coffee shops and as infant food. Based on the favorable response in Malaysia, a similar plant was built in Singapore, where an ice cream facility was opened in 1974.

Encouraged by the success of this joint partnership in Asia, William G. Karnes decided that Europe was beckoning. In April 1961, he, his wife, Virginia, and Juan Metzger went on a tour of Europe, starting in Zurich. Traveling by car, they visited fifteen plants in twenty-one days, calling on chocolate companies in Switzerland, candy companies in Germany, milk and ice cream companies in Belgium, and a spice company in Holland. Although the owners were willing to listen, a major obstacle was a distrust of Americans and American companies. None of the owners wanted to accept Beatrice stock in exchange for majority ownership of their companies. They wanted U.S. dollars and, in several cases, gold, with payment to be made in Switzerland.

Based on what Karnes learned in Europe, Beatrice developed a set of six guidelines for Beatrice's foreign expansion: (1) Acquire leading, profitable companies with exceptionally favorable growth potential and with excellent management willing to stay with the company and retain 10 to 15 percent of the ownership. (2) Confine expansion to fields in which Beatrice had experience and know-how. (3) Operate under a system of decentralized management similar to that which was successful for Beatrice in the United States. This system required a complete management team at each operation, in the field, where it could make day-to-day decisions necessary in adjusting to rapid changes in market conditions. (4) Ensure that management at each individual company consist of resident nationals of the country in which the plant operated. (5) Seek acquisitions in politically stable countries likely to grow at a faster rate economically than the United States. (6) Expand the facilities, product lines, and distribution of each company to facilitate its continued growth.

When Beatrice again approached the companies Karnes had originally contacted, their response to these operating philosophies was positive. However, Beatrice personnel still had to invest a great deal of time in courting the companies, convincing them of the merits of the Beatrice philosophy, and ensuring that there would be no misunderstandings after the acquisition was completed. The Metzgers were of immeasurable assistance. "Joe and Juan Metzger took us by the hand and led us around the world," Karnes noted. Paul T. Kessler, Jr., executive vice president, spent much of his time in Europe, and Executive Vice President John

Hazelton made a number of trips as well. In turn, Beatrice brought the owners of companies in which it was interested to the United States and took them on tours of Beatrice plants engaged in similar businesses. This was a process of getting acquainted and "selling" Beatrice to prospective partners as well as convincing Beatrice personnel that these were people with whom they could work.

Logically, the first major acquisition was a dairy company, Cie Lacsoons, which has its headquarters and main plant in Rotselaar, Belgium, and branch plants in Eeklo and Bierbeek, Belgium. Lacsoons was the largest processor and distributor of fresh milk products in the European Economic Community, and when it joined Beatrice in 1962, its sales were in excess of $18 million. Its extensive product line included fresh milk, buttermilk, yogurt, cream, evaporated milk, sterilized milk, and cheese. Lacsoons distributed through its own routes in the Brussels market and distributors throughout Belgium.

Through Lacsoons, Beatrice contacted Artic of Lot, Belgium, the largest ice cream company in the country. It was operated by Max Willick and his two sons. Following the purchase in 1967, Beatrice introduced many of its new ice cream products to Artic and showed the owners how to sell their products in supermarkets. Both companies prospered under the direction of their previous managements, although Lacsoons became the more profitable. These operations were augmented by the acquisition in 1967 of Dairyworld of Geneva, a worldwide trader of dairy products.

Beatrice entered another field of products allied to its U.S. operations by buying a major interest in A. J. ten Doesschate of Wapenveld, The Netherlands in 1969. Headed by Dolph Buisman, it imported spices from all over the world and marketed them in Holland, Germany, and the Middle East. In addition, it produced nonprescription drugs and drugstore items. It also proved to be a good moneymaker. Subsequently, Stute, a German processor of fruit juices and preserves, joined the company in 1983.

Then Beatrice acquired Gelati Sanson of Verona, Italy, which processed and distributed ice cream and frozen desserts. After it joined Beatrice in 1969, it built the largest, most modern ice cream plant in Italy. To emphasize Beatrice's interest in Sanson, Arthur T. Mussett, who then was the manager of Beatrice's International Dairy Operations headquartered in Brussels, invited the entire Sanson management team headed by Teofilo Sanson to a reception and dinner in Chicago to meet Beatrice executives.

Beatrice went on to acquire Premier Is, with two plants in Denmark in 1969; Marisa, with ice cream plants in Barcelona and on the islands of Mallorca and Menorca in 1967; and Interglas, with ice cream plants in Seville and Las Palmas on the Canary Islands in 1972. Through its Artic subsidiary, Beatrice expanded into Germany and France. These operations made it one of the leading ice cream companies in Europe, with a presence in nearly every major market.

Beatrice had also expanded domestically into the snack foods field, with companies such as Adam's Korn Kurls, Pepi's snacks, and Fisher nuts. Perhaps surprisingly, as its first international acquisition in snack foods, Beatrice chose an Irish company, Tayto, that manufactured potato chips, and bought 85 percent of the company in 1964 for $285,000. Karnes sent Joseph Rogatnick, his European "scout," to call on the owner, Joseph Murphy, whose life would amaze even Horatio Alger. He was a high school dropout with a passion for selling. Before founding Tayto in Dublin in 1954, he sold a variety of products, including lead soldiers, fagots, pens, eggs, tobacco, chocolate, tea, preserves, and even pianos.

One evening, Murphy stopped off at a pub outside of Dublin on his way home and purchased several bags of potato chips imported from England. When he complained that they were stale and soggy, the owner challenged him, "Murphy, you're always bloody complaining. Why don't you go out and make them yourself?"

Shortly thereafter, Murphy started Tayto by scrounging second-hand slicers, second-hand washcloths, second-hand everything including the bathtubs in which he washed the potatoes, and opened a tiny plant in Dublin. His total assets were less than 500 pounds. By 1964, Tayto's business had grown so that it was the leading manufacturer of potato chips in Ireland. Following a favorable report by Rogatnick, Murphy came to Chicago and met with Karnes. "Joe," Karnes told him, "our people tell me your equipment is shoddy and your plant is falling apart. Let's say our fellows went into your plant and beat up everything there with sledgehammers. It wouldn't affect our offer at all. The only things we're really buying from you are five letters, T.A.Y.T.O."

"There were a number of other reasons why we wanted to purchase a majority interest in Tayto," Karnes explained. "The most decisive one was Murphy. He was different. What impressed us the most was his awareness of the importance of sound marketing with emphasis on value and quality. He was a doer, a goer and a winner. He was convinced that with a new plant and additional working capital, the potential for Tayto was unlimited."

Tayto is yet another example of how the application of Beatrice's hands-off policy of decentralized management enabled a company to grow internally. Murphy promptly applied his sales skills to persuade the Republic of Ireland to give his company a grant and special tax incentives to build a new chip plant in Coolock, a suburb of Dublin. The grant represented 40 percent of the $1 million cost. The price of four acres of land was 12,000 pounds, land today worth 400,000 pounds. The plant has been expanded four times since it was opened in 1967.

With adequate financing and a free hand to exercise his marketing skills, Murphy built Tayto into the dominant snack food business in Ireland. He met challenges from competitors such as Perri's, King, and Smith's by stressing freshness and protective packaging, backed by extensive advertising and promotion programs. Ultimately, Perri's went out of business, and Tayto acquired King and Smith's. Murphy introduced new snacks such as peanuts, popcorn, and extruded items such as Korn Kurls. His major creation was a cheese and onion flavored chip that is produced by major snack food companies around the world. The plant was further automated in the 1980s and with new, sophisticated equipment became one of the most efficient snack plants in the Common Market. By 1984, Tayto had 70 percent of the snack food market in Ireland and operated four plants and fifteen distribution centers. Tayto consistently earned more than $1 million annually for Beatrice; its profits for 1987 exceeded $5 million. It also made Murphy a multimillionaire.

Beatrice also sought acquisitions in France. Despite high retail food prices, French food manufacturers and agricultural suppliers had surprisingly low margins. The return on investment for these companies was not up to Beatrice standards, yet money was being made somewhere in the food chain, so Beatrice began studying food distribution companies.

Kessler identified a food wholesaler in Paris, Etablissements Baud, which had been founded by three brothers after World War II. They began their business selling canned goods from a stall in the open market and eventually bought a truck to deliver goods to small shops. The Baud brothers plowed all their profits back into the business and soon had built a sizeable wholesale operation with margins five or six times greater than those common in the United States. After Beatrice acquired Baud in 1969, it built a giant distribution center in a suburb of Paris. Later, with the help of Jean Baud, who managed the business, a supermarket operation, Société Européene de Supermarchés (S.E.S.) in Strasbourg, Alsace-Lorraine, joined Beatrice. Related operations included Aux Planteurs Reunis of Lausanne, an institutional grocery wholesaler.

Beatrice's experience serving the institutional market in the United States through the John Sexton operations led to the acquisition of Nergico, an institutional food distributor in Dijon. Beatrice would also later acquire S. A. Choky, based in Lille, a specialty distributor serving cafes and restaurants throughout France, and Maxime Delrue, an importer and distributor of grocery items to supermarkets and wholesalers. Beatrice thus built a billion-dollar distribution operation in France, with a presence in every important sector of the business.

Following the pattern of other international acquisitions that were in businesses similar to those it operated in the United States, Beatrice purchased major interests in three bottling companies based on favorable results from its RC Cola operations: Winters in Marheeze, The Netherlands, Dwans in Thurles, County Tipperary, Republic of Ireland, and Sunco in Ninove, Belgium. Confectionery companies added included Smith-Kendon confectionery and the Callard and Bowser Group, both based in the United Kingdom and both of which have excellent reputations as marketers of fine English confections and export to nearly ninety countries. Finally, as a complement to its successful U.S. meat company, Eckrich, Beatrice acquired Boizet, a specialty sausage and ham manufacturer in Charlieu, France, and Conservera Campofrio, Spain's leading processed meat company, which was based in Burgos.

Through its policy of buying successful, profitable companies, Beatrice could invest one day and begin making money the next as the managements of these companies ran them with renewed vigor. In contrast, other American companies spent millions of dollars to take American products overseas. They then had to try to educate consumers in these countries to like the products and use them, a slow and costly process that frequently was not successful. Internal growth was another key. In every case, the companies built new plants or upgraded existing facilities and added new products. There were, however, a few failures, for example, O. K. Kaugummi, which manufactured chewing-gum products in a suburb of Hamburg, West Germany was sold after management problems developed. Another was Barzetti, a profitable bakery supply company based in Montova, just east of Milan. Fred Schomer, who had become a vice president of the International Division in 1975, and Tony Luiso, later vice president of International, made frequent visits to the plant to try to solve a series of problems including an unsuccessful effort to expand Barzetti from a regional company to a national one. Another problem was the problem of staffing the additional locations. Ultimately, Barzetti was sold back to the previous owners.

The peripatetic Juan Metzger also played a major role in Beatrice's expansion in South America. While on a trip to Caracas, he met with the owners of Industrias Savoy, which had been founded by three brothers, Rodolfo, Roberto, and Fernando Beer, and an American, John Miller, in 1941 to process and distribute chocolate products. Its plant in Caracas was one of the largest and most modern confectionery plants in South America. What set the company apart was a dominating distribution system and a powerful sales and marketing organization.

By the time Beatrice acquired Savoy in 1964, Savoy had purchased Marlon, a processor of snack foods in Caracas, and annual sales were about 26 million bolivares. A plan was evolved so that Savoy executives and employees were able to purchase shares in the company at a reduced price with favorable financing terms. Ten percent of the company became the property of four hundred employees, the president as well as workers on the factory floor. That program still continues.

Shortly after Beatrice purchased Savoy, the Beers retired, and Peter Bastiansen, a naturalized Venezuelan of Norwegian descent, advanced from sales and marketing director to president. The company then embarked on an ambitious acquisition program during the mid 1960s that enrolled other companies into the group: Industrias Anita of Bogata; Estado, Miranda, a manufacturer of snack foods in Caracas; Carmelos Royal of Caracas, a manufacturer of popular-price hard candies, chewing gum, and related items; Industrias Benco of Caracas, a lithograph and printing company that primarily served other companies in the group as well as outside accounts; Granos de Oriente of Caracas, established to build facilities in the heart of the cocoa bean and peanut growing area of Venezuela to do the initial processing of these products for Savoy companies; and Distribuidor Marsanita of Caracas, created as a distribution company when the growing number of individual products produced by the various companies became too large for the existing distribution systems.

The most important of these was Anita, founded by Winston and Irving Ginstling, who had battled Savoy for dominance of the growing snack market in Venezuela. Savoy chose to operate Anita as a separate subsidiary that continued to market its popular Jack's Snacks brand opposite Marlon's products. Not only did this dual brand approach result in a higher market growth rate, but it also precluded any competitors from gaining a foothold in the market.

In 1984, Savoy acquired Taoro of Caracas, a major processor of pound cakes and fruitcakes, Twinkies, and a broad line of cookies. By then, the Savoy group operated a fleet of more than a thousand trucks and had a sales force of more than a thousand. It served the Venezuelan population of eighteen million from the country's beaches and tropical forests to its high plains. It even operated delivery boats to reach the Indian tribes on the upper Orinoco River. With more than half of Venezuela's population under the age of twenty, the demographics were ideal for a confectionery and snacks company. Under the direction of Cornelio Hoogesteyn since 1978, the group continued to grow, and sales totaled 2 billion bolivares by 1986, seventy-five times the total for 1964. The Savoy name is at least as well known in Venezuela as Coca-Cola is in the United States.

Irving Ginstling, of Anita, was also involved with a snack company in

Bogota, Colombia, acquired by Beatrice in 1966. It and a confectionery company purchased shortly thereafter were combined into one company, Industrias Gran Colombia, the market leader in that country.

One year later, in 1967, Metzger found another good prospect— Productos Chipy, a company that had come out of nowhere to take a strong position in the snack market in Lima, Peru. With a letter of introduction, Metzger opened talks with owner Alberto Katz that quickly led to the acquisition. This company grew rapidly; in 1986, it had a volume increase of more than 70 percent.

Beatrice had been extremely successful in confectionery and snacks in Latin America and was able to make successful acquisitions in Guatamela with a company named Productos René, in Honduras with one named Booquitas Fiestas, and in the Dominican Republic with La Estrella. In a rare circumstance, start-up conditions were built successfully in Panama and Ecuador.

For a long time, Beatrice shunned Brazil and Argentina because of economic conditions. However, in the early seventies, it became involved in a bizarre adventure in the rain forests of Brazil. Karnes and Don L. Grantham learned of a process to extract vegetable oil from a nut that grew wild in the jungle and assigned Schomer, Peter Brown, and an engineer from Taylor Freezer to investigate.

"The man who had this idea was a Texan who had fled to Brazil to avoid extradition for financial dealings of some kind or another," Schomer related. "His concept was to establish a huge babassu nut operation in the wilds of Brazil and ship the oil down the Amazon River. The meat would be sold as cattle feed. The babassu nut, a second cousin to the coconut, yields an oil comparable to that of a coconut. The major problem was that it had such a tough shell it was hard to crack. This fellow's basic idea was to use a machine he had developed to crack the nuts which he would obtain by creating a huge plantation in the interior of Brazil. This would involve a $1 million investment by Beatrice. He told us he was planning to set up co-ops in the jungle where the Indians could bring in the nuts and trade them. The company would be based in Sao Paulo.

"We engaged one of the leading law firms in Sao Paulo to represent us and two of them went with us to Belém, the third largest city in Brazil, located at the mouth of the Amazon. Five of us, including the two lawyers, climbed into a tiny, single engine plane and set out for the interior. All we saw below was jungle and in the middle was the river which has piranha and another flesh-eating fish which is even larger and has two big fangs in its lower jaw that come up through holes in its upper jaw. It was a scary trip. As we were flying along, we saw a lot of small villages and towns. We asked the man who was trying to get us to invest in his scheme what these people were doing there. 'We thought you owned the land,' we said to him. 'Those are squatters,' he said airily."

"We finally landed at a little village," Schomer said. "The hotel there was a one-story building with a butcher shop in the front end. The rooms were the size of a walk-in closet with an old cot, a ramshackle chair, a piece of mirror nailed to the wall and flies.

"Then we were taken to see the machine designed to crack the nuts. It was like an old baseball pitching machine with motors sticking out of it everywhere. It would catapult the nuts against a steel plate, and then workers would gather up the pieces. Peter and I decided not to make the deal. It was too speculative."

Schomer's globe-trotting explorations also took him to South Africa, where Beatrice came close to acquiring interests in confectionery and a snack food company, and to Iran and Nigeria. "We decided against these deals because we considered the political climates too unstable," he explained.

Beatrice also looked at Russia. Or, more correctly, the Russians looked at Beatrice. Through the offices of Bettina Parker, a specialist in Russian business who was associated with the Burson-Marstellar public relations firm, a visit to the United States was arranged for a delegation from Russia's ministry of agriculture, headed by the ninth ranking member of the Communist party in 1976. The objective was to survey Beatrice dairy and meat operations to set up pilot plants in Russia. The Russian government was interested in increasing the efficiency of food production. The delegation toured Beatrice dairy plants and Eckrich operations in the Midwest, then was honored at a banquet in Chicago.

Later, a Beatrice delegation that included William W. Granger, Jr., and Chester Schmidt, along with William Harder of the Fred A. Niles organization, which produced a slide film of Beatrice's dairy and meat operations, went to Moscow. The Americans found the Russian operations to be relatively primitive, but nothing came of the trip. There were no rubles to be made there, and operating restrictions were too limiting.

Logically, the best way for Beatrice to broaden its base in Latin America was through extension of its core dairy and ice cream operations in the United States. However, opportunities were not promising in many countries because of government controls on milk pricing and production and inadequate refrigeration. The acquisition and subsequent development of Holanda of Clavijero, Mexico, typifies how Beatrice was able to apply its decentralized practices while working in cooperation with governments of other nations.

Holanda, the largest ice cream company in Mexico, joined Beatrice in

December 1968. Beatrice purchased 60 percent of the shares of the company from Borden, which had become disillusioned with its investment. The remaining 40 percent was held by the Campero family, with Alberto Campero continuing as general manager. Shortly after the acquisition, Holanda found its growth stymied by new government regulations. It was decreed that any Mexican company majority-owned by foreigners no longer could expand its operation in any way. It could not expand its facilities, its distribution, or even its office. It could not install new equipment.

Holanda was able to increase production through greater efficiencies and longer work shifts, but distribution had to be given to Mexican companies. This resulted in loss of control and lower sales volume and profits because products were sold at a discount to the distributors who also had to earn a profit. Despite all of the restrictions, Beatrice was unwilling to relinquish its majority position in the company.

Still, the company prospered because of sound local management. By 1982, Holanda, which started as a single retail store in 1927, was selling its ice cream products in more than 230 franchised outlets across Mexico. Many of its fifty ice cream flavors also were sold in drug, grocery, and small neighborhood stores. One of the reasons for its growth was its distribution network. Products were shipped to franchised outlets through the country from either Holanda's Mexico City plant or via nine strategic distributor locations in major cities.

When James G. Fransen retired as a vice president and operating director of the Caribbean Dairy Area, supervision of Holanda was assigned to the Latin American Division, headed by André J. Job. A new company called Futura was formed to take over the distribution of Holanda products throughout Mexico. Because 49 percent of Futura was owned by Holanda and 51 percent by the Camperos, it was a Mexican-controlled company, which could expand as it wished. And, because Beatrice was the majority partner of Holanda, it could set transfer prices at will. The senior Campero was appointed general manager of Holanda.

Altesa, a supplier of ice cream cones, stabilizers and flavors, 40 percent of which was owned by Holanda and 60 percent by Altesa's general manager, Carlos Perez, was a synergistic addition.

Several months later, Holanda acquired Barry, a medium-sized ice cream company located in Aquascaliente in the heart of Mexico's dairyland. The owners were dairy farmers who had neither the time nor the knowledge to run the company.

After these acquisitions, Holanda was a "Mexicanized" company that could enjoy full freedom to operate without restrictions. The value of Beatrice's 49 percent interest was, in fact, substantially larger than the 60 percent it held previously. Most important, because the 51 percent was spread among three other groups with different interests, Beatrice retained effective control of the company.

Unfortunately, Campero became ill and retired, and Carlos Perez was appointed general manager. Two years later, Campero, having recovered from his illness, wanted to return as general manager, although Beatrice was satisfied with the job Perez was doing. The company suffered from the infighting, and profits stagnated.

In early 1987, with the encouragement of Beatrice, sale of the Campero, Perez, and Barry shares was arranged. Helados Bing, a rival in one part of Mexico and a well-managed company, acquired the 51 percent majority. However, Beatrice retained a voting veto through the by-laws, which required 53 percent. The general manager of Helados Bing resigned to become general manager of Holanda. Within the next twelve months, Holanda's profits nearly doubled, thus greatly increasing the value of Beatrice's 49 percent interest.

Elsewhere in the Caribbean, Beatrice found leading ice cream companies that increased its presence in Latin America substantially. In San Juan, Puerto Rico, it acquired Montecados Payco, the leader in ice cream and frozen dessert products in the Commonwealth. A major asset was the modern plant's location on a large parcel of land in the heart of the San Juan financial section across from the Chase Manhattan Bank.

With the addition of Cremo in Kingston and North Shore Dairies in Montego Bay, Jamaica, and Frigor in Santo Domingo, Dominican Republic, Beatrice became the dominant ice cream company in the Caribbean. It was not a question of what brand a customer wanted, but what flavor. All of these plants continued to be managed by citizens of their respective countries and were quite profitable.

It wasn't until 1967 that Beatrice entered the Australian economy. A review of dairy operations there discouraged any efforts in that area. Beatrice discovered that dairy plants in Australia were not attractive; practically all are cooperatives and did not meet Beatrice's guidelines.

Instead, its search centered on Red Tulip, a manufacturer of premium quality candies. The company had been founded by William Saunders, who had fled from his candy business in Austria because of conditions in Europe just before World War II. Saunders's choice of a market in which to pioneer was ideal. Although it is the size of the continental United States, Australia has a population of only 15.3 million, but Australians rank second in the world in the per capita consumption of chocolate. Furthermore, 90 percent of the population lives in the three eastern territories, Victoria, New South Wales, and Queensland, and, therefore, is relatively close to Melbourne. Under the direction of Saunders, Brown, and eventually Saunders's son Nick, Red Tulip developed a line of superior continental chocolates distributed from a modern plant in Melbourne to department stores and supermarkets. It also captured more than 80 percent of the after-dinner mint market and dominates the box chocolate assortment business. Part of its success was its introduction of chocolate Easter eggs and bunnies. Easter is to Australians what Valentine's Day is to Americans in terms of gifts of candy.

Encouraged by the enormous success of Red Tulip, Beatrice added six more Australian confectionery companies, including Stark's, Choice Confections, Unicorp, and Europe Strength Foods. Then it acquired Van Camp's chocolates in Auckland on the North Island of New Zealand.

Supporting Red Tulip and its sister confectioners is the largest candy distribution system in Australia, Red Tulip Distribution System, which maintains more than 450,000 square feet of warehouse space in nineteen major locations across the country. It also established an export division to market its products in Japan, China, and other countries in Asia.

Patra Holdings in Melbourne—started by two Thyssen brothers who immigrated from Greece—proved to be another profitable addition. Its principal products are citrus juices, primarily orange and grapefruit. Its location enabled Patra to process fresh orange juice the year around. The oranges were trucked in from groves within a several-hundred-mile-radius to be processed and sold in Melbourne and Sydney.

As it had done everywhere else it had become established, Beatrice branched out into snack foods with Select Chips and PopSnax and into dairy with Yomix yogurt. Later, Manassen Lucchitti, an importer of specialty foods, the Baron's Table specialty meats, and Hearty Beanshoots were added. Also acquired were Henry Berry and Company of Melbourne, a distributor of wholesale specialty groceries, food equipment, and poly-ethylene film, that had plants in Melbourne, Sydney, Adelaide, and Perth; Blue Bird Mills, which made children's clothing; and Marvelwear hosiery.

Long established in Malaysia and Singapore, Beatrice moved into Bangkok, Thailand, with Bireley's orange drinks and noncarbonated beverages and Delite Foods confections and snacks. Despite severe government restrictions it gained an access to Japan by entering into a partnership with Kota Hoketsu, who was engaged in the whaling business, to form Anchor Japan in Tokyo. Anchor distributes food products in Japan under the aggressive management of Yuji "Ted" Sakuma. In 1983, Winner Food Products of Hong Kong, a manufacturer of frozen foods, cooking oil, noodles, and snacks, was acquired.

Almost from the time he became chairman and chief executive officer in 1979, James Dutt had set his marketing hopes on China; the first of his half-dozen visits there was in 1980. The visits came to fruition when the Guangmei Foods Company opened a 140,000-square-foot facility on four and one-half acres in the city of Guangzhou (formerly Canton). The plant initially produced snack foods, fruit juices, and soft drinks both for consumption in China and for export. Subsequently, snack foods—flavored cheese, chicken, seafood, and barbeque puffs—soft drinks, fruit-flavored ices, and sherberts were added to the lines of products.

In April of 1986, a prototype plant was opened in Guangzhou to produce Meadow Gold ice cream. "We're selling everything we make, primarily cones," Charles Diodosio, vice president for China Development, reported at the time. Guangmei Foods is a three-way joint venture by Beatrice, the City of Guangzhou, and the China International Trust and Investment Corporation. With this agreement, Beatrice became the first American food company to establish a permanent joint venture with China.

Surprisingly, Beatrice saved one of the best—and nearest—countries for one of its last quests for international expansion. Through Cedric E. Richie, chair and chief executive officer of the Bank of Nova Scotia and a Beatrice director, Grantham had contacted a number of companies in Canada, but no acquisitions were made until 1969. After that, however, Beatrice made Canadian acquisitions at a whirlwind pace. Dutt was the protagonist for the acquisition program, which began with a small dairy in Kingston, Ontario. Roland Binnington, the owner of that dairy, was widely known and respected in the Canadian dairy industry through his work with the Canadian National Dairy Council. Dutt and Binnington literally took a map of Ontario and laid out a network of dairies for acquisition. Beatrice avoided dairies in the metropolitan areas of Toronto and Ottawa, concentrating instead on those with stronger market positions in smaller towns.

This was precisely the strategy Beatrice had pursued in the early years of its growth in the United States. The strategy was aggressive, but Beatrice was persuasive, and the owners of these Canadian dairies responded to the philosophy of decentralization. Over one three-day period, Dutt obtained hand-shake agreements to acquire three separate dairies—all strong companies. Modern Dairies in Winnipeg, Manitoba, had resisted potential acquirers for years before Beatrice persuaded Donald A. Speirs and his management team to join the group in 1970.

By 1971, ten dairies had been acquired and formed a network that would permit Beatrice to expand throughout Ontario, Manitoba, and, eventually, Quebec. The dairies began employing the name Beatrice as a brand name—the only market in the world where Beatrice is used for product branding. Under the common brand, Beatrice, the Canadian dairies were able to penetrate the large metropolitan markets they had earlier shunned.

Through it all, Beatrice maintained the personal touch. For example, when Binnington attended the first Beatrice meeting after his dairy had been acquired, Karnes, whom Binnington had never met, walked directly up to him, greeted him by name, and welcomed him to the group. "How would you know me?" a surprised Binnington asked. "How would I *not* know you?" Karnes replied.

Next, Beatrice began to diversify into the grocery business in Canada. As a complement to LaChoy in the United States, Beatrice acquired V–H Quality Foods and Mow Sang, Chinese food companies in Montreal. Through its knowledge of the baking business, Beatrice recognized the potential of Colonial cookies in Kitchener, Ontario, which would become the second largest cookie company in Canada. Also acquired was Crescent cheese, a leading maker of processed cheese and yogurt in Montreal. Beatrice ranks as one of the largest and most respected food companies in Canada, and these operations now are owned by Onex, Toronto.

All of these international expansions required special financing, and until 1969, Beatrice had no debt. Its expansion was financed completely by cash, stock, or leases. Domestically, Beatrice acquired substantial amounts of cash in its expansions. However, sellers outside of the United States were not interested in stock. They wanted cash. To provide this, Beatrice sold debentures in the European Common Market. The first series was sold in September 1969 at the rate of 7.25 percent. Additional financing from 1970–73 was obtained by selling convertible subordinate guaranteed debentures at rates from 4.5 to 9 percent.

It was a radical departure from Beatrice's conservative policies of financial management. However, the percentage ratio of debt to net worth was extremely low, and the rewards were high. In the fifteen-year period from fiscal year 1961 through fiscal year 1976, Beatrice built an International Food Division with sales of more than $1 billion, more than twice those of the total sales for the entire company in fiscal year 1961, as well as net earnings after taxes of $31.2 million, more than triple those of the same year. The sales of the International Food Division in fiscal year 1987 were $2.5 billion, with operating income of $147 million. Beatrice operated companies in thirty-one nations and exported to more than a hundred.

CHAPTER EIGHT

The Quest
for Higher Margins

Virtually unheralded, Beatrice had established itself as one of the most progressive companies in the nation in terms of growth in sales and profits and financial stability as the 1960s began. However, the Beatrice operating committee had been closely monitoring all segments of its business on a continuing basis and was concerned about the changes affecting the market for its products, comprised almost entirely of dairy, specialty foods, and agri-products along with its public warehouses.

Competition in dairy and specialty foods was becoming more intense. Growth was slowing, and margins were narrowing. New and established companies were following Beatrice's lead into the ethnic food fields with new chili and pizza products. Others were copying Beatrice's programs for promoting pickles and candy. The committee recognized that if the company was to counter the steady rise in the rate of inflation, maintain or increase its 16 percent return on net worth, and provide shareholders with improving values on their investments, it had to broaden the scope of its diversification program heretofore limited to food products.

Toward this objective, during the sixties the committee began surveying fields outside of foods. The decade became identified later as the beginning of the era of merger mania; companies could be bought initially for only nine to eleven times earnings. By the eighties, companies were offering as much as twenty and thirty times earnings. More than seven thousand mergers were consummated in 1968 alone.

Beatrice formulated a carefully structured plan for acquiring companies outside the food industry after extensive studies by the committee and market specialists. The plan had to follow the same conservative guidelines that had been applied to previous mergers and purchases. It was imperative that the existing management of the acquired company continue to run it, or that qualified successors had been trained. The company had to be a leader in its specialized field and have excellent growth potential. Six fields initially were selected for investment: institutional food service equipment, home and garden accessories, recreation equipment, leisurewear, graphic arts, and agri-products and cryogenics.

Beatrice had been in the acquisition business almost from the day it had been founded. It was a proven professional in the merger game, if not the leader. It also was in strong financial condition. For the fiscal year ended February 28, 1965, sales had increased for the fifteenth consecutive year, and net earnings for the thirteenth year in a row. Sales were up 12 percent to $681 million from the prior year. Net earnings showed a gain of 23 percent to $18 million, and earnings per share had grown by 18 percent to $3.32. The company had no debt, and working capital had risen for the twentieth straight year to $86 million. The stock had been split four times in eight years. Thus, Beatrice stock was a sound investment for owners of companies seeking to establish estates or to secure capital for expansion.

Food Service Equipment

The first venture was into food service equipment. As more women entered the work force, more and more people ate out. Fast-food outlets such as McDonald's, Burger King, Kentucky Fried Chicken, Dairy Queen, and others proliferated, and Beatrice was familiar with the field because of its sales of institutional food products.

Bloomfield Industries was the first acquisition in December of 1964 with more than seven hundred products. Owned by two brothers, Daniel and Harold Bloomfield, it operated a modern plant in Chicago that manufactured Silex coffee brewing and institutional serving equipment, gourmet ware, table service utensils, and stainless steel kitchen and bar service equipment. Its salt and pepper shakers were on thousands of restaurant tables across the country. Bloomfield's sales were about $6 million when Beatrice acquired it. It had a fine sales force that was expanded over the years. Dan Bloomfield often said he worked harder for Beatrice, William G. Karnes, and John Hazelton than he did when he owned the company. However, he prospered too as his Beatrice stock grew in value from splits and price increases. After the Bloomfields retired, the company was capably managed by Louis Pellegrini, whom they had trained.

Taylor Freezer of Rockton, Illinois, was the leader in the manufacture of soft ice cream machines when it joined Beatrice in 1967 at the recommendation of Allan Adams, head of Adams Snack Foods Division in Beloit, Wisconsin. Under the capable direction of Carl Gorychka and Daniel B. Greenwood, Taylor had expanded its market to include all types of food service operations around the world. Its products were in all McDonald's outlets, as well as some of the smallest grocery stores. Among its innovations was a machine that made milk shakes in five seconds.

Other significant additions to this group were: Market Forge Company of Everett, Massachusetts, makers of steam cookers, kettles, convection and microwave ovens, and mobile storage racks for institutional food service outlets and hospital equipment; Wells Manufacturing of South San Francisco, makers of commercial deep-fat fryers and waffle irons; World Dryer of Berkeley, Illinois, makers of electric hand dryers for washrooms in clubs, restaurants, industrial, and commerical operations, airline and rail terminals, and U.S. navy ships; Geerpres Wringer of Muskegon, Michigan, makers of institutional cleaning equipment; and Vogel-Peterson of Elmhurst, Illinois, "The Coat Rack People."

Home and Garden Accessories

Quality was the hallmark of companies formed into the Home and Garden Accessories Group starting in 1965. The first was the Stiffel Company, which manufactures fine residential lamps in Chicago. To capitalize on the trend toward outdoor living, Charmglow of Antioch, Illinois, was acquired in 1967. Its founder, Walter Koziol, told a Chicago bank, "I want Beatrice," and rejected higher offers in favor of Beatrice because of its fine management and decentralized operations.

Others added to the group were: Melnor Industries of Moonachie, New Jersey, makers of water sprinklers and lawn-care equipment; Hekman Furniture of Grand Rapids, Michigan; Hekman Cabinets of Lexington, North Carolina; Indiana Frame and Moulding of LaPorte, Indiana; Max H. Kahn Curtain Corp. of New York City; Beneke Corporation of Columbus, Mississippi, makers of bathroom accessories; Robert H. Peterson Co. of Pasadena, California, makers of fireplace equipment; and John Hancock Furniture of National City, California, makers of redwood furniture.

Anticipating the advent of hardware cooperatives such as Ace and True Value to serve the growing do-it-yourself market, Beatrice next acquired Chicago Specialty Co. of Skokie, Illinois, makers of plumbing supplies; Dearborn Brass of Cedar Rapids, Iowa, makers of plastic and plastic plumbing equipment; Wrightway of Park Forest, Illinois, makers of faucets, shower heads, and water filters; Star Brush of Boston, Massachusetts; Tip Top Brush of Jersey City, New Jersey; and Essex-Graham of Chicago, Illinois, makers of painting supplies.

Sue Marchand became the first woman president of a division when Irvinware, an Astoria, New York-based manufacturer of bar accessories, was added in 1973. United Cabinet of Jasper, Indiana, was acquired the following year, and the name of the manufacturer of quality kitchen and bathroom cabinets was changed to AristOKraft. Liken (the maker of

Delmar woven wood shades) of Huntington Beach, California, was added in 1977.

Recreation Equipment

Beatrice's first venture into the field of recreation equipment was an adventure. The company bought Wally Byam's dream—Airstream—in 1967. In 1934, Byam set out to build a travel trailer that would provide its owner with limitless mobility, the luxury of a private stateroom and the convenience of a fine hotel. What he created was Airstream, a trailer that could—and did—go any place a car could travel. Byam organized the Wally Byam Caravans and Caravan Clubs across the continent. In one notable adventure, he led forty Airstreams on a twelve-thousand-mile trek from Capetown, South Africa, to Cairo, Egypt. In 1964, a caravan of 105 Airstreams left Singapore and covered thirty-four-thousand miles through Cambodia, Thailand, India, the Near East, Scandinavia, and Europe. Specially designed Airstreams were used by NASA for isolation of Apollo 11 and 12 astronauts following their return from the moon. The sleek, light weight trailers of monocoque design were hand-crafted from aluminum and offered all of the creature comforts of home, including air-conditioning, range and refrigerator, aluminum sinks, large comfortable beds, and penthouse baths with tub, shower, and vanity. Airstream's sales in 1967 were $24 million.

After it joined Beatrice, Airstream built plants in Cerritos, California, and Jackson Center and Versailles, Ohio, and expanded its line to include trailers ranging in length from twenty-one to thirty-one feet. Later, it entered the motorhome and minibus markets under the Argosy brand after Arthur R. Costello retired and was succeeded by Charles H. Manchester as president. Bonanza Travelers of Elkhart, Indiana, provided the company with trailers in the medium-price range in 1970.

Beatrice entered new territory with the acquisition of the Morgan Yacht Corporation, St. Petersburg, Florida, in 1967. Founded by the dynamic Charles Morgan, the company was a major producer of fiberglass sailboats ranging from twenty-two to forty-five feet. It also made a sailboat kit for do-it-yourself enthusiasts, as well as custom yachts to order. It built two side-wheel steamboats for Disney World and also expanded into power boats. Morgan used a substantial portion of his payment from Beatrice in 1970 to build *The Heritage*, a twelve-meter boat that he captained in the America's Cup trials. Striker Aluminum Yachts of Fort Lauderdale, Florida, which built the famed *Sportsfisherman*, was purchased in 1971.

In 1953, brothers Hartvig and Harry Holmberg developed a metal and plastic ski that by 1967, when Hart Ski Company of St. Paul, Minnesota, merged with Beatrice, had established a reputation for quality and durability. It offered a lifetime guarantee. With capital provided by Beatrice, the brothers expanded their facilities and product lines and retained Billy Kidd, one of the nation's top skiers, as a consultant. However, foreign competition cut severely into sales, and the company was sold back to the family. Mark Fore/Vatco of Boston gave Beatrice further penetration into the ski market; it produced auto luggage and ski racks as well as auto accessories. Excel of Elgin, Illinois, which made reflectors, pedals, wheel hubs, and multispeed derailleurs for bicycles gave Beatrice access to another burgeoning recreational activity.

Capitalizing on the development of mobile home parks and the rising popularity of these units for vacation homes, the company acquired the following companies: Jacobsen Mobile Homes of Safety Harbor, Florida; Holiday Homes of Lynn and Hamilton, Alabama; New Yorker Homes of Elkhart, Indiana; Seminole, which produced accessories for mobile homes; Pyramid Mobile Homes of Windsor, Ontario; and Reasor of Charleston, Illinois, makers of modular homes.

Leisurewear

Leisurewear was a logical extension of the recreational product group. The company selected E. R. Moore of Niles, Illinois, for its initial entry in 1969. Founded in 1907 as a producer of commencement caps and gowns for rental, Moore expanded into choir and judicial robes, school uniforms, gym suits, and T-shirts and jackets. It operated four manufacturing plants and three distribution centers across the country.

Formed in 1946 by Norman and Wharton Schneider, Allison Manufacturing Company of Allentown, Pennsylvania, was one of the first to market T-shirts and sweatshirts imprinted with mottos and names. Subsequently it expanded into apparel for Boy Scouts; football, basketball, and hockey shirts; and boys' knit pajamas. In 1977, seven years after Allison joined Beatrice, Walt Disney Productions licensed the company to use the famous Disney cartoon characters on T-shirts to be sold to such mass merchandisers as Sears and K–Mart.

The Leisureware Group was steadily augmented by the acquisition of Homemaker of Chicago, Illinois, makers of camping and slumber bags, bedspreads, and comforters; Velva Sheen of Cincinnati, Ohio, makers of printed leisure apparel, including T-shirts and jackets sold to high school and college organizations; Nat Nast of Bonner Springs, Kansas, makers of sportswear, primarily under the Swingster label sold to leading consumer and industrial products companies for public relations purposes;

Monticello of New York City, makers of high-fashion sport shirts; and Dunbrooke Sportswear, a jacket manufacturer.

Beatrice broadened its product lines in the educational market by acquiring Stuckey and Speer of Houston, which made class rings; Sax of Milwaukee, a mail order wholesaler of arts and crafts materials to school art departments; and A. H. Schwab, a St. Louis manufacturer of sandboxes and preschool peg desks.

Graphic Arts

James Weiss's in-depth experience in the printing business was invaluable in guiding Beatrice into the formation of the Graphic Arts Group in 1969. The emphasis, at first, was on photoengraving companies such as Jahn & Ollier and Collins, Miller & Hutchings, both in Chicago; Modern Litho in Grand Rapids, Michigan; Walker Engraving in San Francisco; and Jordan & Horn in Los Angeles. A later acquisition was G. S. Lithographers in Carlstadt, New Jersey.

Beatrice did not overlook the other areas of the graphic arts business. It obtained Weiss's Monson Printing Company and American Typesetting, both based in Chicago. Two major expansions were the acquisition of Day-Timers of East Texas, Pennsylvania, the leader in selling timekeeping diaries to business executives, and Webcraft of North Brunswick, New Jersey. Webcraft's products included catalogs, newspaper and magazine inserts that became a major business in print advertising, lottery tickets, and printed specialties.

The search for higher margins turned Beatrice to the fields of metal and plastic in 1968. In rapid succession, it acquired Accurate Threaded Fasteners of Chicago, a custom manufacturer of industrial fasteners; A-1 Tool of Melrose Park, Illinois, a manufacturer of injection molds for plastic; Acme Die Casting, Northbrook, Illinois, a precision manufacturer of zinc and aluminum castings; Pereles Brothers of Milwaukee, maker of custom-injected plastic moldings for telephone, electronic, and plumbing products; and Hi-temp of Northlake, Illinois, a leader in high-temperature heat treating of metal products.

Agri-products and Cryogenics

Products for the agri-products market were also on the shopping list. Many analysts were startled when Beatrice bought Brillion Iron Works of Brillion, Wisconsin, a leader in the production of gray and ductile iron castings for automotive, farm, and construction equipment use. Its customers included General Motors, Briggs and Stratton, Borg and Beck, and many other leading companies. John Hazelton had the most logical answer to those who questioned the merger with Brillion. "It made good profits," he explained. "It was the most progressive company of its kind in the Midwest. All of its furnaces were heated by electricity, so there was no pollution problem." General Motors officials considered Brillion the finest facility of its kind in the Midwest.

Kelley Manufacturing of Tifton, Georgia, which produced farm tillage tools and cultivators, and Snowco of Omaha, Nebraska, a maker of agricultural equipment and trailers, strengthened Beatrice's position in these markets. Waterloo Industries of Waterloo, Iowa, provided Beatrice with a major position in the production of metal tool boxes and cabinets. One of its customers was Sears, Roebuck.

Mid-West Company of Burr Ridge, Illinois, was engaged in cold-drawn mechanical steel tubing and spring steel forging for a variety of industries, as was Dial Tube Company of Carrollton, Texas. James H. Rhodes of Chicago, marketed industrial steel wool and grinding supplies.

Beatrice's studies also had alerted it to the opportunities emerging in cryogenics, and in 1970 it acquired Minnesota Valley Engineering of New Prague, Minnesota, and Cryogenic Associates of Indianapolis, Indiana. MVE produced cryobiological containers and pressure vessels and pipelines, while Cryogenic Associates fashioned custom cryogenic systems and personal oxygen breathing apparatuses.

Southwestern Investment and Samsonite

Until 1973, Beatrice had confined itself—with the exception of Creameries of America—almost entirely to companies with sales between $10 and $20 million. At the other extreme were a number of small, local dairies that consisted of "a few rusty trucks and some outdated equipment," according to Karnes.

But Beatrice shifted its merger drive into high with the acquisition of Southwestern Investment Company of Amarillo, Texas, on July 24, 1973, and Samsonite Corporation of Denver on August 27. Southwestern, which became a wholly owned subsidiary, was issued 2,434,789 common shares with a market value in excess of $62 million. S.I.C. was engaged in the consumer finance business at 127 locations in Texas, New Mexico, Arizona, Oklahoma, Colorado, and Nebraska. It was in commercial finance business and other operations at eleven locations. It owned two subsidiary insurance companies: Western National Life and Comco, Security Savings and Loan Association in Colorado Springs; two small manufacturing companies, Nunn and Nubro; and Deaf Smith, a custom cattle-feeding facility. Its revenues for its fiscal year ending December 31, 1973, were $70 million, and earnings were $4.2 million.

Southwestern Investment was a good acquisition because of its profitable and growing insurance business; its knowledge and contacts in the insurance business could be helpful to other Beatrice units. This was also true of its contacts and knowledge in the commercial finance business. S.I.C.'s consumer finance business was profitable and expanding rapidly in the growing Southwest; for example, it had more outlets in Texas than any other finance company.

The acquisition of Samsonite Corporation was the culmination of Karnes's and Brown Cannon's long courtship of the Shwayder family, who controlled the company (chapter 12). The merger involved the exchange of 3,795,409 Beatrice common shares equivalent to more than $100 million for all of the Samsonite shares. Samsonite epitomized the type of company Beatrice coveted; it was the worldwide leader in the manufacture of luggage and folding furniture, and all of Beatrice's research showed that the travel industry was booming.

Samsonite rose to the top of its field by applying the Golden Rule to all phases of corporate effort. Other reasons for its success are summarized in a company history, *Jesse Shwayder and the Golden Rule*, published in 1960: concern for human relations; ability, loyalty, and willingness to work hard on the part of all executives; manufacturing products that are different and better than competitors'; advertising nationally on a continuing basis; being aware of retailers' problems; and willingness to invest capital as required for plants, processes, and research.

Samsonite's beginnings were as humble as those of Beatrice. Jesse Shwayder and his father, Isaac, founded the company with $3,500 of borrowed capital in Denver in 1910 to manufacture trunks. In doing so, they were bucking the odds: there were no raw materials; banks would not provide financing; Denver was a small market; they had no manufacturing experience; and there were few skilled workers. Knowing all of this, why did Jesse Shwayder start the Shwayder Trunk Manufacturing Company after a successful term as a sales manager for the Seward Trunk Company of Virginia? "Well, I guess I just wanted to be boss," he explained. "Like most successful businessmen, I'm really a very ordinary person. But this has its advantages. I was too stubborn to admit that I couldn't succeed and so I succeeded."

The first year the company lost $2,000, but finished in the black in 1911 and soon ten employees were making trunks and inexpensive hand luggage while the Shwayders were on the road selling. Sales skyrocketed, primarily because of the adoption of a policy of manufacturing to meet retailers' needs.

One of Shwayder's bread-and-butter items was a $2.50 hand case that looked like every competitor's case and sold for the same price. In 1922, he redesigned it, made it stronger, used shiny metal studs to give it eye appeal, and priced it $4.98 retail. He reasoned that the case was different from his competitors and could be sold at the higher price on its merits. Then he turned his considerable sales skills to promoting the case. Initially, he persuaded the luggage buyer at the Denver May Company store to take two dozen on trial. He met with the store's luggage salespeople and explained why his cases were better than his competitors and that they were guaranteed for a year. The cases sold out in a week. Next, Shwayder persuaded the buyer to put in a window display showing one of these new cases supporting a thousand pounds of flour in sacks. When the display was in place, he sent twenty-five employees to crowd around the window and draw the attention of passers-by. Sales soared.

In 1916, Shwayder had a picture taken that was to become a company trademark and was used in most of its direct mail circulars. It was a photograph of him, his father, and three of his brothers—representing close to a thousand pounds—standing on a plank supported by a Shwayder carrying case. Isaac Shwayder died in 1916, and the picture was retaken in 1923 with all five Shwayder brothers standing on the plank.

Shwayder took his four brothers into the company in the twenties. When asked how he maintained control with his brothers working in key jobs, he explained that "I worked out a formula for keeping peace in the family, I gave all of my brothers stock and odd jobs. But I kept 52 percent of the stock myself, so everybody knew who was boss." Sales climbed steadily from $85,000 in 1918 to $690,000 in 1923 and $1 million in 1926.

The original policy of the Shwayder Trunk Manufacturing Company was to deliver product freight-paid to destination. However, when the railroads doubled freight rates in 1927, the company was forced to look for an eastern manufacturing site to make products for delivery east of the Mississippi River. Shwayder executives located an old Fisher Body plant in Ecorse, Michigan, a suburb of Detroit, and began manufacturing in this leased facility in 1928. Later, they purchased the plant.

The 1929 crash did not affect the company's sales immediately, but by 1932 sales at both plants were down by 50 percent. In its search for ways to keep the plants open, the company tinkered with license plates, "doggie dinettes," sandboxes, stilts, and eventually card tables. Only the card tables were successful—they marked the beginning of the Samson Furniture Division, which later became a very important part of the company's expansion program. It was quite by accident that Shwayder Trunk got in the table business. Maurice Shwayder, while in the Northwest, called on a lumber company in Idaho that had two carloads of card table legs and frames that it was unable to sell. He bought them for little more than the freight to Denver and Ecorse, and thus began the Furniture Division. All that was needed was buy some stays for the legs and adapt the same fiberboard used for suitcases for the tops.

In this same year, 1931, the company's name was changed to Shwayder Brothers, Inc. because it was now more than just a trunk and luggage business. The company also embarked on an extensive campaign of local and national advertising to promote its lines of luggage and furniture. In 1936, the company began to produce folding chairs to sell along with its successful folding tables. The first chairs were wooden, but soon were replaced with tubular steel chairs manufactured in Detroit. At this time, all chairs were produced in Detroit along with tables and luggage; Denver manufactured only luggage and tables.

In early 1941, many of the old-style luggage items were discontinued, and Samsonite Streamlite luggage was introduced. The line of plastic-covered wooden boxes remained for more than fifteen years the bedrock of the Samsonite line and led to the addition of color and fashion for the first time in luggage lines.

During the late thirties and early forties, before Pearl Harbor, the next generation of the Shwayder family began to take an active role in the company management. King Shwayder, Jesse Shwayder's only son, entered the business in the mid-thirties and was sent to Detroit. He returned to Denver in the early sixties and became president of Samsonite. Emmett Heitler and Louis Degen, both sons-in-law of Jesse Shwayder, started in the early forties, and both retired as executive vice presidents of the corporation.

In the early 1930s, the company designed and produced many thousands of metal and board footlockers for the Civilian Conservation Corps camps, and this was the first item the company produced for the armed forces when World War II broke out. Immediately after the start of the war it became impossible for Samsonite to produce civilian items, and so it began to produce a series of products for the military and embarked on its next major expansion program.

The Detroit plant produced Bangalore torpedo casings and metal parts for M-69 and M-74 incendiary bombs that were assembled and finished in Denver. They also produced tank parts for the General Motors tank arsenal. Denver, during the war, produced footlockers, incendiary grenade casings, and M-69 and M-74 incendiary bombs that were filled by the Chemical Warfare Service at various arsenals throughout the country. Much of this production was continued during the Korean War.

By the end of 1952, it became apparent that a new line of luggage was required using jet-age materials with modern design and shape. This eventually led to the development of Samsonite Silhouette made with a magnesium frame and a body covered and trimmed with plastic molded accessories—the most successful line of luggage ever produced. Using the same materials, but with a die-cast magnesium frame, a line of attaché cases was developed that became the best-selling line of business cases in the market.

The company's name was changed in the mid-fifties to the Samsonite Corporation because all of its products were known by the Samsonite brand. It was also decided for maximum efficiency to put only luggage manufacturing and marketing in the Denver operation and all furniture operations in Detroit.

The Furniture Division in Detroit was beginning to outgrow its space. The Pittsburgh plant opened in 1953 to assure a steady steel supply was closed in 1958 because a second plant for chairs only was no longer needed and steel had become readily available. This led to the building of a million-square-foot plant in Murfreesboro, Tennessee, where all the corporation's folding furniture, office furniture, and outdoor furniture could be produced. In the late seventies, the furniture division facilities were augmented by the addition of a table-manufacturing plant in Fort Smith, Arkansas, to produce the laminated particle board used in the furniture operation.

Until 1956, Samsonite had no facilities outside the United States. To capitalize on the potential of the Canadian market and export to the United Kingdom, the company built a plant in Stratford, Ontario. About the same time, it formed Altro, a 50-50 joint venture with the Perez-Alonzo family in Mexico City, which ships luggage, plastic containers, and packaging throughout Mexico and Central America. A plant was built in Oudenaarde, Belgium, and another purchased in Thurout, Belgium, to serve the common market in Europe as well as the Middle East, Scandinavia, and some Eastern Bloc countries.

In the sixties, it became obvious that if Samsonite was to maintain its leadership, it had to enter the rapidly growing soft luggage market. This decision led to the construction of an assembly plant in Nogales, Mexico, and a supply plant in Tucson, Arizona, to take advantage of the Border Industrialization Program.

The roots of the company remain deeply imbedded in Denver, where the Samsonite headquarters are located. It is composed of 1,200,000 feet of luggage assembly facilities, hardware manufacturing, operations, and warehouse space in addition to the corporate offices on a hundred-acre tract near the airport.

However, as important as all of these diverse product lines were to

Beatrice in terms of future internal growth, the primary gains were the people that stayed with them (chapter 10). Among those that advanced to major corporate positions in addition to Weiss and King Shwayder, both of whom became directors, were Theodore Ruwitch from World Dryer, chosen as the first group manager of Manufactured Products, as was Walter Lovejoy from A-1 Tool and Richard W. Hanselman and Edwin Disborough from Samsonite. Others who later became group managers included Douglas A. Bard from Geerpres, John A. Corry from Beneke, Norman Schneider from Allison, Vernon Davidson from Nat Nast, Frederick Phillips from Stiffel, Rudy Buczek from Monson, William Collins from Collins, Miller and Hutchings, and Nolan D. Archibald from Liken.

Beatrice also evaluated many other companies, but did not bid on them for a variety of reasons.

Culligan

Early in 1978, Beatrice issued 2,186,891 common shares to the shareholders of Culligan International Company, Northbrook, Illinois, yet another example of a company that grew from one idea and one product to become the leader in a relatively new industry. Emmett J. Culligan had been raised on a farm and remembered the barrels farmers set out to catch the naturally soft rain water needed for washing clothes. He had no money, but with credit from suppliers, he launched the Culligan Zeolite Company in July 1936 to make zeolite, a synthetic mineral used to soften water by removing minerals, primarily calcium and magnesium. He chose the village of Northbrook, a suburb of Chicago that at the time had a population of eight hundred, because of its several miles of unused streets deserted because of the crash of the stock market in 1929. These streets served as drying basins for the zeolite, which was sold in bulk to assemblers of water-softening equipment.

Household water softeners at that time were bulky, cumbersome to operate, and expensive, ranging in price from $500–$800. The softener consisted of a large tank to hold the zeolite, another for the brine used to regenerate the zeolite, and a cluster of valves. Culligan conceived the idea of providing soft water on a monthly service charge basis, similar to telephone service. The customer would pay between $2 and $2.50 per month for soft water service. The only equipment in the home was a 9-by-42-inch tank of zeolite. The tank would be exchanged every four weeks for a regenerated tank. The exchanged unit would be brought back to the franchised dealer's service center and regenerated for exchange with another exhausted tank.

Then Culligan set about to establish what was to become a worldwide network of franchised dealers. The first two were established in Hagerstown, Maryland, and Wheaton, Illinois, in 1937. At the close of 1939, the company had twenty-five dealers, ten employees, and $420,000 in sales.

Harold Werhane joined Culligan in 1937, Donald Porth in 1938, Samuel Marotta in 1940, and John Gavin in 1941. This quartet and Culligan led the management team for thirty-eight years as the sales in 1979 reached $100 million and the number of employees grew to 2,200. Subsequently, Paul Hylbert, Frank R. Emery, and Donald M. Hintz became key members of management.

World War II caused practically all activity in water treatment to cease, and the company built a chemical plant in San Bernardino, California, to produce silica gel, a dessicant used to protect military equipment from rusting during shipment. Silica gel is closely related to zeolite, therefore, the plant was easily converted to zeolite manufacture on an annual basis after the war.

At the end of 1950, eight hundred Culligan dealers provided soft water service to a million homes. By then, the company also began to extend its product line to other phases of water treatment technology. It developed commercial and industrial units that treat water for iron, sulfur, tannins, acidity, and other elements. Then it introduced a compact water softener with an automatic valve that regenerated itself. It could be either purchased for $330 or rented.

Culligan's exhibit at the Brussels World Exposition in 1958 led to rapid expansion in Europe. Initially, shipments were made from Northbrook to a company-owned distributor in Paris and an independent distributor in Belgium, where Culligan built a plant and office. Distributorships were granted in Spain, Italy, Holland, England, Greece, and West Germany, and a second plant then was built in Cadriano, Italy, a suburb of Bologna. In France alone, ninety independent franchises were opened, with Culligan retaining one on the Ile de France, that covered Paris and its suburbs. In the Orient, distributorships were assigned in Japan and Korea.

Late in the fifties, Culligan began buying out the larger franchised dealers in the United States. These thirty-five franchises contributed substantially to the increases in the domestic volume. Another major development was Culligan's application of new filtering media called cation and anion resins, which used together removed practically all contaminates from water. The company produced large and small units for special uses in which chemically pure water is essential. A compact filter that had as its main components reverse osmosis membranes was introduced in the early seventies to produce pure drinking water without the bottles.

Culligan stock was listed on the over-the-counter market in 1960 and on the New York Stock Exchange seven years later. The company had been courted by many companies over the years, but until Beatrice's offer, management had never considered the timing and conditions right. After the merger, the company continued its steady growth. Under the Culligan and Everpure brands its product line includes practically every type of water conditioning equipment for homes, businesses, institutions, and scientific establishments. When it was acquired as a part of E–II by American Brands in March of 1988, its international sales were $300 million a year.

At their peak in fiscal 1983, when Weiss retired, Beatrice's sales of manufactured products were $2.3 billion and operating earnings were more than $250 million. By then, these operations had been reorganized into three segments: Institutional and Industrial, Consumer Products, and Chemical. There were ninety-nine separate and distinct businesses that operated more than 350 manufacturing plants and employed 23,000 people worldwide.

Before the purchase of Esmark in June 1984 (chapter 18), Beatrice had pruned relatively few of its manufacturing profit centers. Airstream's sales plummeted from $70 million to $30 million, and it and its Henscher Division were sold to Thor Industries. The mobile home units and Bonanza were sold or closed. Lovejoy bought back A-1 Tool and Acme Die Casting and Accurate Threaded Fastener. He and Anthony Girone later purchased Brillion. Hi-Temp and Beneke were also sold to management teams.

Although it had earned a profit of $6.2 million in 1978, Southwestern Investment also was divested at a substantial cash profit in 1979 to a nationwide finance company. Charmglow was purchased by publisher William Rentschler, who later resold it. Morgan Yacht bounced back and forth between a management group and Beatrice and wound up as a part of the Catalina Company. Other companies, such as Striker Yachts, were dissolved.

The huge debt resulting from the $2.7 billion purchase of Esmark in June of 1984 accelerated Beatrice's divestiture program to produce cash to reduce that burden. The food service, foundry, specialty apparel, graphic arts, and cryogenic businesses all were sold, many to former owners or management personnel. These, together with the sales of bakery and cookie facilities, agri-products, wine and spirits, and chemical operations resulted in a pretax gain in fiscal year 1985 of $700 million after loss provisions of $45 million. The after-tax gain was about $386 million. The most valuable of the divisions sold was Specialty Chemicals. How it was developed is discussed in the following chapter.

CHAPTER NINE

Specialties: The Right
Chemistry for Beatrice

When Beatrice announced in September 1984 that its prized Beatrice Chemical Group was for sale, it touched off a hectic bidding war among the world's leading chemical companies. Saddled by the huge debt resulting from the purchase of Esmark in June 1984 (chapter 18) and committed to the mission of concentrating on food and consumer products, Beatrice engaged two investment banking firms, Salomon Brothers and Lazard Freres, to explore the market. The reaction was immediate from more than a score of prospective buyers. "I never thought the response would be what it was," admitted Harry C. Wechsler, president of Beatrice Chemical.

The auction came down to six finalists: Akzo, Amoco, BASF, International Minerals and Chemicals, PPG Industries, and Imperial Chemical Industries (ICI), the British-based chemical giant with a $1 billion a year American subsidiary in Wilmington, Delaware. The winner was ICI, whose bid of $750 million in cash was accepted in December of 1984. The sale was completed early the following year.

What ICI purchased was a group of fourteen specialty companies, most leaders in the fields in which they competed. Sales for fiscal year 1985 were $505 million, which produced $78 million in pretax profits for a return on sales in excess of 14 percent. The division employed 3,450 people, the majority educated in science and technology, most of whom were chemists and chemical engineers. Productivity was high, approximately $140,000 in sales per employee per year.

In the mid-fifties, Beatrice had begun to focus its acquisition eye on the chemical industry. "Many small companies had been formed after World War II and quite a few of them became very profitable in the development of high-tech chemicals for specific, esoteric uses," William G. Karnes said. "The margins were high, and the growth rate rapid for many of them. However, we were never interested in heavy chemicals, many of them commodities, or in competing with giants such as DuPont. We were looking for specialists with sound entrepreneurial management and major segments of sales in the fields in which they were engaged."

The first opportunity knocked when Kidder, Peabody offered Stahl Finish Company of Peabody, Massachusetts, and its sister companies, Polyvinyl Chemical and United Finish Company, to Beatrice in 1965. Stahl was founded in 1926 by Harry Stahl and was being managed by two sons, Louis E. Stahl, president, and Samuel S. Stahl, treasurer, with Felix Levenbach as executive vice president and Joseph Osoff as vice president, sales. The Stahls had extensive contacts in the chemical field, which led to future acquisitions, and Louis Stahl later became president of the Chemical Division. The family was talent-rich: Dolly Stahl, Louis's wife, was a well-known screen writer, and Leslie Stahl, their daughter, became a noted broadcast journalist.

Stahl produced a full line of chemical products for finishing leather, vinyls, and textiles, including resins, pigment dispersions, binders, and introcellulose vinyl and urethane lacquers. Polyvinyl created acrylic emulsion polymers for floor polishes, leather finishes, textile sizes, and paper coatings. It also formulated acrylic solid and solution polymers for paints, inks, adhesives, as well as seamless floors and coatings for vinyls and textiles. Max Potash directed these operations. United Finish, headed by the Stahls, manufactured maintenance paints, automotive and truck paints, and finishes for industrial products.

In all, the companies operated eight plants: three in Peabody, a suburb of Boston, one in Wilmington, Massachusetts, two in Canada, and two in Waalwijk, The Netherlands. Their total annual sales ran to $42 million, and pretax profits were $6.5 million. Late in 1965, Stahl opened a plant in England and later expanded into Mexico, Nicaragua, Italy, Australia, Spain, Venezuela, West Germany, and Singapore.

Stahl's chemists carried on extensive research to develop new products for the treatment of fabrics. One of the most successful was ultra-suede. Stahl established a fashion center in Peabody in 1974 to assist the leather shoe and garment industries in designing new styling and providing greater wearability through chemicals. It advised tanners and footwear manufacturers of new trends in fashion as they applied to a multitude of grains, colors, and textures, and on shoe styling for which these leathers were particularly applicable.

By 1974, two more companies, both based in Peabody, had been added to the group. Permuthane formulated polyurethane resins, coating compounds, pigment dispersions and chips and rotogravure inks. Paule made finishes for the shoe industry. Through its operations in The Netherlands, Stahl was one of the first companies to sell its finishes in the People's Republic of China, a major producer of pigskins, when American products were not permitted entry there.

From this fast-growing base, Beatrice expanded into related fields. In

1967, it acquired Imperial Oil & Grease Company of Los Angeles. Imperial manufactured high-performance metallic solid industrial lubricants, plus oils, greases, synthetic oils, and greases, dry film lubricants, and special application lubricants under the Molub-Alloy and Astrol brands. It was founded in 1945 as the pioneer in the use of metals for lubrication and was headed by George W. Gerber and Robert L. McVicar.

That same year, Farboil Company of Baltimore, Maryland, which made marine and industrial paints and chemical coatings, joined the group. Founded in 1918, it had increased its distribution worldwide, with Farboil products stocked at nearly all of the hundred major ports in the world. One of Farboil's breakthrough developments was the Farbaloy coating system, an antipollution method of applying multilayer coats at one time.

As a logical extension of the operations of Stahl and its associated companies, Beatrice entered the leather-tanning field in 1971 with the acquisition of Pfister & Vogel, which had a state-of-the-art plant in Milwaukee. It had excellent management led by Erhard Buettner, then John J. Justen and reported continuing increases in sales to leading shoe manufacturers across the United States. Its inventory was kept to a minimum because the firm did not purchase hides until it received an order. Subsequently, John J. Riley of Woborn, Massachusetts, which was engaged in side-leather tanning, and Lackawanna Leather of Scranton Pennsylvania, which processed tanned leather for furniture, were added. All three were assigned to the Agri-Products Division, successively directed by Anthony Q. Sanna, Richard Walrack, and Donald G. Stephens.

Another related line of products was flexographic and gravure inks. Founded in 1952 by Karl Behr and two partners in Linden, New Jersey, Converters Ink (CONCO) operated plants in Linden, Atlanta, Chicago, Dallas, and Berkeley when it joined Beatrice in 1970. It also had plants in Toronto, Montreal, Winnipeg, Vancouver, and Calgary. Under the direction of Leon Triberti, it later opened branches in Neenah, Wisconsin, and Cincinnati. H. Blacker Printing Inks, which operated a plant in Hamilton, Ohio, and a branch in El Dorado, Arkansas, was added to this segment of operations in 1976.

The primary market for these ink companies was in the flexible packaging industry for products such as bags for perishable foods, corrugated boxes, candy and gift wraps, and household tissues. Craig Adhesives of Newark, which made aqueous-based adhesives for the paper-converting, food-packaging, laminating, woodworking, and printing industries, increased Beatrice's penetration into these markets, as did Tricon Ink, which formulated lithographic printing inks in Linden, New Jersey.

In 1973, Beatrice found a company in Miami that was a leading specialist in producing coatings and sealants that improve the appearance and durability of concrete and masonry. The sales of Standard Dry Wall's THORO System Products expanded steadily in the United States and in Europe, where it opened a plant in The Mol, Belgium. Headed by Phil Donnelly, it operated plants in Newark, California, Bristol, Pennsylvania, and branches in New Earle, Pennsylvania, and Centerville, Indiana.

With the acquisitions of Dri-Print Foils in 1974, Liquid Nitrogen Processing (LNP) in 1976, and Fiberite in 1980, Beatrice became a major factor in three more highly sophisticated fields.

Based in Rahway, New Jersey, Dri-Print Foils marketed more than six thousand types of foils for the automotive industry, including exterior chrome applications, interior wood grains, and metallic bright decorations, as well as for furniture and decorating applications for packages, handbags, television sets, and even Christmas cards. It also developed the Dri-Form System, which allows the entire surface of a plastic sheet to be decorated and thermoformed in three dimensions in one step.

Recognizing early the enormous potential for growth in the computer and business machine industries, LNP, based in Malvern, Pennsylvania, established programs to formulate, manufacture, and market highly specialized products for the field. It became one of the premier suppliers of engineering thermoplastic compounds for injection-molded composites for computers and peripheral equipment. All the major computer companies were its customers for their structural and internal parts, such as gears, cams, bearings, slides, rollers, frames, and electrical circuitry.

In addition to providing thermoplastic compounds for computer readout terminals, keyboards, and data printers, LNP also supplied products to manufacturers of typewriters, telephones, and telecommunication switching equipment. Managed by Roger Jones, it operated facilities in Santa Ana, California, and Raamdonksveer, The Netherlands.

When the Space Shuttle Columbia successfully completed its maiden voyage in April 1981, Beatrice featured this achievement on the cover of its report to shareholders for the second quarter ended August 31 because its Fiberite Corporation subsidiary, based in Winona, Minnesota, had developed a number of products used on the Columbia. Among them were a high-performance graphite composite that formed the space shuttle's bay doors and an ablative used to fabricate the exit cones and the nozzles used on its booster rockets. The nozzles had to withstand temperatures of up to 6,000 degrees Fahrenheit—heat that would melt steel.

Acquired for $60 million, Fiberite, managed by Rudolph W. Miller and Benjamin A. Miller, produced graphite composites for a variety of commercial applications ranging from jet airplanes to tennis rackets. Fiberite materials were used to form the body of Lear jets to help increase fuel efficiency, as well as by leading automobile manufacturers seeking ways to reduce weight and increase fuel economy. In addition, Fiberite provided products for rockets and other space vehicles, as well as missiles. In 1982, it opened plants in Columbus, Indiana, Texas, and Europe.

Louis Stahl continued on as president of the Beatrice Chemical Division until 1978. Samuel Stahl had died several years earlier, but in the Beatrice tradition, Louis Stahl had trained his successor, Wechsler, who headed the division from 1978 until it was sold in 1985.

Born in Romania, Wechsler came to the United States in 1946 to study polymer chemistry. He earned his Ph.D. in 1948 and went to work for a small chemical company that Borden purchased in the early 1950s. Wechsler, who had developed a process for making polyvinyl chloride, rose to the presidency of Borden's Chemical Division, but left the company when the division was moved to Columbus, Ohio. Aware of his accomplishments in building Borden's chemical business, Beatrice management asked, "Can you do the same for us?" He could and did, starting in 1972. By 1984, he had advanced to the positions of corporate senior vice president and president of Beatrice Chemical.

In the fiscal years from 1972 when it was founded through 1985, the division increased its outside sales from $42 million to $500 million, and its pretax profits from $6.5 million to $70.6 million.

By 1984, Beatrice Chemical had been divided into two divisions, Performance Chemicals and Plastics and Coatings. Performance Chemicals included Polyvinyl, Stahl, Imperial Oil & Grease, Converters Ink, and Farboil. Headed by Jan Dlouhy, it accounted for 56 percent of sales and 65 percent of profits. Plastics and Coatings was comprised of Fiberite Composites, LNP, Fiberite Molding, Dri-Print Foils, and THORO. It was directed by Richard F. Bucher, division president and assistant chief operating officer.

Wechsler noted that over a twelve-year period, the compound growth rate was 19 percent in sales and 19.2 percent in profits; tables 2 and 3 show the growth from 1980 through 1984. He explained the underlying strategies that achieved this progress at a meeting of the Beatrice board of directors in Tampa in June 1984. They were reviewed under four headings:

    1. We provide "chemicals plus," we don't merely sell a chemical (whether it be a commodity or a specialty). We "package" the chemical with customer applications service. Ample technical service is the cornerstone of our approach to business.

    2. Our products are of two kinds: A—products designed to enhance

significantly the value of our customers goods. Leather finishes, waterproofing compounds and others fall into this class. B — performance-tested products, e. g., inks, resins, lubricants, etc., tailor-made to perform under strict service conditions.

3. We are strongly technology driven. Our customers turn to us because our products generally represent the cutting edge of technology in their respective fields.

4. We are international in scope. Virtually all of our international growth has not been by acquisition, but by building from the ground up in ten countries around the world.

Wechsler added that Beatrice Chemical had two manufacturing ventures pending in Japan, with others planned for Taiwan, Singapore, Germany, and several Latin American countries. Weschler cited two areas of concentration in which Beatrice Chemical excelled: innovation and entrepreneurship. "Innovation is the life blood of this group's business," he told the directors. "It usually takes the form of research and development, but the new styling of leather products or the uncovering of new markets for our synthetic resins also qualify as examples of innovation. We are promoting entrepreneurship at the business unit level in an effort to focus on new business ventures through various programs of motivation and reward."

Noting that the chemical specialties business in the United States is one of niches, he pointed out that the group is the leader in the niches in which it competes. Beatrice Chemical was the country's leading supplier of reinforced engineering plastic compounds, as well as the world's leading supplier of leather finishes, including 80 percent of the Canadian market, 45 percent in the U.S. market, 33 percent in Italy, and 35 percent in England.

The Fiberite composites were rated best in the business, and customers included the top companies in the aircraft industry: Boeing, McDonnell Douglas, Lockheed, Northrop Aviation, and British Aerospace. "In the commercial aviation field, we are qualified for 13 major specifications at Boeing, more than any other of our competitors," Wechsler said. "We are the only approved source involving graphite tape for automated lines, a prototype of construction for all future graphite parts"; other outstanding subdivisions were Dri-Print Foils, the largest and most diversified factor in the field; Converters Ink, a leading producer of inks for use in food packaging and flexible packagings; Imperial Oil & Grease, the premier producer of high-performance industrial lubricants; and THORO Systems and Polyvinyl/Permuthane, both ranked as leaders in their respective fields.

Beatrice Chemical was poised for an even greater future in 1984.

Table 2. Beatrice Chemical Balance Sheet, 1980–84
(In Thousands; Unaudited)

	Last Day of February				
	1980	1981	1982	1983	1984
Assets					
Current Assets:					
Cash and short-term investments	$ 6,220	$ 10,236	$ 17,566	$ 15,025	$ 16,824
Receivables	63,645	65,850	73,607	68,395	79,546
Less allowances	(2,460)	(2,277)	(2,875)	(2,539)	(3,299)
Inventories	59,499	57,236	59,263	49,580	60,018
Prepaid expenses	1,126	1,157	1,025	1,102	670
Total current assets	128,030	132,202	148,586	131,563	153,759
Fixed Assets:					
Cost	88,404	89,557	98,486	105,520	109,489
Accumulated depreciation	(26,911)	(28,991)	(31,976)	(35,559)	(38,670)
Net fixed assets	61,493	60,566	66,510	69,961	70,819
Other Assets	2,494	2,201	2,936	2,654	2,994
Total Assets	$192,017	$194,969	$218,032	$204,178	$227,572

	Last Day of February				
	1980	1981	1982	1983	1984
Liabilities and Equity					
Current Liabilities:					
Short-term debt	$6,786	$6,119	$8,714	$8,019	$7,181
Accounts payable	28,116	27,443	34,040	30,918	37,987
Accrued expenses	9,234	11,122	10,359	9,202	13,430
Accrued income taxes	4,225	2,118	5,304	4,061	4,706
Current portion of long-term debt	702	643	844	960	1,038
Intercompany (receivable) payable	(1,361)	(1,834)	(1,256)	(378)	360
Total current liabilities	47,702	45,611	58,005	52,782	64,702
Long-term debt	8,216	7,491	7,905	13,322	12,260
Deferred taxes	1,655	1,969	3,741	4,222	3,300
Other non-current liabilities	567	620	1,163	448	837
Foreign currency translation adjustments	5,255	1,177	(5,039)	(8,548)	(14,157)
Stockholders' equity:					
Beatrice equity	128,559	138,137	152,056	141,740	160,483
Minority interest equity	63	64	201	212	147
Total Liabilities & Equity	$192,017	$194,969	$218,032	$204,178	$227,572

Table 3. Beatrice Chemical Statement of Earnings and Cash Flow, 1980–84
(In Thousands; Unaudited)

	Years Ended Last Day of February				
	1980	1981	1982	1983	1984
Gross outside sales	$297,018	$366,858	$424,894	$400,152	$448,422
Intercompany sales	24,403	25,640	30,061	24,481	28,012
Less discount and allowances	(6,679)	(8,121)	(9,873)	(8,017)	(9,087)
Net sales	314,742	384,377	445,082	416,616	467,347
Operating expenses:					
Cost of sales	204,486	255,022	294,328	277,406	303,889
Selling expense	41,747	47,637	55,627	54,212	58,453
Administrative expense	18,831	25,160	30,970	30,646	34,037
Depreciation expense	4,158	5,794	6,228	6,810	7,325
Total operating expenses	269,222	333,613	387,153	369,074	403,704
Gross operating margin	45,520	50,764	57,929	47,542	63,643
Other (income) expense:					
Interest income	(646)	(879)	(1,699)	(2,064)	(1,051)
Interest expense	1,820	1,894	1,763	2,445	2,513
Other, net	1,500	3,113	(1,861)	304	(649)
Total other (income) expense)	2,674	4,128	(1,797)	685	813

	Years Ended Last Day of February				
	1980	1981	1982	1983	1984
Earnings (loss) before income taxes	42,846	46,636	59,726	46,857	62,830
Income taxes:					
State	2,003	2,217	2,689	2,192	2,967
Federal	17,698	20,026	24,964	21,441	26,785
Investment tax credit	(259)	(329)	(356)	(773)	(328)
Total income taxes	19,442	21,914	27,297	22,860	29,424
Net earnings	23,404	24,722	32,429	23,997	33,406
Depreciation	4,158	5,794	6,228	6,810	7,325
Deferred tax increase (decrease)	489	314	1,772	481	(922)
Net capital expenditures	(5,333)	(6,312)	(14,518)	(11,993)	(9,828)
Change in working capital	(16,700)	(6,263)	(3,990)	11,800	(10,276)
Change in long-term debt	(487)	(725)	414	5,417	(1,062)
Net translation adjustments	1,069	(2,633)	(3,870)	(1,777)	(3,964)
Increase in net assets from purchase of Fiberite	(34,798)	—	—	—	—
Other, net	(156)	247	45	(422)	(16)
Cash to (from) Beatrice Corporate	$(28,354)	$15,144	$18,510	$34,313	$14,663

"Provided we can continue to maintain a climate in which highly competent technicians are allowed to function, and provided we continue to generate new products, there is no practical stopping of (or limitation to) the engine of growth," Wechsler concluded. "Ours is a fast pace, in part because of the rapid rate of obsolescence in many of our products. But our people play the game well and the momentum continues to be in our favor."

That bright future now belongs to ICI. Wechsler, who was scheduled to retire in December 1984 at sixty-five, agreed to stay on to direct the transition. He also acquired Farboil, which was not included in the package that ICI purchased.

CHAPTER TEN

Decentralize and Conquer

Decentralized management was one of the cornerstones upon which Beatrice built its sales and earnings virtually from its founding until 1980. It was the principal reason why Beatrice was able to grow year after year, retain key people including acquired management teams, maintain high morale, and avoid management disasters and major surprises. It was carefully administered, gently nurtured, and constantly practiced by all members of management from the chief executive officer to plant managers and department supervisors.

Various educators, businesspeople, industry analysts, students, and even publishers who have heard the story of Beatrice's decentralization are surprised and even confused by its simplicity. They ask for more details, more guidelines, more procedures to understand decentralized management so they can use it in their own work.

"The truth is that it is simple," William G. Karnes explained. "Its simplicity is definitely one of its strengths. It was kept simple and most of the managers of newly acquired companies found it easy to work with because they could continue to carry on their own methods of management and not have to switch to a new system of complicated policies and rules."

What is decentralized management?

When Karnes succeeded C. H. Haskell as president, the company had but thirteen officers, and only four of them, including Karnes, were headquartered in the General Office. All of the rest were in the field. Under Beatrice's system, there were few levels of management. The basic echelons were the plant managers, the district managers, and subsequently, the division managers, and the general office with the chief executive officer, chief operating officer, secretary, and treasurer.

"Layers of management were kept to three—lines of communication were kept short—so if a problem developed at a plant, we may not have known how to solve it; but at least we quickly knew we had a problem!" Karnes explained.

The primary sources of communication were monthly plant financial reports that were sent to the General Office by the twelfth of the following month. The form was simple but provided a clear picture of sales and profits. The manager could evaluate where a plant was going, and the district or division manager and senior management could quickly spot trouble developing.

Beatrice's system of decentralized management required a complete management team at each operating unit, or profit center, as the company called each of them. The manager of each profit center was its chief executive officer in every sense of business operation. The key was that responsibility was pushed down to the plant level. The responsibility was placed where the sales and profits were generated.

The manager ran the plant on a daily basis, setting prices as long as he or she did not conspire in price-fixing with any competitors. Price-fixing was forbidden, discussed at every sales meeting, and covered regularly by bulletins the Law Department sent to all plants.

The manager could hire and fire and promote people, as well as set pay scales. If help was needed in union negotiations, the General Office was available. The Labor Relations Department was staffed by trained people, most of them former Federal Bureau of Investigation agents schooled in labor relations and abreast of all of the federal and state laws pertaining to the negotiations of contracts.

With a few exceptions, the manager was free to purchase raw materials. Some could be purchased through the General Office, for example, paper products, cartons, cars, trucks, and similar items for which quantity discounts were available.

The manager could advertise and promote products. In operations such as dairy products, he or she was asked to use TV, radio, in-store promotion materials, billboards, and print advertising designed by the Advertising Department in the General Office. However, decisions on placement were made locally, and advertising budgets were based on the products chosen to promote.

Only five controls were placed on each plant manager:

1. The manager could not borrow money. Money had to be requested from the treasurer in the general office. The cash was controlled by a cash management system operated out of the General Office. Cash was drawn down each day from every plant and deposited into one of three general cash funds across the country.

2. The manager could not spend money for capital additions without approval of the division or district manager.

3. The manager was given an inventory quota for the plant and expected to meet the quota by the last day in February, the end of the fiscal year. If the inventory was not kept within certain guidelines, the

manager was penalized by paying interest at the prime rate to the general office.

4. The manager was required to maintain the highest sanitation standards attainable. Under this unique program initiated in the late forties, sanitation experts from state universities were retained to inspect all food plants. The program contributed substantially to quality control and virtually eliminated problems with U.S. Public Health and state health departments.

5. All food plants were required to work closely with the Quality Control Laboratory maintained by the General Office. It assisted the plants by making frequent tests of off-the-line samples sent to the laboratory. One major benefit of the program was that from the 1920s through the 1980s, no serious problems occurred because of contamination or poisoning of food.

With only these few limitations, the management was able to act quickly to meet competitive situations by adjusting prices and distribution, modifying some products, and introducing new ones. The manager did not have to call a district or division manager or the General Office for authorization if the competitive situation in the market made these moves necessary.

Another significant benefit of this system is that the manager and the sales personnel were able to develop close relationships with their customers. Because most Beatrice food plants were located in small and medium-sized cities, such relationships were important and helped position the operation as a good corporate neighbor.

Incentives were an integral part of the system. The manager was paid a base salary plus a bonus based upon the pretax profits of the plant. The system of granting almost full autonomy to each plant was an incentive in itself. The following three examples demonstrate why it worked so well.

Sanna, Inc.

F. Leon Sanna, whose Sanna, Inc., which produced dairy and nondairy products, merged into Beatrice in 1967, offered a number of reasons. "We had reached a point in the company where we realized we needed more capital than we could raise to market and exploit our own product creations," he said. "It takes great resources to develop a market. We were up against big competitors such as General Foods and National Dairy, and we just didn't have the capital to do it. So we decided to play in the big leagues, but we wanted to retain our autonomy, our independence.

"In the first five years with Beatrice, we increased our earnings more than ten times. It's amazing the way they left us alone. Sometimes I was tempted to call them on the phone and ask, 'Hey, are you still there?' It's so easy to meddle in the affairs of a company you own," Sanna added. "But the Beatrice people simply didn't do it. The closest they came to it was making an occasional suggestion. But the final decision was mine to make."

With Beatrice contributing capital as needed, Sanna expanded its facilities in Madison, Wisconsin, and built plants in Cameron and Menomonie, Wisconsin. It increased its product line that includes Swiss Miss instant cocoa mix, Sanalac, and coffee creamers. Its Swiss Miss puddings have become one of the fastest growing product lines in that category.

Vigortone

Early in 1966, Beatrice acquired Vigortone Products, the nation's oldest manufacturer of livestock feeding premixes and animal health products. The family-owned business was headed by Arthur Swartzentruber, a son-in-law of the previous owner. Although the company had been successful over the years, the family wanted to liquidate its holdings and earn income from the proceeds. Beatrice built a new plant for the company in Cedar Rapids, Iowa, as well as plants in Marion, Ohio, and Fremont, Nebraska.

One day while visiting the Cedar Rapids plant, Karnes asked Swartzentruber why the plant was doing so much better than when it was family-owned. Virgortone had increased its sales by 900 percent in ten years at the time.

Schwartzentruber responded, "When we were a family-owned company, I did not want to risk family money to expand the business. I had no particular incentive to expand the business. I was on a salary basis with no bonus arrangement, with no stock options and no pension. After I joined Beatrice, you furnished us with the capital to expand, you gave me a bonus arrangement of a percentage of the pre-tax profits of the company, and you gave me stock options. You also periodically called me into Chicago to attend sales meetings where I saw the enthusiasm and the dedication of other plant managers to Beatrice to grow and expand. Every time the chief executive officer gave a talk, it was about increasing sales and increasing profits where I would benefit along with the company. These were strong incentives to me and prompted me to expand the business along the lines that I was qualified to do, based upon my previous experience. There was no interference from the company other than furnishing the capital and any other assistance I might need out of the general office."

Stiffel Lamps

The Stiffel Lamp Company, located in Chicago, is another illustration of why the system was effective. The company was founded by Theodore Stiffel in the depths of the depression. It maintains a reputation for designing and manufacturing fine lamps. Stiffel had rejected many offers to buy his company until Beatrice's offer; he was fully informed of Beatrice's record and its decentralized policy of leaving management along and, therefore, was receptive.

The offer was 20 percent of the cash down, the balance to be paid over a period of five years. Beatrice actually bought the company in June 1965 with a cash payment out of Stiffel's bank account and then paid most of the balance of the purchase price from the company's earnings during the following five years. Stiffel was assured that he could continue to run the business without interference and could use his own book-keeping system as long as the figures Beatrice needed for its balance sheets and profit and loss statements could be taken from the figures on a monthly basis.

In turn, Stiffel kept his promise of increasing sales by a minimum of 10 percent per year. Consistent with the Beatrice system, he had trained his successors, capable people who had risen from the ranks of his organization and were able after his death to maintain the Stiffel standards of quality.

Another incentive feature of the decentralized system was that it offered opportunities for training and then advancing promising people within the organization. Frequently, a change in managers would result in turning around an unprofitable plant. For example, Beatrice had a food distribution branch in Norfolk, Virginia, that was unprofitable in the forties. The manager died, and a young man who had joined the branch as office and credit manager in 1946 after service with the adjutant general's office of the Army during World War II, was named to replace him.

In a few years, the plant was earning money, and this talented man was promoted to manager of the Washington, D.C. operations in 1958. The next year he advanced to manager of the Meadow Gold plants in Alexandria, Virginia, and Baltimore. He progressed to become an assistant group manager and manager of the Pittsburgh dairy operations, then was named a regional vice president in 1966 and a corporate vice president in 1972. Four years later, he was elected a corporate senior vice president and head of the International Food Division. He was named an executive vice president of the company in 1977, responsible for the domestic dairy, soft drink, agri-products, and international food operations.

This young man was William W. Granger, Jr., who rose to become a director of the company in March of 1979 and vice chairman in 1982. He officially retired as vice chairman in March of 1984 and as a director three months later. Beatrice called upon him for further service (chapter 19).

Another instance of promoting from within the company involved the frozen food plant in Chicago, a pioneer in this field. When the plant's founder died, it had ceased to be profitable, in part because of the increased competition in these products. Karnes called up David Roman from the St. Louis branch to take charge. However, he had been trained in Chicago, starting as a route man. He quickly brought the business back into the black, and it became one of the most profitable of all of the company's specialty food branches.

The Chicago Cold Storage plant offers yet another example. For years it had been floundering. Beatrice searched for the best warehouse operator in its ranks and selected Alex MacTaggart, who had successfully operated an old cold storage plant in Scranton, Pennsylvania. He did so well that he eventually was put in charge of all of the company's cold storage warehouses in addition to managing the Chicago plant.

In 1966, Beatrice bought the Switzer Licorice Company in St. Louis. The family-owned business was being operated by two brothers and not doing well. B. Robert Kill was a young salesman from the LaChoy Chinese foods operations. He had had considerable experience working with food brokers and had developed LaChoy's distribution substantially in several areas. Karnes invited Kill to take over the Switzer plant and made him a promise. If Kill could make $1 million in any one year, Karnes would come to St. Louis and treat every member of the plant to a banquet-style dinner. Inside of eighteen months, the earnings were in excess of $1 million. As Kill later reported, "Karnes went first class, as always. It was a superb dinner with all of the trimmings."

There are many other similar success stories. Almost every company that joined Beatrice grew faster in sales and earnings; many doubled and even tripled their sales and profits in a relatively short time. "We took successful business people who had built companies that made a profit and had fine morale. They were leaders," Karnes said. "We told them, 'Continue to do what you are doing now.' They saw what their new peers in Beatrice were doing and it motivated them to produce more sales and profits. They wanted to be winners, not just for the money, but for the sense of accomplishment, of being a winner with a winning company."

The pattern was the same: put the manager on his or her own, give a free hand, and see how well the manager could do. "Actually, Beatrice never could have operated the 400 profit centers it had throughout the country and in 27 foreign countries on any other basis," Karnes said.

In an interview with Douglas J. Stanard, then corporate secretary, on March 31, 1983, John Hazelton amplified the company's reasons for its commitment to decentralized management. "A plant is good or bad based upon the many decisions made every day by the manager," he said.

Later, Beatrice adopted the decentralized program on a product line basis. For example, when the company put MacTaggart in charge of all public cold storage plants instead of having them supervised by district managers on a geographical basis, profits increased dramatically. The same system was followed in each division as it was formed.

The program also fostered what Beatrice referred to as its "people program." Senior management kept close contact with the plant people, held frequent sales meetings, and gave awards for safety, sanitation, sales and profit increases, and length of service. The effect was that Beatrice developed a team of teams able to use their skills, experience, and creativity to the best advantage to build the company.

Karnes remains convinced that the Beatrice system of decentralized management is still as effective as it was when Beatrice was in its prime despite a more highly complicated economy, more sophisticated accounting procedures, computerization, and stricter government controls. "It will work today if you believe in it, follow it carefully and nurture it," he asserts. "Over the years we had to modify it in certain respects such as in changes in our accounting system, in the formula used in figuring interest from the plants, in the methods of compensation to managers and in the stock option and the pension programs. There also were some minor changes in marketing and advertising techniques. However, we never forgot and never changed the basic principle of decentralized management. Every employee was aware of that and appreciated it. Beatrice was not considered to be the top-paying company on either an hourly or a salary basis, and many employees could have earned more money in another industry. They stayed and gave the company their best because they believed in the system, they knew the company would be fair—and they were proud to be with a winner—the fastest growing food company in the world."

CHAPTER ELEVEN

Decentralized Marketing
and Innovation

Until 1984, not one of the company's nine thousand products was marketed under the Beatrice name, except for Canadian dairy products. Food products were identified by their long-established names; their association with Beatrice Foods was shown in small type on the products' labels. This was because the general company had a substantial, long-term investment in the companies' brand names. The Meadow Gold identity for dairy products dates back to 1901. The Clark name for candies was introduced in 1885; LaChoy Chinese foods, Holloway candies (Milk Duds), and Fisher nuts in 1920; Burny Brothers Bakeries in 1910; and Shedd-Bartush Foods in 1928. Sanna (Swiss Miss) was started in 1935. Culligan was founded in 1936, and Samsonite in 1910. Changing the widely promoted radio commercial to "Hey Beatrice Culligan Man" would not have sold any more water softeners, nor would "A bag named Beatrice" improved on "A bag named Sam."

It wasn't until 1966 that a new corporate symbol was adopted for the entire Beatrice family of foods, but did not replace the many fine brand names that had been household favorites for generations. Rather, it appeared on the label, wrapper, carton, bottle, or cap in "mouse" type, subordinate to the brand.

However, the responsibility for promoting its brand names was entirely that of each profit center. The general manager still was in charge of all marketing and advertising programs, free to hire and fire the sales manager and staff and to budget advertising and sales promotion programs. Under this decentralized marketing system, until 1984, Beatrice divisions or subsidiaries around the world retained more than a hundred advertising agencies and a score of public relations companies.

Contrary to the perception that Beatrice's growth stemmed only from acquisitions and that it was not a marketing-oriented company, these accomplishments were obtained primarily through extensive internal growth, that is, growth in sales and earnings of profit centers that were members of the company at the start of each fiscal year. For example, in fiscal year 1971, internal growth added $91 million in annual sales. In

1977, this had soared to $440 million. In the years from 1973 through 1978, the aggregate increase in internal sales growth totaled $2.2 billion, almost three-quarters of the total gain in sales during that period. The dairy business, for example, grew every year from 1936 to 1980 not only in dollars, but also in units of milk, ice cream, frozen novelties, cottage cheese, and specialty products such as yogurt, egg nog, sour cream, dips, and fruit drinks. Butter poundage sales declined as consumers' concern about cholesterol mounted, and eggs became insignificant in proportion to total sales. Dairy sales for the peak fiscal 1980 were $1.6 billion, and operating earnings topped $72 million. Major factors contributing to this growth were an ever-increasing number of capital investments in new plants and equipment, close quality control, and expanded research and development programs to create new and improved products. The number of dairy plants was gradually reduced as processing was consolidated area by area into state-of-the-art plants such as those in Champaign, Illinois, Englewood, Colorado, Dothan, Alabama, Honolulu and Kauai, Hawaii, and Dannon yogurt plants in New Jersey, Ohio, Florida, Colorado, Texas, and California. In addition, Sanna opened three plants in Wisconsin.

It was imperative that all facilities be maintained at top efficiencies. Beatrice built more than a hundred new plants around the world from 1952 through 1985. Additional investments were necessary to eliminate water, air, and noise pollution and for environmental controls, conservation, and safety. From 1955 through 1985, Beatrice's aggregate capital expenditures totaled almost $2.4 billion.

William G. Karnes and Don L. Grantham repeatedly stressed the necessity for the development of new and substantially improved products, packaging, and sophisticated marketing programs. At sales conferences across the country, Karnes regularly advised Beatrice managers to develop new products. "Five years from now, half of your sales will come from products you don't even make now," he would warn.

The company's central Research and Development Department in Chicago was continually expanding to meet the challenge of satisfying changing consumer needs and preferences. It comprised more than an acre of floor space with eight laboratories, pilot plants, an experimental bakery, taste evaluation areas, and a technical library. It was staffed by trained research and development personnel, including Gerald C. North, Peter P. Noznick, Edward Epstein, Donald Coles, Anthony Luksas, Claude Harper, Jr., and Roy Tjepkema.

The Quality Control Department, initially under the direction of George W. Shadwick, who was followed by George Reeder and Arnold Spurgash, maintained extensive facilities in the Chicago laboratories, and quality control and testing laboratories were established in all regional plant areas to maintain the strictest standards to protect and extend the purity, freshness, and natural flavor of Beatrice food products.

The Engineering Department was charged with finding ways to improve efficiencies. Under the leadership of Gordon Hobbs, Engineering was expanded steadily to include Wallace Rasmussen, Orville Kahrl, Eric "Wally" Volkman, Egon Bohn, Edward Gietl, Richard Tweeten, and Frank Wilderspin.

In 1936, Beatrice established a test kitchen in Chicago headed by a professional home economist who made frequent public appearances across the country under the coined name, "Beatrice Cooke." Pauline Pearson directed a staff that included Ann Lavender, another home economist, in the development of recipes for Beatrice food products and evaluating new ones for flavor, nutritional values, and texture. Her task grew enormously as Beatrice began adding a variety of foods, drinks, flavors, candies, condiments, snacks, and meats after 1954. Other major members such as Eckrich and LaChoy also operated test kitchens and research and development and quality control departments.

Beatrice companies engaged in manufacturing and chemical operations established their own research and development and quality control operations. Grants to institutions such as Purdue University, the Massachusetts Institute of Technology, and the University of Illinois resulted in new products and systems. In addition, outside consultants such as the Battelle Foundation were retained from time to time for special research assignments.

The combined results of all of these efforts was a deluge of new and improved products, services, and systems. The number of new items and lines introduced annually averaged well over four hundred through the seventies. In 1977, there were 523. For example, Stiffel created more than fifty new lamp styles in 1976. Samsonite expanded into softside luggage, Omega attaché cases, patio furniture, and accessories. In less than a decade, softside luggage accounted for one-third of its international sales. Samsonite sold 584,000 Omega attache cases from 1977 through 1980.

Beatrice's product marketing program can be illustrated by the Viva Promotion. In 1968, its studies indicating mounting consumer desires for low-fat, low-calorie foods that still provided nutrition and flavor, Beatrice introduced a line of low-fat dairy products under the Viva brand. Initially, only Viva milk products were marketed under the name. The line was well received and, consequently, was augmented in subsequent years by the addition of Viva low-fat ice cream and novelties, yogurt, sour cream, cottage cheese, and dips. By 1980, Viva accounted for 25 percent of the domestic dairy's total sales volume.

Another product that contributed to growth was Olde Fashioned Ice

Cream in an extensive range of flavors. It was an all-natural product with no additives. The Meadow Gold ice cream flavor of the month campaign was ongoing and supplemented sales of the three major popular standards, vanilla, chocolate and strawberry.

Other noteworthy introductions included Sanna's Swiss Miss puddings, instant cocoa, and sugar-free chocolate drink; Shedd's Country Crock low-fat spreads; Royal Danish imitation dairy products; Meinerz mozzarella, jack, and ricotta cheese for pizza and food processors; cream cheese specialty cheese products by County Line; and ButterKrust's Country Hearth bread.

Fisher Nut increased its sales from $6 million in 1956 to more than $100 million, primarily through food brokers abetted by in-store promotions, TV spots, and new products such as dry-roasted nuts, sunflower seeds, and low-salt nuts.

When Beatrice acquired Eckrich in 1972, its sales of specialty meats totaled $218 million, and distribution was limited to Indiana, Illinois, Ohio, and Michigan. Subsequently, Eckrich modernized three processing plants to state-of-the-art condition and acquired a processing plant in Chicago. It also expanded its lines of specialty meats, added a frozen meat line for the institutional market, and fanned out distribution across the United States. By 1978, sales had tripled, and distribution had been expanded to serve almost 50 percent of the population.

The same success was achieved in other nations. For example, in Spain, Campofrio grew from being primarily a sausage company to luncheon and specialty deli meats, canned hams, and fresh products (chapter 7).

The Marketing "Miracle"

How a tiny, one-product company found ways to compete with such giants in the laundry products field as Proctor & Gamble, Lever Brothers, and Colgate is another example of what a lot of hard work and a little luck can achieve. And the harder Leo Singer, Martin Kaplan, and Bernard Lewis worked, the luckier they became. At the mid-points of their lives, these three men pooled their resources — $200 — and began what was to become the Miracle White Company in the late 1950s. And as in the case of Tayto's Joseph Murphy, they mixed their first product in a bathtub.

In 1959, they were partners in Electronic Water Purifiers, located in the heart of Chicago. They sold and installed iron filters, water filters, water softeners, and salt for regenerating softeners as well as septic aids and other items related to water. Since most of EWP's customers were located in the fast-growing suburbs, they leased the front half of an airplane hanger in the suburb of Lombard. They named the business the Water Conditioning Supermarket, where a customer could find answers to questions about water problems. To attract traffic, they sold hundred-pound bags of salt at 10 cents over cost and became the largest salt distributor in Illinois. But hauling hundred-pound sacks made many customers inquire if there was a water softener that didn't require salt, and the partners' search for alternatives led to exploring several chemical specialties, including glassy phosphates.

One day, Kaplan called Singer and asked him to come over to his house. He had mixed a liquid water softener concentrate in his bathtub. A one-gallon plastic container was hooked to the water inlet to Kaplan's home. The container was filled with the concentrate made from the glassy phosphate; a drop was metered into each gallon of water to soften it.

They called the product "Sure-soft" and initially manufactured forty machines to measure and dispense the softener. Customers were delighted with the machine, when it worked. But problem after problem surfaced. The motor was too small, and the plumbing in some houses was old and complicated, preventing proper suction. The three partners worked seven-day weeks trying to service the customers and solve the problems. Then nature stepped in to provide them with a major break. The pump that supplied the largest volume of Lombard's water fell three thousand feet to the bottom of the well. To compensate, the town tapped into lesser wells that yielded an unpleasant, rusty water. Soon people who lived in Lombard were wearing shirts streaked with rust.

A few days after the accident, a customer came into the partners' office looking for help. Kaplan said that he couldn't fix the customer's unit, which was clogged with rust, but suggested that the customer buy some of the Sure-soft liquid and add some to each load of laundry during its final rinse. Two days later, two customers came to the store and asked to buy some of the miracle washing liquid. They took two gallons. The next day four more customers walked in to buy the product; the following day, six. The partners named the product White and Bright, and by the end of the summer, they had eight hundred customers. Unfortunately, their attorneys told the partners that the rights to the name White and Bright were being contested in court by two large companies. They had no chance of obtaining the trade mark. The search for another name included a list of three hundred provided by the attorneys. Singer rejected them all, to the displeasure of his partners.

The answer came from White and Bright customers. "One day a customer came in and I asked her what she would call the product if the name were changed," Singer related. "She replied, 'I don't know, but it is a miracle in getting laundry white.' Late in the day, I asked another customer the same question. The answer was similar. Toward the end of the day, another woman gave me the same response. At that moment, after hearing our conversation, our cashier turned to me and said, 'Why don't we call it Miracle White?'

"Of course, the lawyers were of the opinion that they couldn't obtain a trade mark for Miracle White because miracle and white were generic words," he added. "In due course, though, the trade mark approval came through. Some years later, Colgate lawyers confided that they had three hundred lawyers locked in a room, their only objective being to formulate new names. How, they asked, did we come up with such a marvelous name?"

After considerable discussion, the partners elected not to patent their formula since the application had to include both the ingredients and the manufacturing process and, therefore, could be copied. "We decided the best patent would be to be first in the market place," Singer explained.

From then on, it was the Miracle White Company. The water conditioning equipment business was sold, and a small store was rented on Armitage Street in Chicago. As the business grew, the company had to move to larger quarters three times before settling into a seventy-thousand-square-foot facility at 4000 W. 40th Street in Chicago after Miracle White joined Beatrice Foods on February 2, 1967.

Supermarkets and grocery stores were the obvious outlets for Miracle White Super Cleaner, but none of the partners had any grocery manufacturing and marketing experience. So they set about developing a marketing policy designed for their special situation.

"Someone remembered that we had installed a water softener for an officer of the Leo Burnett advertising agency," Singer recalled. "We phoned him. His first question was, 'How large is your advertising budget?' Well, we stammered, our first year we might muster up $10,000, but we really didn't know. 'Leo Burnett's minimum budget to take on a client is $100,000 a year,' he said. We thanked him and hung up."

They decided to package Miracle White Super Cleaner in quart, half-gallon, and gallon containers, and chose Lombard as the test market. The deal offered grocers was that they would no longer sell Miracle White out of the showroom in Lombard to consumers. They offered guaranteed sale on first orders. First orders would be on consignment, and the buyers need not pay until the last bottle was sold. Further, the store received one case free with each six cases ordered. The response from Lombard store operators was 100 percent acceptance.

The initial advertising was a six-inch, one-column advertisement in the local newspaper featuring a photo of a cashier at the check-out counter of a local store. The copy was basically a testimonial to how effective

Miracle White was in getting a clean, white, and bright wash. Each week a cashier from another store was quoted.

"The largest Lombard stores began moving five to ten cases a week," Singer said. "We were not experienced enough to realize that the average movement of a product is one case per week per average store."

The program was expanded successfully into other Chicago suburbs, but the company did not dare to enter the Chicago market. "The reason was that when a chain takes on a product, all of its stores will stock it," Singer explained. "Because we didn't support the Chicago stores by advertising in the Chicago newspapers or on radio or television, those stores moved very little product. As a result, the average sale of Miracle White per store throughout the chain was diluted to the point where the space allocated to the product was not profitable to the chain."

The solution to Miracle White's marketing quandary proved to be radio. Singer, Kaplan, and Lewis selected Rockford, Illinois, some sixty miles from Chicago, as a test market using the proven newspaper advertisements featuring store cashiers. Then Singer was lucky again. A store manager told him that a customer had purchased a bottle of Miracle White after hearing about it on "The Party Line." To Singer, a native of Superior, Wisconsin, a party line was a telephone line shared by two or more neighbors to save money. However, this party line was a radio talk show.

"I hustled to radio station WRRR and asked for details," Singer said. "The station manager explained that it was a show where listeners called in to participate in the conversation and ask questions. He said he would guarantee us excellent results if we became an advertiser. I challenged him. How could he guarantee me results, let alone how many people would be listening? 'I'll prove it,' he responded. 'Bring us an executive who can talk about the product and what it does. We'll put him on the air for a half-hour interview. Offer a 25-cent coupon to those who write in!'" Lewis, a good speaker and an expert on removing various stains from clothing, was nominated. The interview resulted in 173 requests for the coupons, and Miracle White had found the high road to marketing success.

The first radio commercial was a fiasco, but the result helped the entire four-person Miracle White team discover the correct approach. "We picked the radio personality we all liked best," Singer said. "She was a sweet-talking, honest-sounding woman named Char on station WRRR. I stopped screwing caps and putting labels on bottles long enough to pay one of Chicago's highest priced free-lance writers $10 to write a one-minute commercial . . . one hell of a wage for a minute's work, I thought." The commercial was terrible. Then someone suggested that the commercial "was terrible because when Char read it, it didn't sound like her."

"That triggered it," said Singer. "I didn't want to risk another $10 to buy a new commercial, so I told Char we had labored over the commercial, but it didn't ring true. Char countered with enthusiasm that she had used Miracle White, and it was the greatest product she'd ever used. Her spontaneous response was so convincing that I quickly told her, 'Just say that and we'll be happy.'

"And from there on, we did just that. We learned that when you buy a personality, use that person's personality. Don't ask her or him to make like a phonograph. We furnished a fact sheet on Miracle White and let the announcer put it in his or her own words. The effect was electric. The warmth came through—the sincerity registered—sales started to go up, and we had more money for advertising."

From there, they took this program to every likely town in Illinois, then moved on to Iowa. Subsequently, they covered the Midwest and next fanned out from coast to coast. "Our advertising strategy for Miracle White was strictly original," Singer declared. "I don't mean that it had never been done before. I mean it was original with us because nobody had ever told us it was being done all of the time. It's called market by market. However, we did add one new technique. With us it was ad by ad and commercial by commercial. Every time an ad took in more than it cost us to run, we spent the difference on another ad. If you think that's a pretty chintzy way to run a business, remember that the first ad we ran cost $65 and that was the entire bank account of the Miracle White Company."

Eventually, sales swelled to the point where an investment in television was justifiable. But radio continued to be a major factor. "The two media worked hand in glove . . . the warmth and intimacy of radio for the heart-to-heart sell . . . the visual impact of the tube for product demonstration and package identification," Singer noted. "I think we sometimes forget in evaluating radio versus television that radio frequently has greater visual impact than television. Every consumer has a television tube built right into his or her brain. One greatly underestimated value of selling by radio is that sometimes, not seeing is believing."

When Miracle White invaded Minnesota, it bought into a talk show featuring local radio personalities Charlie Boone and Roger Erickson, who began promoting the product on WCCO, the CBS outlet in Minneapolis-St. Paul. The advertising was started before there was any product in the stores. "Boone and Erickson kept pitching to the listeners, 'If your store doesn't carry Miracle White, kick the manager in the shins,' " Singer said. "Stores throughout the market had signs in their windows, 'Miracle White is coming. Please be patient.'

"About 10 years later, I was in Minneapolis for a speaking engagement before a group of grocery executives," he said. "After my talk, a man came up to me and declared that I owed him an apology. The reason was that he was one of the store managers who got kicked in the shins. Boone and Erickson found many ways to help promote Miracle White," he continued. "One day Carol Burnett was a guest on their show. Interrupting the interview, Boone said, 'Carol, it's time for a Miracle White commercial. You know about Miracle White, don't you?' Carol replied, 'I use it on sandwiches all the time' "—a comment not as far off base as it might seem. Singer often drank a shot glassful of Miracle White to prove that it was safe to add to drinking water.

Finally, Miracle White was ready to attack New York City, the toughest buyers' market in the country. The approach was the same, but on a far broader scale. Advertising was placed with a number of radio stations that featured celebrities such as Gene Klavan and William B. Williams of WNEW; Herb Oscar Anderson and Bob Fitzsimmons of WHN; and John Grambling, Martha Deane, the McCanns, Jack O'Brien, John Wingate, and Arlene Francis of WOR.

As usual, every distributor rejected Miracle White. There were no orders after the first week the advertising began. By the eighth week, orders flooded in amounting to 94 percent of all of the stores. After Miracle White had achieved national distribution, Arthur Godfrey was retained on Miracle White's first network broadcast. In three years, the company had expanded its distribution from a few outlets in Illinois to more than two hundred thousand grocery stores coast to coast. Sales were in excess of $50 million, and the advertising budget grew to $6 million.

Ahead of their time, Singer and his partners led a campaign against shows of violence on television. They sponsored programs such as Dr. Kehm, who conducted a thirty-minute talk show dealing with child psychology and information helpful in raising children. They also retained Marty Allen, the "Hello, Dere" comedian who put on shows in veterans' hospitals to entertain soldiers wounded in the Vietnam War.

The Singer-Kaplan-Lewis trio introduced another gambit. They promised that if the purchaser wasn't satisfied with the product, he or she would receive "Double Your Money Back," an offer also placed on the package.

"On a percentage basis, the number of people who requested a refund of double the purchase price was infinitesimal," Singer said. "But we gladly made each refund and, with it, we would enclose a stain removal chart and a 25-cent off coupon, hoping they would try Miracle White again. One woman reversed the offer and sent Miracle White double what she spent, $1.75," he added.

After Miracle White joined Beatrice in 1967, it continued to develop its own marketing campaigns under the decentralized system of management, and it expanded its product line to include bleach, First in Fabric softener, and a new formula for Miracle White without phosphates, leading the industry in an environmentally sound decision.

Despite its profitable growth, the company was sold to the Drackett Company of Cincinnati, on January 13, 1977, in part because it was the only Beatrice grocery product that was not a food.

"The Secret Division"

Although its name never appears on a label, package, bottle, jar, or cap, at least one product from the "secret" division of Beatrice is consumed each day by every person in the United States.

The growth of the Specialty Products Division from one product and $1 in sales to the leadership in powdered ingredients for the convenience foods industry is a classic illustration of internal growth through research and development and technical marketing in its truest definition: find a need and provide a product or service to fill it.

By rendering difficult-to-handle ingredients into free-flowing items by spray dehydration, Beatrice built an entirely new industry. Today, the Specialty Products Division's products are used in an almost endless list of convenience foods. Among them are crystal drinks, fruit juices, dehydrated meals, cake, biscuit, bread, doughnut, and cookie mixes, frozen foods, ice cream, dips, canned goods, snacks, candy, pudding mixes, pizzas, whipped toppings, salad dressings, creaming agents, and even a product given to patients in hospitals before they undergo gall bladder x-rays.

Customers include the leaders of the food industry such as General Foods, General Mills, Standard Brands, Hunt-Wesson, Kraft, Pillsbury, Borden, Quaker Oats, and Gerber. Still others are R. J. Reynolds-Nabisco, McCormick, Procter & Gamble, Uncle Ben's, Lipton, Carnation, Green Giant, Pet, Jewel, and A&P.

Why would all of these companies, the majority of them vigorous competitors of Beatrice, purchase products from a rival? The one-word answer is *trust*. All customer relationships were kept in the strictest confidence. The details of any powder created for a specific product for one customer were never revealed to another customer, not even to sister companies in Beatrice. "By adhering to this principle, we built an extremely close relationship with the customer," noted Carl F. Obenauf, who was general manager of the division from 1976 until 1983.

Even the U.S. government was a customer. One of Specialty Products' developments was Trop-Bana banana flakes, which were instrumental in training chimpanzees for space exploration. NASA used the flakes in "monkey pills" to reward the animals when they pulled the proper levers during training. Still other ingredients went to the moon as part of the astronauts' food supply.

All of the division's ingredients were developed under such trade names as Beatreme, Beacreme, Wip-Treme, Lecitreme, Bealite, Liptreme and Chez Tone, among others. Most, including powdered shortenings, powdered butter, powdered sour cream, powdered lecithin, and powdered cheese, are protected by patents. Additional powdered products include emulsifiers, coffee whiteners, cream, soy sauce (LaChoy, of course), vinegar, lactic acid, wine, flavors, chicken and chicken fat, and avocado.

Obenauf remembers that "one customer asked me whether we could render whale meat into free-flowing form. Hell, I didn't know what whale meat looked like, but suggested he send some material to us. We rendered it free flowing. The product was discontinued because the industry turned to beef extract, which we also made."

The tiny seed from which the Specialty Products Division grew was sown in 1930, when C. H. Haskell purchased the Wright and Wagner Dairy, then headed by Charles Wright, Sr., in Beloit, Wisconsin. His son, Homer, however, was the father of the specialty products industry. Homer Wright was an innovator who was interested in other products than those produced by conventional dairies.

In 1941, he tried drying a powdered shortening for a client who had a patent application for powdered shortening and thought he could sell it to the baking mix industry. This was accomplished with limited success, and the Beatrice Research Department in Chicago became involved. Beatrice decided to purchase the patent application and trademark, and the patent was granted. The first customers for the nonfat milk solids and shortenings were manufacturers engaged in the fledgling cake mix business.

"Flako, later purchased by Quaker Oats, Doughnut Corporation of America and Joe Lowe were among the first to enter the mix business," recalled Obenauf, who joined Beatrice in 1951 from Borden. He succeeded Alvin Alton, who had advanced from the Beatrice Research Department to become production manager in 1949 and general manager after Wright retired in 1965.

"The products were spray-dried, high-fat, free-flowing powders which could easily be blended with flour, sugar, leavening agents, colors and flavors to obtain homogenous mixes with reduced mixing time," Obenauf explained. "The ingredients contained a minimum of 73 percent fat with the balance being nonfat milk solids with a maximum of 1.5 percent moisture."

"Powdered shortening can best be pictured as an egg," Alton reported at a meeting of the California Section of the Institute of Food Technologists in 1972, "the liquid portion being the fat and the shell being the non-fat milk solids. First the fats or oils are brought together in a general mixing vat. Then it is pasteurized. The heat applied during pasteurization also liquifies the fat which is necessary for good emulsion formation. The emulsion is formed by brute force, accomplished by using a colloid mill or a positive displacement homogenizer. The preemulsion mixture is forced through a thin screen creating great shear and tearing the large fat globule to a dimension of one to ten microns. The emulsion is then spray dried."

The food industry found these powdered products attractive for a number of reasons. The advantages are that they are powdered, siftable, nongreasy, and free-flowing; mixing is faster; high-speed packaging is implemented; the fat content of the mix can be increased and the mix is still flowable; the powders need no tempering; and waste and clean-up times are reduced.

By 1951, only nine products comprised the Specialty Products Division; seven were powdered shortenings, and two were egg yolk powders. However, sales had reached the $2.5 million level. Beatrice's chief competitors in the market were Borden, Kraft, and Paul Halton. Borden and Halton later withdrew from the field; however Kraft made a product called Sifteen, which was 65 percent liquid cottonseed oil with the balance being nonfat milk solids. Beatrice had a similar product called Beatreme when D. Homer Wright struck a deal with Kraft to manufacture Sifteen. The name *Beatreme* was coined from the words *Beatrice* and *cream* by Alvie Claxton. The egg products were formulated by E. K. Chapin and manufactured and sold by Specialty Products. Chapin also did some of the selling and received a royalty on the powders.

Beatrice's major customers in the early 1950s were Jewel, Duff Baking Mix, Pillsbury-Ballard, Quaker Oats, Eckhart Milling, Standard Milling, and Pioneer Flour Mills. Standard Milling made a biscuit mix under the Ceresota brand. Television weatherman Clint Youle was the spokesperson for the product in Chicago. Pioneer buys more from Specialty Products in a week than it did in all of 1952. Richard DeGregorio, former marketing manager of Specialty Products, became president and chief executive officer of Pioneer.

The foundation had been put in place for further diversification, and in the mid-fifties, the Specialty Products team decided to expand beyond the powdered shortening field into dehydrated sour cream and butter. The reasoning was that gourmet convenience foods such as beef stroganoff could be designed in dehydrated form if these ingredients were available. The National Dairy Council promoted sour cream during the same period. Beatrice's sour cream product was introduced to the industry in 1956, but it took five years before the first commercial product was sold. However, the sour cream concept opened the flood gates for a series of dehydrated grocery and institutional foods. The introduction of high-fat powder with aerating properties made possible the formulation of a wide range of low-moisture items such as whipped toppings, cheese cake, chiffon pie fillings, milk shake mixes, puddings, flavored dips, fruit whips, and Bavarian creme fillings.

Specialty Products developed an intensive marketing program to promote its capabilities. All of its management and sales people are food technologists, chemists, or dairy technologists. They scour the market to determine a need, and then turn to the Research Department to fulfill it. They also are persistent. Obenauf called on General Mills for seven years before he obtained an order.

"Many basic ideas for new products come about as the result of corporate research efforts as well as recommendations from our sales force," Obenauf said. By 1980, there were nine technical sales and service people working out of the Chicago and Beloit facilities. The division also is represented by technical brokers and sales agents throughout the United States, Canada, New Zealand, Australia, and the United Kingdom, as well as a sales office in Vincennes, France, and a marketing company, Beatrice/Dr. Suwelack, in Billerbeck, Germany.

Much of the credit must be accorded to the Beatrice Corporate Research Department, with special recognition to Noznick, Charles Tatter, Alton, Obenauf, DeGregorio, and Jack Warner. Noznick joined the company's corporate research staff in 1946 and was assigned the responsibility for specialty products research in the early fifties. He later became director of research and then director of the company's corporate Science and Technology Department.

The development of dehydrated cheddar cheese powder is another example of the teamwork involving research, sales, and production. A customer requested a cheddar powder to be formulated for a new macaroni and cheese item. The competitors could not meet the customer's requirements. Specialty Products did. Today, it dehydrates not only cheddar, but also blue romano, parmesan, and bakers cheese (cottage cheese). It developed nuggets in varying flavors from fruits to cheese for use in baking mixes, baked goods, and casseroles. To meet the growing demand, Alton established a cheddar cheese plant in Beloit in 1977 to ensure adequate supplies of raw materials. It also contributed to the division's profits. Subsequently, an imitation cheese powder was created.

In typical Beatrice style, the division has expanded its main plant many times. It also has been augmented by the addition of Malcolm Condensing Company of St. George, Ontario, Dell Food Specialties of Beloit, and Meat Industry Suppliers of Northbrook, Illinois.

Under the direction of Graham Malcolm, Malcolm Condensing, acquired in 1969, has steadily expanded its production of spray-dried specialties and its manufacture of milk products such as sweetened condensed whole milk and skim milk, evaporated skim, and skim milk powder. The latter was developed in conjunction with Sanna for which the division makes a number of ingredients. Malcolm Condensing has a basic intake of about fifty million pounds a year; it had increased its sales from $2.2 million to $10 million per year by 1977.

Dell Foods, headed by David Nuciforo, was integrated into the division in August 1975. It formulates and blends coating agents for the snack food industry and uses many of the products manufactured by the parent plant in Beloit as ingredients. Meat Industry Suppliers, managed by Frank Westberg, joined the group in March 1978. It formulates special spice blends—both in liquid and dry forms—for the processed meat industry. The Suwelack operation produces spray-dried products for the Beatrice/Suwelack marketing organization in Europe.

The headquarters plant has a relatively small intake of less than a hundred million pounds of milk per year, which it receives from producers within a radius of twenty miles. It ships some bulk milk to a local dairy in Rockford, Illinois, in order to qualify under federal market orders. It also expanded into blending and packaging equipment as additional special marketing tools. Working with Archie Meinerz and Robert Burns of Meinerz Cheese in New Berlin, Wisconsin, it began manufacturing cream cheese.

When the Food and Drug Administration banned various red and yellow coloring agents used in food processing in the late seventies, the division developed "colors by nature" manufactured from beets and other foods in a joint venture with Aunt Nellie's.

After the leveraged buyout by KKR in 1986, the Specialty Products Division was folded into E II Holdings, and the name was changed to Beatreme Food Ingredients. The Beatrice Research Department was closed, and the division has a staff of twenty research scientists in the Beloit plant. Warner, who joined the division in 1969, was named president when Obenauf retired in 1983, and the growth continued. By the end of fiscal year 1986, sales were approximately $100 million, compared to $44 million in 1978, and the product line had increased to six hundred. In September of 1988, Kerry Foods Inc. agreed to buy Beatreme for $130 million. Kerry is a unit of Irish-based Kerry Group PLC.

"We had a great time," Obenauf reminisced. "As I often said, 'The ridiculous is our business.' We enjoyed every minute of our work, especially when the product reached the retail trade. It all came about because of the foresight and faith of Homer Wright. He believed. I doubt that Beatrice management ever knew how much research expense Homer buried. He even paid for some of the margarine project expense at Champaign. One great advantage I had was that I never had to apologize for a product. Homer and Al Alton saw to it that we never violated a customer's confidence. Perhaps that is why the doors were always open to us. I wish Homer had lived to see where his imagination took us."

Advertising, Sales Promotions, and Contests

Although the Specialty Products Division did little advertising, and that primarily in trade magazines targeted to food technologists, Beatrice was a leader in advertising its proliferating arsenal of consumer products. For example, it was the first dairy company to advertise butter in national magazines. But because Meadow Gold, and later Viva, became national brands for milk, ice cream, butter, and other dairy products, the Marketing Department created the advertising campaigns centrally in the general office. These campaigns included radio and television commercials, billboards, free-standing newspaper inserts, and point-of-purchase materials for use by local plant managers.

In the early years, William East, a son-in-law of C. H. Haskell, was a director of these operations, and he was succeeded by Roy Ricksham, who expanded the department to include Harold Bogigian, Anthony Grady, Harold J. Berns, and Frederick Gross. Successors included Charles S. Morgan, Joseph Major, and Patrick Keenan. Things were not always perfect. For example, when Beatrice went home to Beatrice, Nebraska, to observe its seventy-fifth anniversary by holding its annual meeting there in 1972, the directors were greeted by a billboard that read, "Welcome Beatice."

Meadow Gold was one of the first dairy companies to use television. In the early fifties, it sponsored a half-hour show featuring the cowboy singer Bob Atcher and Don Williams's animal puppets. Other TV spots were produced for advertising ice cream. Subsequently, similar programs were sponsored for Louis Sherry ice cream in New York. Meadow Gold products also were promoted in the early sixties by the newly formed Major League Baseball Players Association and the American Football League Players Association. Featured were such stars as Pete Rose, Harmon Killebrew, Bill Freehan, and Ben Davidson. Killebrew would not endorse candy, so John Hoermann, division manager of Confections and Snacks, persuaded Blackhawk hockey star Bobby Hull to promote Milk Duds.

Well aware that recipes are always of paramount interest to consumers, full-color advertisements featuring "Beatrice Cooke's Mealtime Adventures" were placed in publications such as the *Ladies Home Journal,* the *Saturday Evening Post, McCall's, True Story,* and *Life.* These were supplemented by radio and newspaper advertisements and recipe pamphlets. Requests for recipes grew to a total of more than 150,000 per year. Pearson's culinary skills were attested to by the boards of directors, who looked forward to the special luncheons she prepared when meetings were held in Chicago. She also regularly conducted taste panels for various consumer groups.

A monumental symbol of the company's marketing momentum was the lighting of one of the largest and most distinctive signs in the world in 1968. Located atop the Ma Brown plant, the double-sided sign, as high as a thirteen-story building, was erected on Chicago's heavily trafficked Kennedy Expressway to be viewed by more than seven hundred thousand travelers daily. The sign combined the corporate logo with the product advertising with three changing pictorials on each side and a message changer alongside of them. It can be seen from Chicago's Loop, four miles away. The sign was updated in 1983.

Another program that combined public service with marketing was the Dairy Division's sponsorship of Marching Bands of America. The program, later directed by Garry Beckner, assisted high school bands across the country in raising funds for instruments, uniforms, and trips to regional and national competitions by providing Meadow Gold and Viva products coupons that the bands could redeem for cash. This program later was expanded to other food divisions. The company also sponsored the annual national championship competition among high school bands at Whitewater, Wisconsin, and performances by the winners at the Orange Bowl football parade in Miami on New Year's Eve.

Beatrice used a variety of in-house awards and contests to honor managers and sales managers for superior accomplishments. Contests were a long-established practice for motivating profit center managers to use every appropriate marketing tool available. On display in the reception center of Beatrice's general offices at 2 North LaSalle Street in Chicago until 1988 were 264 plaques honoring profit center managers for outstanding performances during the month of April. This Hall of Champions program was inaugurated in 1973. Each winner's picture, company, title and year of achievement were etched on a copper plate on the plaque. Stars were added for success in subsequent years. A duplicate plaque and additional stars were sent to each "champion." That was the only prize. The program graphically demonstrates one of the keys to Beatrice's remarkable internal growth performance.

The first contest was President's Month, developed in 1946 in honor of the birthday of C. H. Haskell in July. The sole award a plant received for achieving or exceeding its sales quota for July was a plaque that the president presented at the annual sales meetings held late in the year. The contest was held each year from 1946 to 1980, and sales in July increased over those of the previous July every year during that time. The only part the president had in the program was the presentation of the awards. As the company expanded, the District Managers' Month Contest was introduced. Again, the only prizes were gold, silver, and bronze trophies in recognition of the district managers whose plants showed the largest increase in sales and profits during October.

Peer recognition was the motivation. "Managers and district managers would call me up before the results were announced and ask, 'Did I win?'" recalled Harry Berns who was in charge of contests. "They didn't care about a prize. They wanted to be winners."

"These contests generated a great deal of enthusiasm and increased effort on the part of the plants," Karnes related. "They were constant reminders to the district managers, plant managers and their sales staffs of the importance of increasing sales."

In order to stimulate first-quarter—March, April, and May—sales, Beatrice ran a special contest in the seventies offering Cadillac cars to the wives of plant managers. The winners and their spouses were invited to a meeting in Chicago, where the keys to twenty-six cars parked outside were awarded.

As they were formed, divisions organized their own contests. For example, the Dairy Division staged a Fruit Ade Contest in July, an Egg Nog Contest in December, and a New Customer Contest in September. Prizes were awarded to the winning sales managers. The International Division started a Gold Cup Contest, with the winners also receiving cash prizes. In all contests, the plant or profit center competed against itself. It set a goal of a certain percent of increase in sales over the same period of the prior year.

A meeting of 750 members of the non-foods divisions at the Doral Country Club in Miami in 1972 illustrates how effective these contests were in motivating managers. After Karnes had awarded sixty-three President's Month plaques, he invited the winners to have individual pictures taken of him presenting their plaques to them. Every winner— many of them millionaires as a result of Beatrice stock they had received for their companies—patiently awaited his or her turn.

Another popular award was membership in the President's Honor Club. A number of these memberships were awarded annually at the various sales meetings to employees of the company below the rank of manager whom their supervisors had judged to have made outstanding contributions to the company during the year. The award was a special jeweled ring and a pendant for the honoree's spouse. Most of the winners later rose to senior positions in management, and they always wore their rings.

Beatrice established the William G. Karnes Community Service Award in 1983; it was presented to Beatrice operations to recognize their efforts to improve the quality of life in the communities in which they are located. A $5,000 contribution to local organizations benefiting from these activities is part of the award, and the winning plant receives a plaque. These contests and special awards focussed the attention of all members of the company on the ultimate objective, internal growth. A quarter of a century of increased sales and earnings documents that these methods worked.

In later years, Beatrice expanded its marketing efforts to a number of constructive programs, for example, the organization of the Music Bowl competitions for high school bands in regions across the country. Another innovation was the consolidation of its product displays into one display covering almost twelve-thousand square feet, a recommendation first made by Daniel Bloomfield of Bloomfield Industries in 1963.

The company sponsored workshops, entertainment, and social events at a growing number of conventions, including the Food Marketing Institute, the National Restaurant Association, the National American Wholesale Grocers Association, IGA, Piggly Wiggly, and the National Home Center show, among others. Beatrice also sponsored America's Marathon/Chicago, the Western Golf tournament, a racing car program, a bicycle classic in Texas, the Summer Olympics, the Lyric Opera in Chicago, and spots on telecasts of the 1984 Olympics.

CHAPTER TWELVE

Negotiating
Friendly Mergers

Each of the more than four hundred mergers, acquisitions, and purchases that Beatrice negotiated was completed with a friendly smile, sometimes amid a few tears, and a handshake. Beatrice never was a raider. Every acquisition was structured so that it was of greatest benefit to both the seller and to Beatrice. Each one was different, adjusted to the wishes of the seller—within reason—and to the type of products and services being acquired. Types of acquisitions negotiated included statutory mergers, stock-for-stock exchanges, stock-for-assets exchanges, poolings of interests, triangular mergers, and cash payments. One of William G. Karnes's favorites was what he termed a "nothing deal" (p. 133).

The negotiations varied in each case. However, Beatrice followed general guidelines in initiating and completing its mergers. First, Beatrice identified which field of business it wanted to enter next. Almost without exception for the larger mergers, Beatrice would pinpoint the company it wanted in that particular business. It would study the company, obtain all figures available, and determine the company's distribution area and reputation. Above all, Beatrice researched information about the quality of the company's management. The ultimate criteria were the reputations of the seller's people and brand names.

When it was determined that a company met Beatrice's standards, a representative of the company, usually Karnes and later Director of Corporate Development Lee Schlytter, or both, would call to arrange a meeting with the owners. Schlytter had joined the company in 1941 as an accountant in Montana, and advanced through the Internal Auditing Department to become a vice president and a director. He concentrated almost exclusively on mergers and acquisitions and was excellent with figures, as well as creative and imaginative. He quickly won people's confidence. When Schlytter retired, Richard W. Truelick assumed his duties. He, in turn, was succeeded by P. Robert McClure.

Usually, Beatrice had to make several calls before the prospect would consent to a meeting. As was to be expected, there were frequent instances when the company contacted showed no interest. However, as Beatrice's reputation for fair play became more widely known, more and more companies either came calling or asked banks and accounting firms to introduce them to Beatrice.

Beatrice paid few brokers' fees, and those it did pay were to brokers representing the seller and, in most cases, it was the seller's obligation to pay the fee—an arrangement also true for some large companies that investment bankers brought to Beatrice.

At a 1973 seminar, Karnes summarized his approach to negotiating mergers. "Once we have determined that there is a mutual interest in joining forces, we hold several meetings where we get to know each other," he said. "We chat about each others' philosophies. We discuss how we intend to operate the business and whether we can get along with each other. Then we talk about the price we'll pay. We make the first offer. We believe the initial price should be a fair price. It may not be our final price, but one which can be negotiated upward, if necessary. We did not ask the potential seller what his price was."

Many of the larger companies acquired were either family-owned or family-owned companies that had gone public, for example, Peter Eckrich & Sons, Samsonite, and Melnor Sprinkler. All negotiations were confidential, and Karnes and Schlytter met only with the principals of a company. They made frequent trips to cities where the companies had headquarters, and meetings would be held at a remote hotel or at the airport. Thus, if negotiations fell through, as many did, no one was hurt.

When an agreement in principle had been reached with a listed company, it was announced immediately in accordance with Securities and Exchange Commission and New York Stock Exchange regulations. In all cases, Beatrice officials met with employees of the new affiliate to introduce them to Beatrice, assure them that neither their jobs nor their benefits were in jeopardy, and answer questions. Beatrice also participated in the preparation of all news releases and related literature that went to various publics and customers in order to avoid rumors and the possibility of competitors spreading false stories.

In a number of situations—Eckrich was one—Beatrice struck out on its first overtures, then ultimately completed a deal several months or even several years later. Karnes talked to three different Eckrich presidents before the company showed interest. He met first with Henry Eckrich; the answer was a flat no. Karnes was told that the company was going public. After it did, Karnes contacted Richard Eckrich, but there was still no interest. However, when Henry Eckrich died, his estate encountered problems in selling his large block of stock because the market was too thin. Then Eckrich took the initiative. Richard and Donald Eckrich were ready to talk. The deal was consummated in 1972, with Eckrich stockholders receiving 1,918,235 shares of Beatrice common stock for their shares in a pooling of interests merger.

Karnes's persistence also paid off in the ultimate acquisition of John Sexton & Co. of Chicago, a leading purveyor of foods and related products to restaurants and other institutions. Initially, he met with one of John Sexton's daughters and her son. Then, he talked to Thomas Sexton, John Sexton's son, president of the company. None of them was interested. Some time later, T. Mackin Sexton became president, and Karnes invited him to lunch. Mackin told Karnes, "I have just been elected president of the company I've been working for all of my life. I still have a home in Pittsburgh. I have just bought another in Winnetka, Illinois. The answer is no."

However, Karnes and Schlytter were not to be deterred. Some months later, Schlytter created an attractive offer of preferred stock for Sexton. He and Karnes then called Mackin, and this time Sexton responded favorably. Mackin and William Sexton met with Karnes at the Chicago Athletic Club and worked out a deal that was completed in December of 1968.

Sexton was bought entirely on the basis of its balance sheet, profit and loss statements, and reputation as a leading company in its industry; Beatrice knew that the Sexton management was "our kind of people." Beatrice representatives never called on any of the company's nineteen branches. Of course, both Sexton and Eckrich were carefully audited by Beatrice's internal auditors before the completion of the mergers.

The acquisition of Samsonite in 1973 was the consummation of a long series of conferences to become acquainted with the members of the Shwayder family, the principal owners of the company (chapter 8). The first contact was with Emmett Heitler, a member of the family and active in management. Meetings were held with Heitler, King Shwayder, the chairman, and Louis Degan, another family member. Eventually, the family indicated interest, and the deal was effected, with Samsonite exchanging its stock for 3,795,409 shares of Beatrice common stock.

Eckrich, Sexton, and Samsonite were relatively large mergers, but Beatrice also made many smaller ones, especially in the fifties and sixties. Gordon Swaney recalls one day when Karnes scored what might be termed a "three-bagger" in baseball parlance. "He started out from his home in Illinois and called on a pizza plant in Indiana in the morning. Next he stopped at a dairy in Fort Wayne, Indiana. On the way home he called on a small maker of Oriental soy sauce in Columbia City, Indiana. Eventually, he completed deals for all three of them. Three in one day, a first for Bill Karnes."

Often the acquisition teams traveled on shoestring expense accounts.

In one instance shortly after World War II, C. H. Haskell sent Alvie Claxton and Karnes on several scouting missions to the southern states to check on dairy plants that might be available. Beatrice had a number of leads, and in one trip Claxton and Karnes called on four different plants in Tennessee and Alabama and completed the purchase of two in Alabama. It was just before Thanksgiving, and both men wanted to get home, so they went into the railroad station to purchase tickets. Claxton thought Karnes had money, and Karnes thought Claxton had money. Luckily, pooling their combined cash, they were able to buy two upper berths on the Panama Limited from Tupelo, Mississippi, back to Chicago in time for Thanksgiving.

Why were dairy companies that were family-owned, many for several generations, willing to join Beatrice? In some cases, the merger was made to settle an estate, in others to obtain working capital to expand. And others had no continuity of management. Although the present owners were willing to stay, no one in the family wanted to inherit the businesses. The best way for the owner to capitalize on a career's work was to merge with Beatrice.

A similar problem persuaded Rosarita Mexican Foods to join Beatrice. Robert Davenport, the owner of the Mesa, Arizona, based company and his wife had been killed when his private plane crashed, leaving several young children. The deal Beatrice worked out provided for their education and future security. Rosarita had fine professional management headed by Paul "Cleve" Langston that would continue.

"One reason why Karnes was so successful in effecting mergers was that he traveled a lot, made a lot of telephone calls," John Hazelton explained in a March 31, 1983, interview. "People liked Karnes. He'd tell them something and they'd believe him. I'd tell them something, and they'd think I was lying. He used to give them everything they wanted. I'd try to chisel them down."

Hazelton frequently teased Karnes about the time he "gave away the store." One day in 1948, Hazelton called Karnes, who was then Haskell's assistant, and told him that a dairy in Tiffin, Ohio, was for sale. He also advised him that a competing dairy was looking at it. However if Karnes came to Tiffin the next day, Hazelton thought Beatrice could buy it. Karnes said:

> The next morning, I checked with Haskell, and he gave us permission to buy it if it looked okay. I got on a train to Lima, Ohio, from where Earl Campbell, our manager there, drove me to Tiffin. We met Hazelton and went down to see the publisher of the newspaper, who was the executor for the estate of the owner of the dairy. The publisher knew nothing about the

dairy but gave us two annual reports. We told him that if he would give us about an hour to study the reports, we would have an offer for him. John warned me that we had to work out the deal that night because the rival dairy was so interested that it had several people checking equipment and even counting the milk bottles. We met with the publisher that night and gave him a cash offer which we intended to include only the equipment, good will and rental of the building. He said, "Does this also include the inventory?" John and I looked at each other for a second and replied with an instant "Yes." The editor accepted our offer, and we also got the inventory. Right after he left us, John chided me. "You gave away the retail store."

The dairy owned a retail store in downtown Tiffin. I told John we didn't like retail stores, but he said we could have gotten the store, too. We went out to look at the plant after we made the deal, and I told John, "They're going to have to paint the plant before we buy it." The next day, John called up the publisher and told him he would have to have the plant painted before we would go ahead with the deal. He agreed to do so. Then John called me about a week later and said, "We're in trouble." . . . the dairy had 130 employees, about twice as many as we had at a plant in Newcastle, Indiana, which was about the same size. However, Hazelton worked that [problem] out over time, and the plant became quite profitable, even without the store I gave away.

Harry Niemiec, an executive vice president and director of Beatrice, offered an additional explanation of why Karnes's negotiating technique was so effective. "Karnes created an atmosphere wherein people felt secure in merging with Beatrice," he observed. "Most of the businesses were privately owned. The owners had built their businesses, and their lives were wrapped up in them. Large corporations intimidated them to some degree. Bill Karnes gave them comfort and confidence."

After it was determined that both parties of a proposed merger could work together, Beatrice outlined its management policies, indicated how the company would be managed, explained its decentralized management system, interest and cash management programs, salary and bonus arrangements, pension plans, and stock options. Then Beatrice sought assurances that the present management would stay and that there was back-up management to operate the company in the years ahead. If the present management was not willing to stay, Karnes was not interested. Only after all such matters had been discussed was the price mentioned.

Beatrice used various formulas for mergers. Originally, most of the acquisitions were made for cash because the owners were in the dairy business and were quite small. In those situations, it was cash for the equipment, good will, and the lease of the building. In many cases, Beatrice used the seller's cash in the bank to make the down payment.

This benefited both parties. If the seller took the cash out before the merger, it was classified as a dividend. If the seller received it as a purchase price, it was taxable as a capital gain.

In later years, Beatrice developed what it called "the nothing deal." Beatrice would lease the equipment, trucks, and buildings; pay cash for the receivables; and use the first day's sales receipts from the new affiliate to open a bank account. It had a leasing arrangement with a Chicago bank; the bank would buy trucks, and Beatrice would lease them. Next, Beatrice would work out an equipment-leasing deal with the bank or insurance company similar to the truck arrangement. However, Beatrice would carry the lease on the building.

Beatrice would recover its original cash payment when the receivables (the money owed the company acquired) had paid themselves out. Therefore, the total investment that Beatrice would have would be the obligation on the leases. For tax reasons and for a guaranteed cash flow over a long period, this type of transaction, backed by Beatrice, was also beneficial to the seller. The rental income carried on for fifteen to twenty years. In all cases, Beatrice had an option to renew at a fixed formula.

A nothing deal that Karnes remembers well involved a dairy that Beatrice bought in Montana. The district manager told Karnes that he definitely wanted the dairy and to please not offer a "nothing deal."

"So we met with the owner and tried different approaches of cash and stock," Karnes related. "Finally the owner said, 'I hear you make deals where you rent everything.' And I asked, 'Is that the kind of a deal you want?'

" 'Very definitely,' he said. 'I want to leave the income to my children over a period of years. I don't want them to have all of the cash at once.' So we leased the trucks and the equipment and the building and bought the receivables on a guaranteed basis. It turned out to be one of the best nothing deals we ever made."

As the company grew in sales volume, so did the size of many of its mergers, and stock was used or traded, depending upon whether the company was privately or publicly owned. As a result of these mergers, Beatrice "sold" a large amount of stock at high prices because the common stock was selling at from sixteen to twenty times earnings and, at one time, as high as twenty-six times earnings. Beatrice also acquired a lot of cash from these transactions because many of the companies were quite liquid. In effect, Beatrice was trading its stock for cash with a minimum of expense.

Karnes chuckles as he recalls one transaction with a large company in the South. At the closing, the principal stockholder told Karnes that when his wife and daughter signed the agreement, they both burst into tears. "Don't worry, when they cash their large dividend checks in the future, they'll be crying all the way to the bank," Karnes reassured him. In fact, had they held their stock until the leveraged buyout in 1986, they would have seen an appreciation of more than 250 percent in the value of their stock. One seller, who sold four associated companies in Texas to Beatrice in 1967, kept his stock until the buyout in 1986 and, through two 2-for-1 stock splits and the buyout, cashed in his stock at four times what it was worth in 1967.

Divestitures were almost unknown during the Karnes-Hazelton-Grantham era. "When you bought a company, you made it grow, made it more profitable," observed Swaney. "That was the company policy. We were not junkmen who bought a company and then sold off the parts for cash."

International mergers were made for cash because there was no tax advantage for the foreign sellers in accepting stock. Beatrice issued convertible subordinated debentures in the European market to provide the necessary cash, as noted previously. Generally, the same guidelines were followed in acquiring foreign companies as in the United States, with the exception that Beatrice insisted that the seller and remaining managers retain between 15–20 percent of the company. They had a right to "put" this stock to Beatrice over a period of years, and Beatrice had a call on the sellers to buy the stock in the foreign subsidiary over a period of time. Many of them held their stock until the buyout in 1986. Karnes recalls pleading with one owner overseas to hold onto his stock. He didn't. "He sold before the buyout. It cost him a bundle."

It was Beatrice's policy not to acquire companies that were losing money, companies where the management would not stay, or companies that had no backup for present management. Profits and management were always very important; in fact, they were paramount. Beatrice always had a few plants that were not making money, and it didn't need more. Its goal in its expansion program was always to increase the rate of return on its equity to offset growing inflation and enable Beatrice to increase dividends on its stock.

Even if a company was making money and had management, it did not always qualify for acquisition. It did not qualify if sales were not increasing, or if it was in a limited or a declining market. It did not qualify by Karnes's standards if its product was basically a commodity, or the product's price was determined by a national or world market, as in the case of coffee. It did not qualify if its competitors were giant companies, as in the cereal business. Karnes did not like large acquisitions in which a wrong guess could hurt the company, as it did in the case of Tropicana and Esmark.

To illustrate some of the acquisition guidelines, a comparison of two acquisitions is perhaps helpful: Dannon Yogurt, an ideal acquisition, and Company X, which presented many problems.

Dannon Yogurt	*Company X*
Profits: Fine gross margins, one of the best of all Beatrice food products; always a cash producer.	Profits: Profits depended on pricing set by foreign competition and the extent of research into new products; losses in some years.
Management: Excellent management. Father backed up by son who stayed with the company until they retired.	Management: Founder left the company at time of merger. Several unsuccessful managers followed.
Product: Unique, a growing niche in the food business.	Product: Very competitive with a high obsolescence factor. Required intensive advertising and marketing in an ever-changing market.
Competition: Time of purchase and during the twenty-five years with Beatrice, practically no national competition; always held top position in U.S. market.	Competition: Several large competitors in the United States plus foreign competition from large aggressive companies; share of market very small.
Growth: Tremendous growth over thirty years and still growing. Per capita yogurt consumption in 1960 .26 pounds per person, increasing to 4 pounds per person in 1987.	Growth: Some growth over the years but highly dependent on developing new products. Products had high degree of obsolescence.
Investment: Purchased for Beatrice stock. No good will, fine return on stock issued. Produced sufficient cash flow to expand Dannon and build five plants across the United States; held 20 percent of entire market.	Investment: Multiple very high, total cost contained substantial amount of good will. Net effect was to add nothing to (and actually reduced) Beatrice earnings per share; Beatrice also had to invest additional monies in capital improvements as well.

What is true about Dannon is true about a host of Beatrice companies such as LaChoy, Fisher Nut, Eckrich meats, County Line Cheese, Sanna, Taylor Freezer, Stiffel, Brown-Miller, Vigortone, and the entire Chemical Division as well as many international companies.

Beatrice's expansion program was to augment its growth by buying smaller, profitable companies that immediately added to the sales and cash flow.

The next step was to finance these companies with their unique products and encourage their management to grow—to create jobs and new products, build plants, and expand these regional companies into companies with national distribution. The resulting profits would provide increasing dividends for Beatrice shareholders. This provided stability and balance over thirty years to support six stock splits and many dividend increases during that period. Acquisitions such as Company X did not contribute.

Every major concern was covered to make the transition from an independent company into Beatrice as smooth and painless as possible. For example, Beatrice would assume the pension plans of the acquired company and, over time, would freeze the assets in these pension plans and enroll the same people under the Beatrice pension plan, which usually was better. Thus, the individual would be covered by two pension plans when he or she retired. If the acquired company had a better pension plan or a good profit-sharing plan, Beatrice would continue it.

The merger steps Beatrice used can be summarized in ten guidelines. (1) Survey the industry and pick the best company. (2) Obtain as much information as possible, particularly about reputation and people. (3) Make your own contacts. Beatrice used few brokers. (4) Use first meetings to get acquainted and to see if management philosophies are compatible. (5) Keep negotiations secret and confidential. (6) Avoid unfriendly mergers because management must stay, and backup management must be available. (7) Use the type of compensation in each acquisition that fits the seller's needs—cash, lease, or stock. (8) Make the first price offer and do not ask for the seller's price. (9) Be present at the announcement after a deal was completed to tell Beatrice's story to the employees and the public. (10) Use Beatrice's own internal auditors to audit the deals before closing.

An extremely important benefit came from the practices of considering only friendly mergers, using its own auditors to make the initial audit, and treating management fairly after the agreement was signed. Beatrice never had a lawsuit filed by the seller or any of the company's shareholders. When several shareholders of a large company with which Beatrice was negotiating threatened a lawsuit, Beatrice quickly withdrew its offer. It didn't want just a family—it wanted a happy family.

George E. Haskell set the basic policies that led to Beatrice's growth.

C. H. Haskell, Beatrice president from 1928–52.

William G. Karnes

John F. Hazelton, Sr.

From left: Harold F. Stotzer, Walter L. Dilger, and Don L. Grantham, Chicago, 1967.

George A. Gardella

Don L. Grantham

From left: Alvie J. Claxton, Charles H. Patten, and Aaron Marcus.

Lewis Komminsk

William G. Mitchell

John T. McGreer

Carl Hansen

Wallace N. Rasmussen

Edward M. Muldoon

Brown W. Cannon

Louis Nielson

Harry Niemiec

John J. McRobbie

Paul T. Kessler, Jr.

Gordon E. Swaney

William W. Granger, Jr.

Donald P. Eckrich

James L. Dutt

Juan E. Metzger

Anthony Luiso

Robert Cooper

Richard A. Voell

Carl F. Obenauf

Harry C. Wechsler

John P. Fox, Jr.

Louis E. Stahl

Homer Wright

From left: John H. Coleman, Jay G. Neubauer, and Edward M. Muldoon.

Frederich B. Rentschler

Donald P. Kelly

Leo Singer

Roland M. Binnington

From left: R. Wilbur Daeschner, Gerald C. North, and Fred K. Schomer

CHAPTER THIRTEEN

People, a Company's Finest Resource

Times don't change; people change them. And companies don't grow; people build them. Through all of the years since the founding of Beatrice, William G. Karnes and his predecessors recognized that the most successful companies are those in which all employees play a meaningful part.

"We are a people-oriented company," Karnes advised attendees at the fiftieth anniversary convention of the Phi Eta Sigma honor fraternity at the University of Illinois in 1973.

> We believe people are our greatest resource. The success of Beatrice is the result of the efforts of all of the men and women. Our company believes it has certain responsibilities it must fulfill every day. We must create wealth so that the countries in which we operate can grow. We do this by providing more and more productive and meaningful jobs as well as by earning profits that yield taxes to support governments. We also feel we must free each individual employee from economic personal concerns—a home he can call his own, creature comforts for his family and himself, economic security. But there is much more to it than that, however. We believe we must provide our employees with the opportunity to grow, to develop their talents and know-how. We must offer them challenges. Our decentralized system of management encourages each individual to capitalize on his abilities, make the most of his skills, satisfy his ambitions. We don't say our system is the answer for every company. But it is successful for us.

Karnes cited two principal qualities that Beatrice looked for in the men and women it hired and those it considered for promotion: "They must be people-oriented, be able to get along with other people and motivate them; they must be profit-minded. Our system puts its faith in people," he said. "Our philosophy is that the best way to get a job done is to pick a good man or woman who has demonstrated these two qualities, give him or her the authority to do the job, offer rewarding incentives, and hold that person responsible for accomplishing it. . . . It's not necessary to get along with a computer. But it is important to get along with the people who operate the computer."

One measure of a company is the people it keeps. Beatrice provided motivational incentives designed to retain valued employees. These incentives were augmented, and others were added as the company grew. One of course, was money. Managers received a base salary plus a bonus based on a percentage of their plants' pretax profits.

Another incentive was a firm policy of promoting from within the company, both vertically and horizontally. Until 1980, every district manager and subsequently every division manager was promoted from within Beatrice. "People knew that if they did a good job, advancement was possible," Karnes said. "It was incumbent on management people at all levels to train their successors." Any employee could even aspire to be Number One. Every chief executive officer during the company's entire history as a corporation had invested his entire business life with Beatrice. All started from low-ranking—and low-paying—jobs and worked their way up to the top of the executive ladder.

A pension plan was introduced in 1944. Over the years, it was continually improved so that by the 1980s it was one of the best in the food industry. The first stock option plan was adopted in 1957. It, too, was continually modified and expanded to include more and more people. Karnes believes Beatrice probably extended its options program to more levels of management than most companies. Included were all plant managers and many at the second echelon of plants. In later years, management incentive plans were devised that were built around the return of profits on investment, such as a phantom stock plan. Members of the general office staff were included in all of these plans.

These programs were successful in encouraging people to stay with the company and contribute to their fullest capabilities. They also generated enthusiasm and maintained a high standard of morale. Turnover of managers and officers was negligible; during the twenty-five-year period when Karnes was chief executive officer, the company lost only one officer whom it did not want to lose. Even though salaries were not high in comparison with other companies in the food industry, there was general enthusiasm throughout the company because Beatrice was a winner, and people were proud to be affiliated with it.

Every district and division manager was a profit-maker. Each also could train and motivate people and build them to become management material. Outstanding examples over the years were John F. Hazelton, C. H. Haskell, John T. McGreer, Don L. Grantham, Brown W. Cannon, Alvie Claxton, Charles McConnell, Carl Hansen, Jay Neubauer, William W. Granger, Jr., Edward Comegys, Sr., Paul McClure, John Conners, Lewis Komminsk, E.A. Walker, Edward M. Muldoon, George Gardella, Donald Eckrich, Harry Niemiec, James Weiss, Louis Stahl, and Harry Wechsler.

All advanced from humble beginnings. Weiss, for example, started his business career with 60 cents in the 1930s. He repaired a broken-down mimeograph machine and went into the printing business. He was a high school drop-out who later studied nights and weekends at schools such as the Lewis Institute, the Illinois Institute of Technology, and the Art Institute of Chicago. Then he expanded from printing into the candy business. It did so well that he sold it for $6 million to Beatrice in 1965.

It was Weiss, not the candy and printing businesses, that Beatrice bought. He rose to become an executive vice president and director of the company and became responsible for all manufactured products. So did Niemiec, who started as a salesman for Mario's Olives in Detroit. Grantham, who became president, began his career working in the office of a dairy plant in Mattoon, Illinois.

In 1978 in an interview by Don Gussow, editor-in-chief of his Magazines for Industry Publishing Company, Weiss was asked, "What do you think is the key to success for the independent entrepreneurs who join Beatrice Foods when selling Beatrice their companies?" Weiss replied:

> From a long-range viewpoint the bottom line, the profitability of the business, is the basic determing factor, but it is not the only element of success for the former entrepreneur who merges his company with Beatrice Foods. The healthy, friendly but pragmatic interrelationship between the independent entrepreneur and the members of senior management at the local operating unit as well as his relationship with the person to whom he reports as well as his relationship with corporate level management is a key to his and Beatrice's success. Mr. Karnes always says, "People are our most important asset. We do it with people or we don't do it at all." I totally agree with Mr. Karnes and his philosophy of management, and it is my responsibility to create the ideal environment for these people to prosper.

For Karnes, working with Haskell and McGreer was an enlightening experience. "Both were warm, understanding men who took the time to help and teach young company people," he recalled. "They were demanding, as they had to be, but for a job well done there was always a pat on the back. They managed in a positive way, not by fear or threats." That continued to be the Beatrice way under Karnes, whose office door was never closed.

"In delegating responsibility and demanding accountability of the plant managers, Haskell and his management team did not seek to create an authoritarian climate within the plant," Karnes noted. "Quite the contrary. Haskell constantly urged his managers to develop a team spirit within the plant and use positive techniques of motivation."

Haskell frequently wrote "Dear Manager" letters on the subject. In a letter dated December 5, 1945, he said: "I am very pleased to say that there seems to be a general awakening among managers concerning the importance of relationships between management and employees. I have recently received several requests for a guide or code of conduct for supervisors, foremen, sales managers and managers in their relationships with employees under their supervision."

The letter also included a list of do's and don't's developed from recommendations of several company committees. They included: (1) ask, don't order; (2) give full credit for a job well done; (3) know how to correct people, don't carry a grudge; and (4) don't be afraid to give responsibility.

Haskell concluded, "The code of conduct is a simple statement of common sense. I'm sure there isn't anything in it that you haven't agreed with all along. Yet, like the Ten Commandments, we've got to do more than agree with them. We've got to live with them."

Karnes subscribed fully to these policies that had prevailed before him. In an article in the *New York Times* on Sunday, March 19, 1972, entitled "Head of a People Company," James N. Nagle wrote, "Mr. Karnes' calm disposition doesn't diminish the respect in which he is held by employees. He has rarely been heard to raise his voice and no one can recall having heard him swear." One of his closest associates describes him as "an extremely sensitive person who has a feeling for people and knows how to get the best out of them."

Richard A. Voell, formerly executive vice president of Beatrice, wrote in the December 1987 *Focus*, the house paper of the Rockefeller group,

When I was at Beatrice, Beatrice was a $350 million domestic dairy company in 1958. The chief executive, Bill Karnes, said that we are to go for $1 billion. That sounded like an unreachable goal at first, but in 10 years we did it. When we got to a billion in 1968, he said now we are going to become the largest food company in the world. And between 1968 and 1978, we went from $1 billion to $9 billion in sales. We had the largest running record of any company on the New York Stock Exchange—25 years of uninterrupted increases in sales earnings and earnings per shares. We passed all the players on the field. We outran every competitor. Yet Beatrice Foods was a collection of ordinary people; it wasn't a collection of stars.

Now let me recall what Karnes did. He put together a diverse team of people who respected each other, people who had great consideration and tolerance for differences of opinion—the diametric opposite of an organization where everybody is a paper cutout or a replica of one another.

Beatrice was an excellent example of the value of balance. It was a diverse, but balanced team: Beatrice didn't have any dominating concentrations of 30, 40 or 60-year olds. It didn't have all Ph.D.'s or M.B.A.'s or all accountants or all marketers. Beatrice was a mix of backgrounds, education, experience; people working in an environment of mutual respect with their varying talents and strengths complementing each other for the success of the organization.

What was remarkable at Beatrice was the teammates' genuine affection as well as respect for each other. They recognized that the key to success was not taking the other guy's piece of pie but enlarging the pie by working together to build more opportunities. People didn't say, "Okay, here's our company and for me to get from here to there I've got to knock this guy out or knock that guy out." What they said instead was, "Let's expand our opportunities by building a more successful company."

This policy of treating people as part of the "family" was manifested in various, meaningful ways. Top officials always attended sales meetings and made a point of greeting managers by their first names and, in almost all instances, knew the names of managers' spouses. Awards at the meetings always were presented by a senior officer. Haskell, Karnes, Grantham, Hazelton, Rassmusen, and Dutt attended these meetings to demonstrate their interest in those present. The awards weren't dealt out like a hand of poker; each presentation was preceded by a thumbnail citation of the individual's accomplishments.

As another example of the people-to-people philosophy of the company, management personnel and their spouses in the area were invited to a dinner on the night before an annual meeting. In a practice more memorable than an impersonal speech, Karnes made it a practice to introduce everyone present by name. As many as two hundred would attend a meeting, but Karnes never missed, not only on names but also on ad-libbing a few comments about their efforts in behalf of the company. This procedure was especially effective at a meeting in Brussels, Belgium, in 1973, attended by company directors and most of the European management and their spouses.

There were other personal touches that mirrored the human relationships that the company considered invaluable. Karnes personally signed and sent birthday cards to management people; it was mandatory that members of top management attend funerals for management people; and many weddings of their children were attended by representatives of the General Office. On the day before Christmas, Karnes personally went around the General Office and to plants in the Chicago area to wish Merry Christmas to every employee and to shake his or her hand. He even gave all General Office employees the afternoon off following the annual Christmas party. He went back to work.

It was always a source of personal pain to Karnes when an officer or management person had to be dismissed for lack of performance. These occasions were rare, but the esprit de corps of the company was evidenced in the fact that the employee remained friendly and supportive of the company. There never was a lawsuit resulting from the dismissal of an employee while Karnes was in charge.

The value of all these people-oriented programs can be illustrated by two instances after Beatrice began spinning off divisions. After Beatrice sold its Shedd operations in 1984 to Lever Brothers, which had been contracting with Shedd to manufacture Imperial margarine, a Beatrice official encountered an executive of Lever Brothers. "Boy," the Lever Brothers executive volunteered, "Shedd is a great operation with a fine group of people."

On another occasion, after the sale of Meadow Gold Dairy Division to Borden in December 1986, another Beatrice representative met a Borden officer at a trade show. "We bought Meadow Gold to give us distribution in markets in which we were not operating," the Borden employee said. "We didn't recognize how many great management people we are getting."

CHAPTER FOURTEEN

Keep Owners
and Market Informed

The obvious way to keep the shareholders—the actual owners of a company—happy is to increase the market price of the stock and the dividends. Equally important to Beatrice since its first shareholders' meeting just before the turn of the century had been to keep them informed on an ongoing basis. The principal ways used to communicate with shareholders were through annual and interim reports, supplemented by annual meetings and letters from the chief executive officer about special actions deemed significant.

In the early years, the annual meeting of Beatrice shareholders could have been held around a kitchen table. Until the early forties, only ten people attended in addition to the directors. Usually, they were the same ten people.

However, the number of shareholders was increasing steadily, principally because C. H. Haskell issued additional common stock to raise capital. Recognizing this, the company sent invitations to the 1941 annual meeting to shareholders in the Chicago area. One of the attractions was a lunch that featured company products. About sixty gathered in the theater of the company's Chicago State Street plant.

In 1944, after Beatrice had moved its headquarters to 120 South LaSalle Street, it scheduled the annual meeting in the Grand Ballroom of the Palmer House. The invitation list was expanded to include not only shareholders in the area, but also bankers, local customers, and the press. The meeting was widely reported in the Chicago newspapers and a number of business magazines. More than three hundred were present to hear Haskell conduct the business of the meeting, introduce the directors, review the results of the previous year's operations, and answer questions. A company motion picture was shown. After lunch, gift packages of the company's food products were distributed.

Basically, this format was used for all future meetings until 1986, when the company was taken private by a leveraged buyout.

Attendance grew each year as the number of shareholders steadily increased. In 1951, the meeting at the Palmer House drew 375 shareholders and guests. At the close of fiscal year 1952, there were 6,498 common shareholders and 1,316 preferred shareholders. It is significant that 54 percent of the shareholders were women and only 5 percent were institutions and insurance corporations.

The meetings—and the luncheons—were so well received that Beatrice decided to hold them in other cities as the number of shareholders in other states became significant. The first was in New York City in 1949, and the next meeting there was held in 1957. Subsequent meetings were held in Boston, Denver, Dallas, Milwaukee, Lincoln, Beatrice, Los Angeles, San Francisco, Tampa, Nashville, and San Diego.

Several of the meetings are worth discussing in greater detail. What other major company ever held an outdoor barbecue for its shareholders and guests or featured a high school marching band? In observance of its diamond jubilee annual meeting, the company decided to "go home" to Beatrice, Nebraska, in 1972, but because Beatrice had only one small motel, the directors and their wives met in Lincoln, forty miles north. The morning of the meeting, they, bankers and investment analysts from Lincoln, and members of the media boarded a special train for the short trip. At Beatrice, they were met by Nebraska Governor J. James Exon and Robert Sargent, mayor of Beatrice, and escorted in antique cars amid forty floats and marching bands through the town's main streets. All stores had window displays of Beatrice products, and prizes were awarded to the winners. Everyone involved wore seventy-fifth anniversary badges. After the annual meeting in the city auditorium, the entire population of Gage County was invited to a western barbecue. More than three thousand were served a wide selection of Meadow Gold products, as well as beef that had been pit-barbequed for three days.

In 1976, the last meeting at which William G. Karnes presided, more than a thousand were present in the Arie Crown Theatre in Chicago's McCormick Place. They were serenaded by a two-hundred-piece marching band from Conant High School of Hoffman Estates, Illinois, at the close of the meeting. By 1976, Beatrice stock was held by more than forty-three thousand persons and institutions.

By 1985, Karnes had attended fifty consecutive annual meetings. Until he retired, the agenda was essentially the same. The first business at many meetings in the 1960s and 1970s was to announce that the stock had closed at a new high on the previous day and that the directors had increased the dividend again that morning—a point at which the shareholders always rose to give management a standing ovation.

As Karnes often said, "After these two announcements and the election of the directors, why not close the meeting and invite the shareholders to an early lunch?" In the twenty-five annual meetings that

Karnes conducted while he was chief executive officer, no one ever asked him about the earnings' origins. Shareholders were satisfied that the earnings were there, that their stock was worth more, and that their dividends were greater. Over the quarter of a century, there were six stock splits.

As the nationwide interest in Beatrice increased, the meetings began to attract what the financial press termed "corporate gadflies" such as Lewis D. Gilbert and his brother, John, Wilma Soss, and Martin Glotzer. In Karnes's opinion, Lewis Gilbert in particular was a constructive force in the corporate communications of many major companies in the United States. However, Karnes did not agree with all of Gilbert's recommendations. Usually, a Beatrice representative met with Gilbert before the meeting to assure that the meeting would proceed with dispatch. Gilbert was always cooperative. At least two rehearsals were held before each annual meeting, and Karnes and members of the senior management team would review a two-hundred-page document prepared in anticipation of any possible questions from the floor.

At Karnes's final meeting as chairman, Gilbert presented a resolution complimenting the company on its excellent shareholder relations. On two other occasions, when Karnes was elected to the boards of other companies, Gilbert congratulated their managements on selecting a director who really understood shareholder relations.

Karnes firmly believed that it was obligatory for a chief executive officer to publicize the progress of the company as widely as possible. Steady increases in the price-earnings ratio not only were of benefit to all the shareholders, but they also made Beatrice's common stock more attractive to those companies targeted as merger candidates. To these ends, the company cultivated security analysts across the United States as well as in foreign countries from Europe to Japan. In the mid-fifties and sixties, security analysts began paying closer attention to this "sleepy dairy firm from the Midwest." As many as thirty analysts began following Beatrice's progress in the sixties. At first, Karnes handled most of these calls, but eventually, George Zulanas, an accountant, was assigned all contacts with analysts.

In addition, Karnes and other senior officers began meeting regularly with societies that were members of the Financial Analysts Federation. As many as eighteen presentations a year were made in cities such as New York, Chicago, Boston, Philadelphia, Detroit, Atlanta, Dallas, Houston, Denver, Minneapolis, Los Angeles, San Francisco, San Diego, Pittsburgh, Sarasota, and Fort Lauderdale. Later Beatrice increased its exposure to the financial community by sponsoring conferences around the country to which analysts, bankers, and other investment specialists were invited.

To assure that its financial rating was triple A, Beatrice also met at least once a year with representatives from Standard & Poor's, Moody's Investor Service, and Babson. Management insisted that all personnel always tell the truth and not dissemble. The figures were never inflated; predictions were forbidden. "We just gave them all the facts," Karnes said.

Interest also mounted steadily in the media in direct proportion to the company's growth. Karnes met frequently with writers from the *Wall Street Journal*, *Business Week*, *Forbes*, and major newspapers in the United States. In 1976, *Fortune* published an eight-page feature on the company—the first time it had done so since 1936.

The company did little institutional advertising. Although its brand names, including Meadow Gold, Dannon, LaChoy, Samsonite, Culligan, and Eckrich were advertised heavily, their association with Beatrice was almost invisible. However, the name of Beatrice Foods was well known on Wall Street and in the financial circles. "We operated on the theory of having as many reliable sources as possible to spread the good word about us—employees, shareholders, customers, analysts, brokers, bankers, retirement funds managers and many others," Karnes said. "It was effective and relatively inexpensive. It was the most effective advertising of Beatrice we could do."

Karnes bristled whenever security analysts and writers identified Beatrice as a conglomerate after it began adding non-food companies. "We are a diversified, international company with our primary emphasis on food," he asserted. In fact, foods accounted for 75 percent of sales in fiscal year 1977.

The company's major document, of course, was its annual report. Karnes had received his indoctrination into the intricacies and time demands of annual reports in March 1952, when he was in Champaign, Illinois, and was informed of C. H. Haskell's death. He spent the time on the return train trip to Chicago drafting the annual report, which was due at the printers.

Karnes frequently offered the opinion that "you could print the annual report on bathroom tissue if the numbers were good," however, his actions were diametrically counter to his words.

Beatrice won a number of awards for its annual report, which became more and more detailed and sophisticated. Beatrice began printing it in four colors in the mid-sixties, and the number of pages grew as the company grew and Securities and Exchange Commission and New York Stock Exchange requirements increased. Karnes also believed that all figures should be reported on a historical basis to show true growth, rather than restate them for poolings of interests' mergers. Finally, he compromised by having them reported both ways in 1966.

The annual report was supplemented by interim reports. Beatrice was one of the first major companies to issue quarterly reports, which consisted of a message from the president, a profit and loss statement (unaudited) comparing the current quarter with the same quarter in the previous year, and information about the company's progress, such as development of new products, new facilities, and promotions. Subsequently, coupons offering discounts on selected consumer products were inserted in the reports. The dividend was included with each report, which increased the probability that it would be read. These reports only presented details of what had been accomplished. No projections or predictions were ever made.

The result of these practices was that the price of Beatrice stock climbed through the years. It ranged from between eleven and twenty times earnings, and in 1962 rose to twenty-six times earnings, an extremely high multiple at the time. The multiple also was boosted by frequent increases in dividends and six stock splits from 1952 to 1977. The dividend was raised ten times between 1965 and 1977. A share of Beatrice common stock that sold for $20 on the market in 1952 was worth $80 in 1977.

Unfortunately, some of these practices were abandoned after 1980, and a share of Beatrice common stock that was worth $28 in July 1976 was only valued at $29 in August 1985, even though a bull market started in 1982, and Beatrice dividends per share were doubled during the period. This lack of stock price improvement indicates that policies followed in earlier years, although relatively inexpensive, were highly effective.

CHAPTER FIFTEEN

The Financial Formula
Was KISS

Shortly after he became president of Beatrice, William G. Karnes received a visit from the treasurer of the company. "Our cash balance at the bank is under $2 million," the concerned treasurer advised Karnes. "What shall we do about it?" After he recovered from shock, Karnes asked the treasurer to explain. "We always maintain a cash balance of $2 million in the bank," the treasurer said.

"In 1952, that was big money for us," Karnes recalled. " 'However, we are not going to leave that much money in the bank—we are going to put it to work!' I told him. I asked him to invest it in treasury bills or similar securities that were safe and paid interest. The return on our investment in treasury bills was enough to pay for the cost of the entire treasurer's department for a year." Karnes was ultra-conservative in cash management, but $2 million was excessive even for him. Karnes also regarded debt as an anathema. Robert W. France, who later became treasurer, remembers that he finally was allowed to open a line of credit at one of the banks with which Beatrice dealt. "It was for a minimal sum and never used," he reported.

Beatrice's accounting and auditing systems had not changed much since 1909 when C. H. Haskell teamed with J. H. Greenhalgh to introduce uniform systems for all profit centers. However, as the number of profit centers around the world multiplied, the company's system for financial controls was reviewed in depth in the mid-1950s. Despite Beatrice's long-established policy of decentralization and its strict hands off philosophy, it was deemed necessary to establish a strong system of accounting controls. Rather than devising elaborate accounting systems with detail reporting and monitoring, Beatrice did just the opposite. Basically, the company used the "KISS formula": Keep It Short and Simple.

The keystone in maintaining controls was a simplified system of financial reporting. The structure was pyramidal, and the reports were basic. In early 1976, there were more than four hundred individual profit center managers. They reported to fourteen divisional vice presidents who worked directly with Karnes and Don L. Grantham.

The accounting reports used by the profit centers were the monthly reports (MRs) due in the Corporate Office by the tenth of the following month. Copies were also sent to the district managers and the division vice presidents. These reports were basic, consisting primarily of a balance sheet, income statement, some details of expenses, and a product line profit report (fig. 3). The accounting system needed to produce such reports was also simple and required no large accounting department and, for many smaller profit centers, required only a part-time bookkeeper.

As Beatrice grew and new companies were acquired, all adopted these same basic financial reports. The change-over procedures used to put these "new Beatrice" companies on the standard Beatrice MR reports were done by the Internal Audit Department. This department also made sure that the proper acquisition cut-off day transactions were recorded, and that the Beatrice philosophy of conservative accounting procedures was adhered to.

The Internal Auditing Department, together with the company's outside auditors, made sure that all the major profit centers were visited and audited at least once a year. The smaller profit centers were audited on a random rotating basis at least once every few years unless there were reasons to believe more frequent audits were necessary. This procedure, although required by law, did not result in any interference with corporate's basic hands-off policy.

The audits were primary operational audits in addition to being financial. The auditors usually had a wide range of knowledge and personal experiences from visiting other Beatrice and non-Beatrice plants and were generally well respected by the operational staff. In fact, many of the auditors moved from the Auditing Department to operations. For example, Anthony Luiso started as an internal auditor in 1971 and progressed through the ranks all the way to executive vice president of all food operations in 1984.

The auditors' comments and suggestions were taken seriously and were reviewed and discussed with management, and action was taken on these recommendations. The result was that almost all profit centers benefited from a visit from the internal audit staff.

The Corporate Accounting Department and the Auditing Department worked closely together, and there was considerable personnel movement between them. Because of Beatrice's hands-off policy, the Corporate Accounting Department did no financial analysis on the individual profit centers. Corporate Accounting, therefore, requested only financial information necessary to carry out its responsibilities—primarily taxes and external reporting. If any questions arose about a profit center's MRs, the answers had to come from the operating staff or the Corporate Auditing

Figure 3. Monthly Report Form
(Cents Omitted from This Report)

PLANT NO |1|3| |2|8|2| |9|

PLANT NAME   EXPENSE FOR THE MONTH OF January 30, 1977

INF. NO.	MR.1 LINE	ACCOUNT CLASSIFICATION	A CURRENT DATE 01/02/77	B BASE DATE 02/28/73	C INCREASE (DECREASE)
1		ASSETS			
2					
3	2	Cash (Exclude Central Banking Cash)	14 277	591 069	
4	4	Accounts and Notes Receivable (Gross)	10 068 704	5 165 607	
5	6	Inventories	8 740 869	5 287 715	
6	7	Prepaid Expenses	462 153	487 173	
7	23	Non Current Receivables (Net)	44 500	60 755	
8	26	Other Non Current Assets	169 320	166 865	
9					
10		TOTAL ASSETS	19 499 823	11 759 184	7 740 639
11		LIABILITIES			
12					
13	31	Accounts Payable	7 143 519	4 631 272	
14	33	Accrued Taxes (Except Taxes on Income)	557 310	443 206	
15	34	Other Reserves and Accruals	3 507 514	1 968 237	
16	43	Other Intercompany	177 747	(7 326 016)	
17					
18		TOTAL LIABILITIES	11 386 090	(283 301)	(11 669 391)
19		NET WORKING CAPITAL (Line 10 minus Line 18)	8 113 733	12 042 485	(3 928 752)
20		FIXED ASSETS			
21					
22	21	Net Fixed Assets (Reported on Balance Sheet)	37 167 835	26 408 165	
23		Value of Leased Real Prop. (From Gen. Off.)	3 950 077	1 367 910	
24					
25		TOTAL FIXED ASSETS	41 117 912	27 776 075	13 341 837
26		NET ASSETS (Line 19 plus Line 25)	49 231 645	39 818 560	9 413 085
27					
28		INTEREST COMPUTATION			
29		INC (DEC) IN NET WORKING CAPITAL (Line 19 Column C)	(3 928 752)	.69 %	(27 108)
30		INC (DEC) IN TOTAL FIXED ASSETS (Line 25 Column C)	13 341 837	.19 %	25 350
31		NET ASSETS AT BASE DATE (Line 26 Column B)	39 818 560	.19 %	75 655
32					
33		GROSS INTEREST (Lines 29, 30 & 31)			73 897
34					
35		NET CASH GENERATED FROM			
36		EARNINGS SINCE BASE DATE			
37		Pre-Tax Earnings (3 YEARS 10 MONTHS)	55 562 261		
38		Add: Interest Paid–General Office (Same Period)	(265 922)		
39					
40		ADJUSTED PRE–TAX EARNINGS (Lines 37 & 38)	55 296 339		
41		LESS: Federal Income Tax @ 48% of Line 40	26 542 243		
42		AFTER–TAX EARNINGS (Line 40 minus Line 41)	28 754 096		
43		LESS: Provision for Dividends @ 42% of Line 42	12 076 720		
44					
45		NET CASH GENERATED (Line 42 minus Line 43)	16 677 376	.69 %	115 074
46		NET INTEREST CHARGE THIS MONTH (Line 33 minus Line 45)			(41 177)
47		LESS: Interest on long-term debt (This Month)			740
48					
49		ADJUSTED GENERAL COMPANY INTEREST EXPENSE (INCOME) NEXT MONTH			(41 917)

Department. Except in rare instances, the profit centers' financial statements were not questioned by the Corporate Accounting Department. Requests for data and paper work were kept to a minimum.

This KISS philosophy also applied to other areas of the company. Even though Beatrice kept a tight control on capital expenditures by requiring approval on all requests over $2,500, the vehicle for approval of such a request was a one-page document, an "XG-3B." The most complicated part of this form was its name—whose origins are a mystery—the only space-age terminology Beatrice ever used. The form itself also was basic, with 80 percent of it blank space where the profit center manager prepared a narrative statement explaining what this project was and why it was needed. No formal justification was required. Approval rested more on the trust and credibility of the various levels of management than on pure estimated financial numbers. With the management emphasis on profits and cash flow, everyone knew the importance of putting money only where it would get the largest return.

The basic accounting reports were simple and easy to read, therefore, it follows that the Corporate Office procedures for consolidating this information were also simple and easy to understand. The primary report issued by the Corporate Accounting Department was the sales and earnings (S & E) report, a manual report listing each profit center's sales and earnings for the current month and year-to-date compared to the prior year and projections. This summary was issued as often as twice a day.

The report was so critical that it was not uncommon to see Karnes in the Accounting Department around 2 or 3 P.M. to get a "feel" on how the numbers were coming in. George Zulanas, the Accounting Department manager, always teased Karnes by telling him, "We've got a nice report for you today." Indeed, they never really had any bad news.

Even the consolidation of all financial data for the annual report or for the detailed S.E.C. reports was done by a simple basic manual monthly report recap procedure. As the company grew and more profit centers were added, the procedures remained simple and uncomplicated. When the international profit centers were consolidated for the first time in fiscal year 1970, it was decided to lag their results for two months because of the problems of different accounting rules, procedures, customs, and currencies. Their financial year generally ended on December 31 and was consolidated with the domestic year at the end of February. Their first month (January) was consolidated with the domestic first month (March).

This and other KISS procedures meant that the Corporate Office did not require a large number of people or a high-powered computer system to carry out its responsibilities. The accounting and auditing staffs never missed a deadline. Karnes took great pride in the fact that Beatrice had grown to a multibillion dollar business, but that the corporate office staff had remained at fewer than a hundred people including top management levels. He always kept his own expenses down to the bare minimum and let his staff know how important it was to keep costs low.

Until 1979, the General Office was not elaborate. It included 185 people on one and one-quarter floors at 120 South LaSalle Street in Chicago. Karnes was president for ten years before the company bought him a car, and that was at the insistence of the directors. Karnes told the directors "If you furnish me with a car, you will have all officials of the company wanting cars." The purpose of his decision was to set a good example for the plants, to stress the importance of tight financial controls, and to operate without frills.

Karnes frequently observed that the bag boy who received a 50 cent tip for carrying two sacks of groceries from the supermarket check-out counter to the customer's car made more than the net profit on the sale of those foods for the manufacturer and retailer combined. This penny-pinching mentality was in part dictated by the fact that profit margins on dairy products were minimal, less than 2 percent for milk and less than 1 percent for butter. Karnes also would not allow any of the "corporate overhead expenses" to be charged to the profit centers. This could not be done, not only because of Beatrice's decentralization and hands-off philosophy, but also because Karnes believed the profit centers should not be charged with any expense that they could not control.

In fact, even when it was evident that large savings could accrue to Beatrice if certain new procedures were adopted, these procedures were not forced upon the profit centers. There had to be an acceptance by the profit center and, in effect, they had to show there would be a bottom-line improvement before any such procedures were adopted.

The Beatrice KISS philosophy was abandoned only when it proved to be not cost-justified, for example, the company's intercompany interest-cash management program. Beatrice had been on a central banking program since the early 1960s, as had been many other large corporations in the United States. Under this program, all profit centers deposited and disbursed all monies from a central bank or banks. In addition, all large disbursements such as taxes and certain expenses were made from a central source to avoid a manual and costly need to transfer funds from one unit to another.

With such a central banking program, Beatrice charged the profit centers intercompany interest based upon a month-end balance sheet computation. In computing what the interest would be, the profit center began by figuring what then were its total net assets at a base date. Then it computed the increase in fixed assets and in current assets, primarily inventories and receivables. The profit center then paid a low interest rate on the base assets and the increase in fixed assets and a higher, more current interest rate on the increase in current assets. Credit at the higher rate also was given for the after-tax, after-dividend net earnings generated at the profit center since the base date.

The effect of this formula was that if the profit center manager did not manage assets wisely, the profit center paid an interest charge, whereas those profit centers that kept a close watch on inventories and receivables and, of course, made a profit, paid no interest and could even generate interest income.

Haskell, Karnes, John Hazelton, and Don L. Grantham indoctrinated the entire management corps with the importance of keeping inventories and receivables at absolute minimums consistent with sound operations. Inventory quotas were established by the General Office three months before the end of the fiscal year. All managers were keenly aware that the top officers would react negatively to any excesses over quotas. Plant managers were also well aware that they were not to report a loss for excess inventories on the last day of the fiscal year. Karnes told them pointedly that he would "not accept any weather reports." By "weather report," he meant one that began with "We would have had a good year, but. . . . "

Policies had been long-established to require that reasonable operating reserves were to be set up during the year. Rigid rules dictated that obsolete inventories such as cartons and other paper items and ingredients had to be written off at the end of the year. Excess inventories would cost each manager personally because write-offs would affect interest charges each month.

Although partially effective, this banking program still left a lot of cash in hundreds of bank accounts scattered throughout the United States and gave little incentive to the profit center to manage its cash or balance sheet aggressively, except at month-end.

This program was overhauled around 1968 so that the General Office acted as a central banker for the profit centers, which were then in a daily debit or credit position with the General Office. This created an incentive to the profit center to remit cash to the General Office as quickly as possible in order to earn interest on a daily basis or, conversely, to limit its use of borrowed funds in order to reduce interest charges. Both interest income and interest expense were calculated in arriving at the profit center's net income upon which management bonuses were based.

Through special arrangements with the central bank, the majority of the record-keeping work was done by the bank with little or no charge to the profit center or the General Office. Although no separate "bank accounts" were established for each profit center, the bank was able to compute actual daily receipts and disbursements and a "theoretical" cash balance for each profit center. The General Office imputed certain "allocated" disbursements to each profit center, such as payroll and income taxes, specific salaries, bonuses, and other direct and indirect profit center expenses.

In order to preserve both short-term and long-term components to the capitalization of the profit centers, the system continued to move the base date forward every year and to make use of the historical intercompany interest rate on a portion of the profit center's net assets, which were deemed to be "long-term capital." Thus, no profit center was burdened with "excess debt" charges.

The system was eminently successful. In the first six months of implementation, more than $50 million in free cash were generated in the U.S. operations alone. The system was expanded to operations in both Canada and Great Britain. Here again, Beatrice was a pioneer in such an expansion, even though it was easier to institute centralized cash management because central banks existed in those countries. Therefore, Beatrice was able to establish a system in Canada in which each operating profit center maintained its own account with the Royal Bank of Canada. The bank simply netted the debits and credits on an internal bookkeeping system on a daily basis, transparent to the profit center but generating monthly interest charges or credits based on daily activities.

The advantage, compared to the United States, where there are no national banks, was in the elimination of the need to transfer funds physically between hundreds of various depository accounts in separate banks and, instead, to carry out the whole system through the electronic network of a single bank.

When Fred Schomer made an initial trip around England to visit Beatrice's profit centers and branches of the U.K.'s Westminster Bank to explain this pioneering system, the reactions ranged all the way from "Wonderful, I'm glad we're taking the lead in such a progressive step" to "Terrible. How could you give away the bank's profit on the float like this?"

The most effective incentive for financial control of all was, of course, compensation. Beatrice's policy was to pay managers a flat salary plus a percentage of the pretax profits of their plants, generally around 2 percent. The General Office made no charge on the pretax profits except for the monthly internal interest charge, which the managers could control. Managers were repeatedly reminded that the profits they made at their plants and the salaries and bonuses they received were definitely in their hands.

At all general meetings, sales meetings and operating meetings as well as by frequent written reminders from the general office, three basic things were stressed: product quality; importance of increasing sales; and the absolute necessity of making a profit.

These financial policies and controls were major reasons why Beatrice was able to increase its profits every quarter over the comparable quarter of the preceding year for 120 consecutive quarters from March 1952 to February 28, 1982. There is no record of any major company being able to accomplish such an achievement during the same period.

Beatrice borrowed no money and had no debt from 1936 to 1969, not even short-term debt. It issued its first debentures to finance international expansion in 1969. Even with extensive expansion around the world, which produced $1.2 billion in international sales by 1976, the company had a debt ratio of only 20 percent of its net worth. In 1975, it was one of the few industrial companies that was rated triple A by both Standard & Poor's and Moody's. Over the twenty-five-year period from 1952–77, Beatrice increased its working capital annually, and each dollar of working capital produced $10 in sales each year. Without risking the financial stability of the company and by adhering to a conservative debt ratio, Beatrice still was able to expand its sales from $229 million in 1952 to $9.2 billion in 1982. This continuous growth record had many positive benefits for Beatrice shareholders. From the late fifties through the seventies, its common stock sold at between sixteen and twenty-two times earnings.

Beatrice paid a dividend on its common stock every year except in the depression years of 1934 and 1935. A share of common stock that sold for $50 in 1986 had a value of $2 in 1940 after adjustments for six stock splits from 1940 to 1985 — the ultimate payoff of sound financial policies and controls.

M227

CHAPTER SIXTEEN

Beatrice and the
Federal Trade Commission

William G. Karnes had repeatedly demonstrated his diplomatic skills in negotiations with companies Beatrice was wooing, unions, and government agencies. Those experiences were to prepare him for the sternest test he had ever faced as the company's chief executive. In 1953, Beatrice had received oral approval of the acquisition of Creameries of America from Joseph Sheehy, an official of the Federal Trade Commission (chapter 3). The lesson to be re-learned was that when dealing with a government agency, "Get it in writing."

Beatrice was alerted that the Federal Trade Commission was adopting a hard-line policy against dairy mergers when the FTC first brought an action against Foremost Dairies charging violation of section 7 of the Clayton Antitrust Act. Foremost had been highly active in acquiring dairy companies throughout the country, many of which overlapped in the dairy markets in the San Francisco Bay area of California and in Florida. Essentially, the FTC charged that these acquisitions tended to reduce or eliminate competition in the dairy business.

On October 16, 1956, three years after the FTC had reviewed the Creameries merger and three weeks before the second presidential election between Dwight D. Eisenhower and Adlai E. Stevenson, the FTC filed separate but similar complaints against National Dairy, Borden, and Beatrice charging each of them with violations of section 7 of the Clayton Act. The complaint against Beatrice challenged 175 dairy acquisitions. Seventy-seven were challenged under section 7 of the Clayton Act, and the remaining ninety-eight under section 5 of the FTC act because the latter companies were not corporations or engaged in interstate commerce. All of the Creameries plants were included in this action.

The hearings in the Beatrice case were prolonged over seven years, and the initial opinion of John Louis, the hearing examiner, was not issued until March 2, 1964. Upon appeal to the commission, its final order was entered on December 10, 1965. This order required divestiture within eighteen months of four of the five acquisitions found to be illegal and prohibited Beatrice from making any further acquisitions of milk or ice cream companies for ten years. The four divestitures were major companies and included all of the Creameries plants in the western states, as well as the milk and ice cream plant in Hawaii: Greenbriar Dairy Products Company in West Virginia, Durham Dairy Products Company in North Carolina, and Community Creamery in Missoula, Montana. The FTC also ordered the divestiture of Dahl Cro-Ma in Hilo, Hawaii, which had been destroyed by a tidal wave several years earlier.

Beatrice filed its appeal of the decision with the U.S. Court of Appeals for the Ninth Circuit in San Francisco. Now, Beatrice had to make a major decision. To proceed further with litigation would have been expensive; the printing of the appeal would have cost thousands of dollars alone. Further, Beatrice would have risked losing highly profitable plants in Hawaii, Utah, Idaho, Colorado, and Northern California.

It was decided that Karnes would go before the commission and offer a settlement plan. He had been involved in the purchase of every one of the companies involved in the decision, had testified many times at the commission hearings, and was fully informed about the facts surrounding the mergers as well as the legal aspects of the case. Although such a hearing is extremely unusual, it was arranged that Karnes would appear before the full commission in Washington, D.C. The commission was composed of Paul Rand Dixon, chair, and Commissioners Mary Gardiner Jones, Everette MacIntyre, Philip Elman, and John R. Reilly.

Typically, Karnes had done his homework. He devised three plans with the help of John P. Fox, Jr., the company's general counsel, and his staff, and Edward Foote, a brilliant lawyer with Winston & Strawn in Chicago, Beatrice's outside counsel. He then rehearsed his presentation, which included a series of charts and graphs, thoroughly for twelve hours in his closed conference room and continued refining his presentation on the train to Washington.

Karnes had met most of the commissioners a number of times previously, and he was on friendly terms with them. He had barely launched into his Settlement Plan No. 1 when one of the commissioners left the table and disappeared behind a screen at the back of the room. This occurred four times during Karnes's discussion, and he grew concerned with what seemed to be the commissioner's apparent lack of interest—he later learned that the commissioner was taking coffee breaks.

The consent decree proposed by Beatrice was the divestiture of plants and related facilities in Pasadena, California; Cedar City, Utah; Las Vegas, Nevada; Price's Creameries in El Paso, Texas, and Roswell, New Mexico; and Valley Dairy in Albuquerque, New Mexico, as well as the operations in Glendale, Arizona. All of these operations, which spanned a distribution market through most of the West, were to be sold within eighteen months to a single purchaser, who would form a viable, competitive dairy operation. The settlement also called for the separate divestiture of a dairy in Morgantown, West Virginia, and prohibited Beatrice from acquiring any domestic dairy company without prior commission approval for ten years.

On June 7, 1967, the FTC accepted by majority vote the modified consent order offered by Beatrice. In a letter to shareholders, Karnes wrote, "The settlement in our opinion meets all the criteria important to your company in that the order does not impose serious restrictions upon future growth and the agreement eliminates further prolonged litigation." After outlining the terms of the order, he added that "The dairy operations to be divested represent three percent of the sales and a lesser percent of the net earnings of Beatrice Foods Co. for the fiscal year ended February 28, 1967."

He noted that the settlement did not prohibit the company from effecting mergers with domestic companies not engaged in the fluid milk and ice cream business. "Without acquiring any major milk or ice cream operations in the United States since June 1961, our sales of these dairy products have continued to grow steadily. This growth, achieved through internal development, is faster than the national average. We are confident we will continue in the future to maintain our growth in fluid milk and ice cream sales."

In addition to avoiding the high costs of litigation, including thousands of hours of time, the decision permitted Beatrice to retain plants with great growth potentials in Idaho, Utah, Colorado, West Virginia, and Montana, as well as in Hawaii where it was the leading distributor of milk and ice cream. The plants designated for divestiture were sold to a single purchaser effective January 31, 1969; Morgantown had been sold on November 30, 1968.

This was not the first investigation of Beatrice by various federal agencies, nor was it the last. Beatrice, along with other major dairies, was involved in the "ice cream case" in the late thirties and early forties, an industry action brought by the FTC against ice cream manufacturers that charged them with attempting to eliminate competition by price discrimination and the loaning of ice cream cabinet equipment. The case dragged on for many years and finally was settled with no serious impact on the industry.

Beatrice repeatedly, in meeting after meeting and bulletin after bulletin, warned its plant managers, sales managers, and salespersons to avoid price-fixing and to comply with the various federal and state laws prohibiting unfair competition. Unfortunately, not everybody listened or paid attention to the bulletins. This industrywide problem still continues.

Beatrice was involved in a series of complaints by the FTC and the Department of Justice alleging price-fixing of milk in various cities. In the 1940s, a case was brought against all the dairies in Dubuque, Iowa, and the local union. Beatrice's milk plant manager there was accused of price-fixing. The case was settled, the manager paid a fine, and an injunction was issued against him and the company. Shortly thereafter, the government brought another case against the company and the same manager for alleged price-fixing. The company determined that there had been no price-fixing the second time, and the case was tried in the federal court, where a jury found the company and the manager not guilty.

In the late 1950s, a similar price-fixing case was filed against the company, the district manager, and three plant managers in Montana. After considerable negotiation and hearings, the case was settled by an injunction and fines of the district manager and three managers. In the 1960s, another case was brought against the district manager and two managers in Utah. After lengthy litigation, it, too, was settled with injunctions and fines of the district manager and two managers.

Almost three years later, Beatrice was challenged yet again by the FTC. On April 30, 1970, the FTC issued a complaint charging that the acquisition of John Sexton & Co. would lessen competition substantially and tend to create a monopoly or to restrain trade in the institutional dry grocery wholesale industry. Beatrice had acquired Sexton on December 20, 1968 (p. 130).

Beatrice vigorously contested the commission's allegations, arguing that beginning in 1958, the institutional dry grocery trade had shown a substantial increase, largely accounted for by the growth in the number of "multi-unit food service operations" (MUFSO accounts) such as fast-food franchises and the increasing number of people who ate away from home. Beatrice introduced evidence that MUFSO sales had doubled from $9 billion in 1965 to $18 billion in 1970 and that many major food companies were already in this rapidly expanding industry.

In spite of these arguments, a hearing examiner, Andrew Goodhope, entered an initial decision on May 14, 1971, holding that Beatrice's acquisition of Sexton constituted a violation of section 7 of the Clayton Act. The examiner's order would require Beatrice to sell Sexton within six months and forbade Beatrice to acquire any institutional dry grocery business for ten years without prior FTC approval.

Both Beatrice and counsel supporting the complaint filed cross appeals from the hearing examiner's initial decision. The commission then was comprised of Miles W. Kirkpatrick, chair, Dixon, MacIntyre, Jones, and David S. Jennison, Jr. On February 28, 1972, the commission reversed the initial decision of the hearing examiner and ordered dismissal of the complaint.

Commissioner Jennison issued a unanimous opinion holding that the elimination of a food company as a potential entrant in the institutional dry grocery wholesaling business by its acquisition of the largest such wholesaler in both the relevant and national markets did not have sufficient effect on competition because of the number of other potential entrants and the ease with which entry could be accomplished. The complaint's counsel cannot appeal a ruling from the FTC commissioners.

The decision that the acquisition of Sexton was not illegal allowed Beatrice to establish a competitive position in institutional foods, the fastest growing segment of the food business. Beatrice later put Sexton in the frozen food business, and it opened additional branches across the continent and in Hawaii.

In 1973, Beatrice was able to obtain clearance for its merger with Peter Eckrich & Sons at a hearing before the administrative officials of the FTC in Washington.

The company encountered no problems with the acquisition of Culligan, but the acquisition of Tropicana Products on July 11, 1978, led the FTC to issue an injunction in June of 1978 against the proposed transaction. The FTC alleged that the acquisition violated the antitrust laws. The deal was completed in August following the expiration of the injunction.

Tropicana was the largest processor of fresh and frozen orange juice in the United States (chapter 5). Over the years, Beatrice had sold small quantities of orange juice and orange concentrate off of its milk trucks, products reconstituted from frozen orange juice at the company's milk plants. The sales volume was minimal, representing less than 1 percent of the annual orange juice consumption in the United States. Major competitors were Coca-Cola, which owns Minute Maid, and Procter & Gamble, which markets Citrus Hill. The case was argued until June 17, 1983, when the FTC dismissed it. By 1984, the FTC had become far more permissive; there was no challenge of the Esmark acquisition in 1984.

Karnes points out that all of these cases were handled by Foote, who was a major factor in designing the defenses, planning the strategies, and following through as the trial attorney. Karnes, of course, was the principal witness. It should be recognized that Beatrice was a leader in negotiations with the government. While many other leading food companies were unwilling to effect major acquisitions because of fear of actions by the federal government, Beatrice elected to step forward in areas where its management believed there were no violations of laws. It obtained companies such as Creameries of America, Sexton, Samsonite, Eckrich, Culligan, and Tropicana, among many others, to move ahead of all other food-related companies in America at a critical economic time. The companies were acquired at favorable prices, and the growth resulting from their consolidation under the Beatrice policies of decentralization and careful financial controls enabled them to expand rapidly.

CHAPTER SEVENTEEN

The Wars of Succession

In anticipation of their planned retirement in 1976, William Karnes, chairman, and Don Grantham, president, early in 1974 began preparing for an orderly succession. But the untimely death of Brown W. Cannon played a hand in the management plan for the future.

The first major step toward setting up the line of succession was taken on March 5, 1974, when three new executive vice presidents and a senior vice president were elected. The new executive vice presidents were Cannon, William G. Mitchell, and Wallace N. Rasmussen. The senior vice president was E. A. "Johnny" Walker.

Rasmussen was named president of all food operations. Cannon moved from the Dairy Division to become president of all manufacturing and chemical operations, and Walker took charge of dairy and agri-products operations. Cannon, who joined the company as an auditor in 1940, had been a director since 1950, and Rasmussen's service with the company dated from 1934. He became a director in 1970.

Mitchell, who started with the company as an attorney in the Law Department in 1958, was elected a director in 1974. Walker began his career in the Salt Lake City dairy plant in 1936 and was elected a director in 1972.

Behind them was a skilled management team that included Paul T. Kessler, Jr., executive vice president of the Chemical, Educational and Consumer Arts, International Grocery, and Confectionery divisions; Harry Niemiec, executive vice president directing the Grocery and Confectionery divisions and the Bakery Group; and Juan E. Metzger, vice president, International Group manager, Yogurt-Specialty Dairy Products Group.

Other key operating officers included William W. Granger, Jr., vice president supervising the Eastern Dairy Region; Gordon E. Swaney, vice president and assistant general manager of the Grocery Division; Donald P. Eckrich, president of the Specialty Meat Division; and James G. Fransen, assistant vice president and assistant to the president in addition to serving as operating director of the Caribbean Dairy Area. Two other Beatrice veterans, Carl T. E. Sutherland and Leo J. Himmelsbach, were assistant vice presidents and group managers. In all, only twenty-three officers directed the corporation with more than $4 billion in sales operating throughout the United States and in twenty-seven foreign countries. Kessler, Metzger, and Niemiec were also directors, as was Eckrich.

The consensus was that Cannon, fifty-eight, and Rasmussen, sixty, were the leading contenders for the top job. They were men of contrasting styles. Rasmussen's academic credentials did not go past a high school diploma, although he was an inveterate reader of business publications. He was a burly, blunt man driven by a will to overwhelm others. Cannon was a scratch golfer who played with Lawson Little on a college championship team at Stanford University, where he earned an A.B. degree. Subsequently, he was graduated from Harvard Business School with an M.B.A. After graduating from Harvard, Cannon, a personable, outgoing man with a fine sense of humor, began working for Beatrice as a member of its internal audit staff. During World War II, he served in the Navy and after his discharge went to work for the Denver dairy, eventually becoming its manager. When he was thirty-five, he was promoted to vice president and district manager of all western dairy plants and was elected a director in 1950. Cannon's belief in the Beatrice decentralized system of management was fixed in granite as is illustrated by the following story that he told at a dairy meeting.

There were two high school football teams which had established an intense rivalry over a score of years. However, one of them had suffered the indignities of ten consecutive losses. The two teams met for their annual contest with the perennial winners again heavily favored. With two minutes left in the game, the score was tied and the underdogs had the ball on their own two-yard line. The coach called time out and huddled with his quarterback.

"Here's what I want you to do," the coach told his quarterback. "On the first play, you carry the ball over center. On the next two plays, you do the same thing. Then you punt the ball. If you don't follow my orders to the letter, you're off the team. Kick on the fourth down."

On the first play, the quarterback smashed over center and ran for forty-eight yards. On the next play, he went twenty more yards. On the third play, he drove to the opponent's two-yard line. Then he stepped back and punted the ball out of the stadium.

"What were you thinking of when you punted the ball from their two-yard line?" screamed the coach.

"I was thinking what a dumb coach I have," the youth replied.

The moral of that story, ladies and gentlemen, is don't overcoach.

Cannon was in fact offered the opportunity to buy the Denver franchise of the American Football League by merely assuming the club's debts. Although it was a great opportunity, he decided to remain with Beatrice. Unfortunately, Cannon died of cancer on August 8, 1975, a great loss to Beatrice. Richard A. Voell, then forty, was a protégé of Cannon's who was to play a major role in the subsequent struggle for power. Voell joined the company as a salesman for Hawaii dairy operations in 1958, became a vice president in 1973, and an executive vice president in 1975.

The untimely death of Cannon spurred the board of directors to adjust its long-ange thinking. In a few weeks, it designated Mitchell as chairman, Rasmussen as president and chief executive officer, and to bolster management ranks, James Weiss was promoted to executive vice president. Subsequently, in February 1977, Weiss became a member of the board of directors as well.

"Designating successors at this time will accomplish two things," Beatrice explained in its quarterly report for the period ended November 30, 1975. "It will enable the designated officers to assume their responsibilities gradually while present officers are there to advise and assist them. Also there will be no interruption in the smooth flow of operations throughout your company." Things were not smooth for very long.

Rasmussen, the son of a saddlemaker, was born on a farm near Beatrice, Nebraska. In 1931, he left home after he graduated from high school at the age of sixteen. He worked on a ranch in the Mojave Desert, peddled handbills in Los Angeles for 10 cents a thousand, and did various odd jobs before returning to Lincoln, where he got a job pulling four-hundred-pound blocks of ice for refrigerated cars at the company's plant there in 1934. He advanced through various engineering positions there and was promoted to the Vincennes, Indiana, plant in 1937. He moved up the ranks and was named manager of the Nashville, Tennessee, plant in 1955 and group manager of the Southern Dairy Group in 1957. He proved to be such a successful profit producer that the company had to put a cap on his salary; he was making more money than his bosses. Rasmussen next became a regional vice president in 1965, and then executive vice president in 1974.

On the other side, Mitchell, forty-four, had no line experience. His background paralleled that of Karnes in many ways. After graduating from the University of Oklahoma, he received his law degree from Northwestern University. He advanced through various legal and administrative assignments, working very closely with Walter L. Dilger, general counsel and secretary of the company for more than thirty years, and who had hired Karnes in 1936. When Dilger retired in 1965, Mitchell was elected corporate secretary. He then became a vice president and chief financial officer in 1973 and an executive vice president in 1974. Mitchell was well acquainted with the financial institutions with which Beatrice dealt; he had been involved in many acquisitions. He also had the ability to motivate people and to work with all kinds of people—employees, bankers, stock analysts, and the media.

When it came to picking a successor, Karnes said that he, having been chief executive officer for twenty-four years and sixty-five at the time, definitely felt that he should retire. He had installed the rule requiring retirement at sixty-five some years earlier, and his wife had serious health problems—in fact, she had lung surgery within a year after his retirement.

Karnes felt that people such as Rasmussen, Mitchell, Dutt, Voell, Eckrich, Walker, Weiss and many others who had been with the company for many years and had worked with the decentralized program knew what made Beatrice run and the importance of handling and working with people. Karnes had great confidence in the ability of these younger men, all of whom had come up through the ranks as he had and had shown ability and knowledge and belief in the Beatrice management principles. He was sure that they could carry on. There had been very little dissension in the ranks when C. H. Haskell and Karnes were chief executive officers, a period of forty-eight years of almost continuous growth. All of the younger men still with the company when Karnes and Grantham left in 1976 had proven their abilities to get along with and motivate people.

Rasmussen, who had three years to retirement, had a great deal of operating experience and had proved that he could handle and motivate people in his various regions very well. Managers who reported to him respected him, although he was forceful and demanded performance. However, the economy in the late 1970s required tighter operations, greater productivity as competition in the food business was increasing. It seemed natural that during these three years, Rasmussen, as the senior executive, should direct the company and train and mold the several younger men to take over for the future.

Karnes and Grantham talked to Rasmussen about working with the young men and molding them so that after the three years it could be determined by Rasmussen and the board who would carry on into the future.

When Karnes and Grantham retired in July 1976, Beatrice's sales at the end of that fiscal year were $5.7 billion, and net earnings were $206 million, both all-time highs. In fact, Beatrice registered the highest earnings of any food company in the United States at the end of that fiscal year in February 1977. The stock was selling at twenty-seven after a two-for-one split just eighteen months prior. The return on average equity was 17.2 percent, also a record for the company. It was one of the few companies rated triple A by both Standard & Poor's and Moody's. The dividend payout was only 38 percent of per share earnings, and the ratio of debt to equity was 23 percent.

A report by Value Line in June 1977 covering the fiscal year ending February 28, 1977, stated:

> Beatrice Foods is now the nation's largest food company. In terms of net income it moved into first place in 1974, displacing General Foods. In terms of sales it became the leader last year, overshadowing Esmark and Kraft, Inc. Becoming number one in the U.S. was not achieved overnight but rather is the result of steady, uninterrupted growth of sales and net income for 25 consecutive years. Moreover, this well-managed, financially strong company is expected to maintain its preeminent position in the foreseeable future. Largely due to accelerated internal growth, annual earnings gains of 12% or better on average through 1981 are in prospect vs. 11% on average over the last five years and 10% over the past decade. And dividend increases promise to be larger and more frequent, too. As a result Beatrice Foods could easily double in price by 1980.

But Beatrice stock did not double by 1980. It did not double for lack of sales and profit increases or lack of increases in dividends, but apparently because of policy changes by management, the type and cost of acquisitions being made, personnel changes, and possibly because of an unfortunate "boardroom battle" in 1979.

However, when the new management took over in July 1976, the struggle between Mitchell and Rasmussen was joined. Mitchell wanted to consolidate the string of acquisitions that Karnes, Hazelton, and Grantham had assembled. Rasmussen believed that Beatrice should continue making acquisitions. By September 1977, just fifteen months after Karnes and Grantham had retired, Mitchell was gone, ousted at a special meeting of the board of directors held in a secluded restaurant in a suburb of Chicago; Karnes was in Europe at the time with his family. He was called in Zurich late the night before the meeting and so was unable to reach Chicago in time to attend. Mitchell received a settlement of his various benefits and became president of Centel Corporation of Chicago, a position he held until he retired in 1987.

"I'm dedicated to outshining the last management," Rasmussen told *Chicago Tribune* writer George Lazarus in a September 1977 article. As an article in the February 19, 1978 issue of *Forbes* entitled, "The Man Who Came to Dinner" commented, "From then on Rasmussen had a free hand and he used it to make himself chairman, and, according to one ousted executive 'to clean out anyone who had a close connection with Karnes.' "

Once he had won the showdown with Mitchell, Rasmussen quickly named his own team to key posts. Directors elected James L. Dutt, then fifty-two, as president and chief operating officer, Voell as deputy chairman and chief corporate officer, and Eckrich, fifty-three, as vice chairman. Eckrich also continued as president of domestic grocery operations. To Rasmussen's credit, he did not attempt to retool the Beatrice decentralized system of management to any major degree. Annual sales increased each year from 1976 through 1979 to $7.5 billion, net earnings rose from $174.5 million to $261 million, and earnings per share climbed from $1.84 to $2.60.

However, in his zeal to efface the memories of Karnes, he began to discard many of the people whom he regarded as loyal to Karnes; a number of them were fired or else retired. Others were to follow, and the spirit of camaraderie began to disappear throughout the company. "You have a job for life," Rasmussen had told one junior officer, who was soon told on a Friday morning to be gone by 5 P.M. that same day.

Under Rasmussen, the company continued making acquisitions, but on a grander scale. Financial analysts and long-term members of Beatrice's staff questioned two of them in particular. The first, in 1977, was Harman International Industries for 3,590,087 shares of common stock. Karnes warned officers of the company that it was inadvisable to try to compete with the Japanese in the stereo equipment business, which was changing rapidly, and he was opposed to taking over a company that would not have the founder and president staying with it.

The second was the acquisition of Tropicana, Inc. for $490 million in the summer of 1978, which diluted the company's earnings by 5 cents a share in the 1979 fiscal year and 3 cents in 1980. Further, it generated a large amount of goodwill. It was basically in a commodity business, which was highly competitive and weather dependent.

When Rasmussen was elected president and chief executive officer, he was viewed by many as an interim boss serving in a caretaker role until he reached the mandatory retirement age of sixty-five in July 1979. However, after Mitchell was forced out, Rasmussen effected another stratagem to extend his stewardship. He persuaded the board to amend the retirement rule in December 1978. But the board then began having second thoughts and reversed itself in March 1979, reinstating Rasmussen's retirement in July. It also asked him to designate a successor. Mitchell's ouster and Rasmussen's policies had bothered some of the outside directors.

It is relevant to the subsequent battle in the Beatrice boardroom to explain that the Securities and Exchange Commission had been prodding companies to increase the number of outside directors on corporate boards. At the end of the 1977 fiscal year (February 28, 1977), thirteen of Beatrice's directors were insiders and only six were outsiders. The insiders included Karnes, Grantham, Mitchell, Rasmussen, Eckrich, Metzger, Niemiec, Schlytter, Sexton, Shwayder, Voell, Dutt, and Weiss. Dutt had been elected to the board on December 7, 1976, and Weiss on February 14, 1977. Four of these, Karnes, Grantham, Schlytter, and Shwayder, were retired. The outsiders were John H. Coleman, former deputy chairman of the Royal Bank of Canada; G. A. Costanzo, vice chairman of Citibank; Bernard A. Monaghan, president and chief executive officer of Vulcan Materials Company; Durward B. Varner, president of the University of Nebraska; Omer G. Voss, executive vice president of International Harvester; and Flavel A. Wright, partner in the law firm of Cline, Williams, Wright, Johnson & Oldfather of Lincoln, Nebraska.

One year later, the balance of the board had shifted to eleven "ins" and eight "outs." Mitchell was gone, as was Schlytter, who had retired. Joining the outside group were Jayne Baker Spain, senior vice president for corporate affairs for Gulf Oil Corporation; Russell L. Wagner, president of NLT Corp., a Nashville insurance firm and long-time friend of Rasmussen; and John H. Williams, chairman and chief executive officer of The Williams Companies of Tulsa.

Karnes had no objection to a majority of the board being outsiders. The only reason that a number of management officers were put on the board was because of the wide diversification of Beatrice. He believed that the major divisions of the company such as Dairy, Grocery, Manufactured Products, and Chemicals should be represented on the board and report and inform the directors about the progress of their divisions. The number of outside directors had been increasing over the years.

Rasmussen asked Varner to chair a new committee of three outside directors—Costanzo, Williams, and himself—called the Corporate Governance Committee to help in the selection of all directors and officers. The first recommendation of the committee was that the board be composed of a majority of outside directors.

In the fall of 1978, the Corporate Governance Committee met in New York City with Rasmussen to discuss his retirement. It had agreed to let him stay until December 31, 1979 and to continue his benefits until the end of the fiscal year, February 28, 1980. Later, when Rasmussen refused to name a successor, the committee decided that he should retire in mid-July 1979 and that Voell should be his successor. That decision marked the start of what the *Chicago Tribune* described in an article on Sunday, May 13, 1979, as a "bitter boardroom brawl." A lawsuit was filed on May 7 in the United States District Court by a retired director.

The suit disclosed that on March 6, 1979, Beatrice directors unanimously approved a directors' slate composed of only six inside directors and ten outsiders. Karnes, Grantham, Shwayder, Metzger, Sexton, and Niemiec would not be reslated. Karnes welcomed this because his advice was seldom asked, and, when given, was ignored.

In addition to recommending Voell as the new chairman and chief executive officer, the committee also believed that the combination of Voell, Dutt, and Eckrich would form the nucleus of a strong operations team. They didn't reckon with the ambitions of Dutt and Eckrich. Rasmussen testified in court that he never agreed with the committee's selection. At a March 5, 1979, meeting with all nine outside directors, before the regular board meeting, he told them, "You are making a mistake. Voell is not ready. He does not have the support of the troops. We have the responsibility to keep this company in strong hands. . . . You're forcing something that will be bad for this company. There will be resignations."

Rasmussen testified that he had the impression that he was to retire in July. Varner said this was not so. "It was agreed—unanimously—by the nine outside directors to recommend that Mr. Voell be named chairman and CEO, effective January 1, 1980," Varner reported, according to the *Tribune* article of May 13.

Instead of meeting with the outside directors at a breakfast, on March 6 Rasmussen sent them a handwritten note tendering his resignation effective July 11. Later in the day, all the directors met in a regular board meeting and approved the heavily independent slate of outside directors for the next year. They also approved the election of William W. Granger, Jr., to the board. That raised the number of inside directors to twelve, ten of whom backed Dutt. At this March 6 meeting of the board, the Corporate Governance Committee made no report to the full board about Rasmussen's successor, or about Rasmussen's retirement date. Later, on the afternoon of March 6 after the board meeting, Varner called on Karnes to tell him of the committee's selection of Voell. "Karnes responded with outrage," a Beatrice attorney told the court. "How dare you do such a thing without putting it to the vote of all directors?"

That evening Dutt asked to meet with Karnes. The conference was held at the University Club in Chicago. To Karnes's surprise, Eckrich accompanied Dutt. What they told Karnes, in effect, is that if Voell was elected chairman, they, along with Weiss, would resign and there might be a proxy fight. Varner thought his side had the majority. He was counting on the votes of the nine outside directors, plus Voell and Shwayder. Rasmussen told him he would vote with the majority. On Sunday, March 11, the ten inside directors supporting Dutt met at the

Union League Club in Chicago. Rasmussen attended this meeting. Two outside directors, Spain and Wagner, joined them.

Karnes had no previous preference about who should be chairman at that time. He had not been asked for a recommendation. He had been retired for three years. However, because Rasmussen apparently did not want to retire and did not recommend a successor, and because the selection of Voell would trigger several resignations of important key people, he believed that Dutt would be the best choice because of his overall experience in the dairy and international operations and also, an important consideration, he had the support of the operating officers and managers in the field.

Karnes tried during the Union League Club meeting to bring the two factions together, to keep all of the directors on the board, and to keep Voell in the company. He communicated by telephone with the outside director group several times during the meeting. Unfortunately, it was too late. The action of the Corporate Governance Committee and others had caused deep feelings and irreconcilable differences. It was a sad day for Beatrice.

At a specially called board meeting on Monday, March 12, attended by all twenty-one directors at the Hyatt Regency Hotel, Rasmussen opened the meeting with a prayer calling on "The Almighty for guidance in our discussions and deliberations." He then recognized Weiss who presented several motions. One was to elect Dutt chairman and chief executive officer; another rescinded the previously approved slate of directors and offered a new slate to be presented to shareholders.

Still another motion was to establish the office of chairman of the executive committee of the board, a post to which Rasmussen was elected effective after his retirement on July 11. The board also rescinded the director retirement policy under which Karnes, Grantham, and others would have had to leave the board, as well as approval of the slate of sixteen nominees approved at the March 6 meeting. The vote again was twelve to eight. Then it approved a slate of seventeen nominees with Karnes, Grantham, Metzger, Sexton, and Niemiec back on the ballot; Varner, Williams, and Voell were omitted. Karnes agreed to stay just one more year to help with the transition. The board also changed the name of the Corporate Governance and Nominating Committee to the Nominating Committee. Karnes and Grantham replaced Varner and Williams on the committee. On May 16, the company sent out a revised proxy statement superseding the one sent May 2. The details of the series of meetings were reported in the revised proxy statement.

When the March 12 meeting was over, Voell resigned, as did Varner and Williams. Voell received a handsome settlement and then became president of Penn Central and in March 1982, became the head of New York's Rockefeller Center. Karnes asked to—and did—retire from the board the following June 1980.

Karnes said that it was a great disappointment to him to see what happened to management after he retired. Many of the people who had been with the company a long time were wrongly considered "Karnes's people" and were either retired or fired. Employee morale tended to be hurt when new outside people with no background on the history and policies of Beatrice were chosen, asked to fill key positions, and placed over Beatrice people with seniority and experience. Further, Rasmussen at first refused to retire on schedule or to designate a successor, a lack of leadership that led to an unfortunate board of directors battle in picking the new chief executive officer. This was the first major disagreement of a Beatrice board in its ninety-year history.

The Corporate Governance Committee also shares part of the blame for the event. The members proceeded on their own to negotiate with Rasmussen, changing his retirement date and picking a succeeding chairman and chief executive officer without ever bringing their recommendation to the whole board. A chief executive officer is not chosen by a committee or by a minority of a board of directors. It was the responsibility of the whole board of twenty-one directors. As a result, Beatrice suffered; it lost a good man, Voell, and received bad publicity which hurt its credibility with the investment community.

On July 11, 1979, Rasmussen abdicated in favor of Dutt but continued as a director and chairman of the executive committee. He retired from the board in June 1981, along with Grantham, Niemiec, Sexton, Coleman, and Wright. Following the annual meeting in Denver on June 6, 1979, the line of succession was in order. Dutt was in command with a favorable board. He was backed by a seasoned management team that included Eckrich as president and John D. Conners, Granger, Niemiec, and Weiss as executive vice presidents.

Morale, which one Beatrice executive had described as "gone to hell," would be restored to a high level of confidence throughout the ranks. Dutt, fifty-five, was an amiable, soft-spoken man who had started with the company in 1947 in a part-time job as a checker of ice cream packages going through the Meadow Gold line at the Topeka, Kansas plant while attending Washburn University. He had paid his training dues as administrative assistant to the executive vice president, John Hazelton, in the General Office starting in 1956 after working as a company auditor for several years.

In 1961, Hazelton sent him to Dayton, Ohio, to manage the dairy plant there. His supervisor was John F. Hazelton, Jr. While he was at

Dayton, Dutt earned an M.B.A. from the University of Dayton. He advanced to assistant general sales manager for the Dairy Division in 1967, and then assistant director of marketing and director of marketing services and new products in 1968. That experience was to influence his subsequent actions as chairman and chief executive officer. He became a corporate vice president and director of International Dairy Operations in 1974, and president of International Food Operations in 1975. In 1976, he was elected a director and assigned the additional responsibilities of supervising the Dairy and Soft Drink and Agri-Products Division. The next year, in 1977, he became president and chief operating officer. Dutt's office door was open, and he frequently went out for coffee and doughnuts with his lower-echelon workers at mid-morning.

The new management team of Dutt and Eckrich declared its commitment to the policies that had built Beatrice. In a section of the 1980 annual report entitled "Management Perspectives," Dutt was quoted as follows: "Beatrice Foods is a company built on three basic principles: diversification, decentralization and balance. Beatrice's strength traditionally has come from our decentralized operating units and the people who run them. It's a growth formula that has proven itself for the past 28 years and one we're going to stick with." Sales, earnings and earnings per common share rose steadily to $8.3 billion, $290 million and $2.67, respectively for fiscal year ended February 28, 1980.

According to the 1981 annual report, the same discipline prevailed. On page 68 in a section entitled "Beatrice in the Future," was the following statement:

> For all the success of its interrelated operating traditions and diverse worldwide operations, Beatrice remains a mix of the traditional and the contemporary. Contemporary in its ability to anticipate consumer needs and trends, and to respond to them with quality, cost-competitive products and services; traditional in that Beatrice management remains dedicated to fostering the company's growth through its time-tested operating philosophies.
>
> Among these, Beatrice will continue to emphasize decentralization. As James L. Dutt, chairman and chief executive officer says, "It is a tribute to the founders of Beatrice that they established a principle that is as relevant and effective in the 1980s as it was in the 1890s. While products, marketing techniques and production methods often change, our commitment to leaving the decisions in the hands of the local managers continues to hold firm."

Sales rose to $8.8 billion, net earnings to $304 million and primary earnings of $2.94 per share, all records, in fiscal year 1981. By then, the company employed about eighty thousand people at operations in more than ninety countries.

However, a series of subtle changes was being effected by Dutt in those years that led to a dramatic alteration of traditional policies in 1982. This alteration was to accelerate in the next three years. In 1979, the company moved its headquarters to Two North LaSalle in Chicago. There it occupied luxurious offices atop a steel and glass structure just completed on the site of the landmark LaSalle Hotel. In contrast to the one-and-one-half small floors that Beatrice's corporate office had occupied since 1946 at 120 South LaSalle, these offices were the epitome of elegance. The staff swelled to such a size that four and one-half floors were required.

Over the years, Haskell, Karnes, Hazelton, and Grantham believed that corporate officials and the general office image and expenses should set the tone for the entire company. Officers' salaries were kept comparatively low. Haskell never had a company car in his twenty-four years as president. Karnes and Hazelton did not have company cars for ten years after taking office and only then were given company cars at the insistence of the board. The general office was kept small and unpretentious for various reasons. First, it provided an example for the plants on how to control expenses. Second, it was kept small so that the four officers in Chicago could be close to what was happening at the plants. Lines of communication were short so that if a Beatrice plant had a problem, they would know about it quickly. Short lines of communication also allowed the General Office personnel to watch the sales trends, expense trends, and the use of cash at the plants. Karnes always said, "You don't make any money in the General Office, you only spend it; so keep it small and efficient. You can't keep putting pressure on plant management to hold down expenses if the general office is not watching its expenses."

Before Dutt became chief executive officer, no company airplanes were used by General Office personnel. Beatrice could never justify the cost of using a company plane; any Beatrice plant in the United States could be reached from the General Office by commercial plane in three hours or less. From 1952 to 1979, Beatrice board meetings were held at private clubs such as the Mid America or Metropolitan Clubs in Chicago, where lunch was served. Therefore, the company did not pay rent on a large board room when it was not being used. These and many more measures set a good example for Beatrice plant managers who were operating on small margins and battling rising inflationary prices and wage increases during this thirty-year growing period.

Beginning in 1980, Dutt paid lip service to decentralized management as a keystone for future growth, while he was changing the strategies of management. Ultimately, they were restructured so radically that Beatrice disappeared from view as a corporate entity and became privately held.

Sales for fiscal year 1982 were up 3 percent to $9 billion, while net earnings rose 28 percent to $390 million and primary net earnings per share were increased 29 percent to $3.80. It was significant that only Dutt signed the letter to shareholders in the annual report. Eckrich did not, as he had in the prior three years.

In 1982, Dutt's agenda, which had been hidden, surfaced. He embarked on fulfilling his vision of building Beatrice into the nation's largest diversified food company. One major phase was an asset redeployment program which had been initiated in 1979. Essentially, this meant selling companies that didn't meet the financial goals he had set and acquiring those with greater potential. His objectives were to raise return on equity to 18 percent and boost revenues 5 percent in real dollars and profit growth to 16 percent per year. Among the first to go were most of the segments of Harman International, Airstream, Morgan Yachts, South-western Investment Company, and Dannon yogurt. Krispy Kreme Dough-nuts and Buxton were divested in 1982.

Dutt was after bigger game. After a $170 million stock-for-stock offer to Bob Evans Farms fell through, he set his sights on beverages. Initially, the company showed an interest in Pepsi-Cola, but switched to Coke. On January 13, 1982, Dutt acquired the beverages segment of Northwest Industries for $580 million, $450 million of which was good will. The deal included the Coca-Cola Bottling Company of Los Angeles and The Buckingham Corporation, a major importer of wines and liquors such as Cutty Sark scotch. The purchase price was more than fifteen times earnings. The Royal Crown operations were sold for an after-tax gain of $32.4 million. Subsequently, the Coca-Cola Bottling Company of San Diego was acquired for three million shares. This was followed by the addition of the Coca-Cola Bottling Company of San Bernardino and a number of Coca-Cola bottlers in the Midwest.

Another change effected in 1982 was to switch from Last-In-First-Out (LIFO) inventory accounting to First-In-First-Out (FIFO) for many domes-tic operations. But even more important was the decline in morale, as Dutt became increasingly autocratic, arbitrary, and isolated from his managers.

In an article in the June 11, 1984 issue of *Industry Week* entitled "Can Dutt Do It?" Bryan Moskal wrote, "James L. Dutt, chairman and CEO of Beatrice Foods Co., is a man who won't be outdone.

"A framed cartoon behind his desk in Chicago illustrates his new management style. It shows the head of a company at a table flanked by his management team. The caption reads: 'All of those opposed signify by saying, I quit.' "

Then came the first sign of a crack in Beatrice's solid financial foundation.

For thirty consecutive years, the shareholders and analysts following Beatrice had seen the company report record years with each quarter surpassing the comparable quarter of the prior year in sales and earnings. In the report for the first quarter of fiscal year 1983, dated June 24, 1982, the company reported that net earnings had plunged 35 percent to $71.3 million from the prior year. Primary earnings per common share were down 36 percent to 68 cents from $1.06. Sales were up 2 percent to $2.3 billion.

"Net earnings in the prior year include a one-time gain reflecting· a change in accounting principle for investment tax credit," Dutt explained. "Excluding the gain, net earnings declined 7 percent." The recession was blamed, but Beatrice had proved to be "recession proof" through six similar economic declines.

On September 1, 1982, Eckrich, then fifty-eight, resigned as president and as a director. Eckrich cited personal reasons for resigning, although many felt that he was not in accord with Dutt's restructuring plans or with the increasing centralization of the company. In a statement, Eckrich said, "I've enjoyed my association with Beatrice Foods in Chicago since our merger in 1972. However, my roots and family remain in Fort Wayne, Indiana, where the Eckrich Company was founded, and it's my desire to return to that area where I've spent so much of my life." He later became president and chief executive officer of Central Soya in Fort Wayne and retired in 1988. Dutt added the role of president to his list of titles, but later eliminated the position. There were more resignations to come. Less than six months after Eckrich resigned, James Weiss, executive vice president and a director in charge of all non-food businesses, with sales aggregating $2.3 billion and pre-tax earnings of $350 million, resigned.

The non-food businesses included three major segments: Chemical Division, Consumer Arts Division, and Industrial Division. All told, there were more than a hundred independently operating businesses, approximately one-third of which were in foreign countries. Each business was run by an able president-manager, who was totally responsible for his business. These businesses were highly complex and best run by Beatrice's proven, decentralized philosophy. Weiss had learned well under Karnes's and Grantham's tutelage and was a firm believer in Beatrice methodology, but Dutt had started to insist that these businesses be consolidated. Dutt wanted Weiss to end up with five or six consolidated operating businesses and to eliminate the very heart of them—the whole layer of entrepreneurial managers. He wanted to centralize what could not be centralized without devastating effect.

Weiss knew through hard-won experience that this would never work and tried to dissuade Dutt. But Dutt persisted and began encouraging his staff people to force implementation of the plan, which created great discontent and demoralization within the operating companies. Weiss knew that implementation would have a negative effect on the operating managers and that Beatrice, a jewel of a company, was about to come apart. He said that he did not want to be a party to the dismemberment, and so he left on February 11, 1983.

From 1980 through July of 1985, thirty-nine of fifty-eight executives who had been with the company in 1980 had resigned, retired, or "been thrown overboard" as one newspaper phrased it. In addition to Eckrich, Weiss, Niemiec, and Metzger, the list included Duane D. Daggett, Walter R. Lovejoy, and James E. Murphy, all senior vice presidents, and eight vice presidents. Among them were Kenneth A. Barnebey, Edwin D. Disborough, James G. Fransen, Joseph E. Quinlan, Gordon E. Swaney, R. Wilbur Daeschner, P. Robert McClure, Jr., and William J. Polidoro. George J. Zulanas, Jr., had been transferred to Tropicana.

William J. Powers, head of the Confectionery Division, had retired and his successor, B. Robert Kill, later resigned. Richard A. Walrack was reassigned to Tropicana as general manager, and subsequently returned to Hawaii to manage the dairy operations there. Gone, too, were such division executives as Walter L. Baker, Peter Brown, William C. Burkhardt, Chester W. Schmidt, Wayne H. Tingey, Norman M. Schneider, and Culligan's two top executives, John A. Gavin and Donald L. Porth. The situation was exacerbated when Theodore R. Ruwitch, vice president and assistant to the chairman, died in December 1982.

To shore up the eroding staff, Granger was named vice chairman; J. J. McRobbie, formerly president of LaChoy, was elected a senior vice president and director of corporate marketing; William E. Reidy was named a senior vice president and director of strategy, succeeding Ronald B. Williams, Jr., who had been terminated earlier as director of corporate planning; and Anthony Luiso, president of the International Division, was promoted to senior vice president.

For the 1983 fiscal year, sales were up slightly to $9.2 billion, but net earnings dropped from $390 million the previous year to $43 million as a result of special charges of $278 million during the year and gains of $77 million for special items in the preceding year. Earnings per share sank to 27 cents from $3.90. Long-term debt was $772 million compared to $197 million in 1973.

In the 1983 annual report, Dutt announced a giant step toward changing the course of Beatrice. "Fiscal 1983 was a turning point for Beatrice," he said in the letter to shareholders. "During the year, your company embarked on a new strategic course built around a total commitment to marketing. This new plan calls for transforming Beatrice into a unified, directed marketing company with real power in the markets we serve and with the skills needed to enter new markets successfully."

Dutt explained his ambitious plan in greater detail in his address to the shareholders at the eighty-sixth annual meeting held in Chicago on June 9, 1983.

> Marketing will be the decisive element in the company's future program of internal growth, while acquisitions will play a smaller role. [Subsequent developments belied that statement.]
>
> Our future is in the marketplace, and we're taking the steps needed to transform Beatrice into the total marketing company the future demands.
>
> The early retirement program has begun, and the final results will be known after July 1.
>
> Substantial progress has been made in the divestiture program. To date, we've sold four companies, and active negotiations are underway for the sale of more than half of the companies included in the reserve.
>
> But to make the most of the opportunities our clout in the marketplace offers, we recognized that it would be necessary to realign our domestic profit centers, bringing them together into larger business units organized along marketing lines.
>
> In the past, our system of a number of small, regional profit centers worked well. But to be competitive and to grow in the future, we need broader product lines, with national marketing and advertising and with national distribution systems.
>
> In fact, this critical aspect of our program is ahead of schedule.
>
> A total of approximately 30 principal marketing areas has been identified, and our domestic profit centers now are being formed into new business units to serve those markets.
>
> And it's important to know that this realignment is not a mere consolidation of numbers. The result will be a much smaller number of free-standing and self-supporting businesses operating in the company's principal marketing areas. These new "businesses of Beatrice" will be larger, cohesive business units with more autonomy, responsibility and accountability. Above all, they will be strong, competitive marketing companies.

Dutt then explained that these new business units would be structured along marketing lines into six operating groups: Refrigerated Food/ Distribution Services, Beverage, Grocery, Consumer/Commercial, Specialty Chemical, and International Food (the total comprised twenty-seven operating units).

"To be sure that we have in place the strongest and most efficient management team possible, we're announcing a comprehensive new management structure for Beatrice," Dutt continued. "I believe this structure addresses the needs of the future and better addresses a changing market environment."

Dutt advised the shareholders that the first step was to form an Office of the Chairman composed of himself, Granger, and Conners, both vice chairmen, and Reidy. Also formed was the Office of the Chief Operating Officer composed of six senior operating executives with Dutt as chairman: Richard L. Chisholm, Thomas P. Kemp, Nolan D. Archibald, Luiso, and Harry Wechsler. One vacancy remained to be filled.

"I believe that out of the new structure we've put in place will flow the next generation of management for Beatrice Foods," Dutt said.

"This combination makes for a new Beatrice Foods. A Beatrice Foods that, in my opinion, is on the verge of experiencing the best years this company has ever seen."

For more than eighty years, Beatrice was regarded as a sleepy Midwest company that seldom made the headlines and then only in positive terms. Its continuing record of increases in sales and earnings was duly reported by the media. From time to time, Karnes would meet with reporters of the *Wall Street Journal, Business Week, Forbes, Dun's,* and the Chicago *Tribune, Sun-Times,* and *Daily News.* The conferences were friendly and the subsequent reports glowing, as were those resulting from meetings with security analysts.

Then, the media started to focus increasing attention on the company after Dutt won out in the battle for the lead part in the Beatrice drama in 1979. However, Dutt and his public relations staff succeeded in antagonizing many editors and reporters who received either limited access to him or no attention at all from him. The Chicago press became more and more negative. For example, the *Wall Street Journal* ran a feature article written by Sue Shellenbarger on September 27, 1983:

> After a lunch of Beatrice Foods Co.'s cold cuts and frozen pudding bars, 450 Beatrice managers sat back to hear a speech by James L. Dutt, the company's chairman.
>
> If, as they appeared to be, the Beatrice people were in good spirits at the beginning of Mr. Dutt's talk, they were hardly jolly at the end of it. The usually low-key Mr. Dutt's tone was grim. "He came down like a lead pipe," one observer says.
>
> "We're changing the company. With change comes uncertainty. Nothing would please me more than to tell you today exactly how things are going to work out, and exactly how each of us will fit into the picture. I can't do that. We must be honest with ourselves and face reality. We can't run this company tomorrow by following yesterday's game plan."
>
> The theme of Mr. Dutt's speech and of his recent tenure as chairman is that he is giving himself two years in which to transform the sprawling food, consumer and industrial products holding company with $9.19 billion in annual sales into a consolidated marketing giant on the order

of Procter & Gamble. That means discarding a longstanding strategy of decentralization and growth by acquisition. For Beatrice, whose name many employees still pronounce Bee-AT-riss, after the small Nebraska town of its origin, the metamorphosis is proving to be painful.

In his first months as CEO, he says now he was uncertain about strategy. Asked early in his tenure how he planned to manage Beatrice's sprawling businesses, he said, "I didn't know what to say, so I indicated we're not going to change anything; but the more I got into it, the more I realized that the company was unmanageable. Many companies were drifting, lacked momentum and direction. In Beatrice markets the degree of sophistication of management and the qualifications of people running the business were changing, and we weren't changing with it."

"Beatrice acts like a company that's gotten mad at itself," says John P. Larson, an analyst with Blunt, Ellis, and Loewi, a brokerage firm based in Milwaukee.

Fiscal year 1984 was a year of financial recovery and further realignment of management. Granger retired as a vice chairman and director on June 5, 1984. Reuben E. Berry, senior vice president, management resources, and Luiso were added to the office of chairman and McRobbie, senior vice president, Grocery, and William S. Mowry, Jr., senior vice president, International Foods, joined the operating team.

At the 1984 annual meeting, the company was renamed Beatrice Companies and a new identity was designed. This symbol, the name *Beatrice* in sans serif italic type on a red stripe, was to be added to all packaging, signage, trucks, brand advertising, and promotions, to be backed by an extensive television and print media campaign. The number of advertising agencies representing various Beatrice operations was consolidated to ten from more than a hundred, and the number of brokers serving various companies was reduced.

Sales rose only 2 percent to $9.3 billion, but earnings rebounded sharply to $433 million from $43 million for 1983. Primary earnings per share soared to $4.23 from 27 cents. In addition, money obtained from divestitures was used to purchase ten million shares of the company's stock at $34 per common share. It was oversubscribed, but the market price which had climbed from the low $20s to as high as $36 per share, dipped back to as low as $28 in 1985.

As further evidence of Dutt's determination to change the direction of the company, are quotations from his address to New York security analysts on July 24, 1984:

> More than two years ago, we began to reposition Beatrice. That process began after a year to a year and a half of very serious thinking, planning and studying within the company. We recognized the fact that markets

were changing our ability as a decentralized company, to respond to various needs in the marketplace. Our inability to respond to these needs and to react competitively to other national companies caused great concern. The company needed a focus, and needed to move out of a number of markets and a number of the companies that we were in. So we began to divest operations.

We accumulated a good deal of money, and a lot of talk began in the marketplace about a stock buy-back. But we had more important things to do at that time; namely, to buy Coca-Cola of Los Angeles.

We moved from Royal Crown Cola, which was in the number five marketing position, to the number one marketer of beverages. We also moved into the number one Coca-Cola operation in the United States and perhaps in the world. This was a very difficult transaction because we bought one company and sold the other at the same time. But it was the right thing to do, and the right time to do it.

We bought the biggest and the best at what is now the lowest price that since has been paid for a Coke bottling franchise. The business today, two years later, has doubled its profits. We have moved from the number two position in the Los Angeles/Southern California market to a strong number one position. This was made possible through the combined efforts of Beatrice and Coca-Cola U.S.A. We now have one of the finest franchises in the world.

We were responding to a changing environment, and we made the fundamental decision to position the company for the future. Our cornerstones are these four commandments which continue to dictate our strategy at Beatrice:

To make Beatrice the premier worldwide marketer of food and consumer products. Those words are very specific and very clear; they state the goal and the strategy of the company.

To build national presence and brand franchises.

To gain more direct access to the consumer.

To place top quality people throughout our organization.

And we are doing all of these things.

To achieve our goals, we have realigned our entire organization from 430 business units down to 28.

We also have made substantial progress with our second divestiture program. In the past 18 months, we have sold more than 30 companies including some large operations like Shedd's margarine business, John Sexton & Co. and the U.S. confectionery operations. We realized $76 million in gains on the sale of those businesses and we reduced the divestiture reserve by about $23 million.

We have certainly demonstrated our ability to divest companies, and I think this is one of our real strengths. We have divested certain operations much quicker than we first indicated, and we have also achieved much higher prices than we first anticipated.

We are reorganizing our entire food broker organization to almost one-eighth of what it was. This gives us tremendous leverage with our broker operations in the United States.

We have begun investing much more heavily in advertising and marketing activities. This marketing investment is producing profitable results.

We have realigned our U.S. advertising agencies. A few years ago we had more than 140 agencies. Now we have about 10 world-class advertising agencies working for us. This also provides real leverage.

We have adopted a new corporate identity program. This program will be used on consumer packaging to associate the Beatrice name with quality and with value. The quality/value image should make the introduction of new brands easier, as well as open many new markets for us.

We have adopted a new name, BEATRICE COMPANIES, INC., which really tells what Beatrice is—a group of free standing companies all working together. Yet, with all the changes we have made, our operations have held up very well. We have been able to build the company in spite of selling sizeable portions of it.

We have experienced substantial market share gains with Tropicana, Fisher Nut and Swiss Miss. And the Soft Drinks Division certainly exemplified another good, strong market share in a very, very competitive industry.

The program of consolidating and focusing the company has moved far ahead of our original two-year schedule. So far ahead, in fact, that we felt we had to stand back and decide what the company needed in this new configuration to achieve our corporate objectives and to become a premier worldwide marketer.

We determined that first we had to have a very good, strong national distribution system. Second, we had to have an aggressive national sales organization—not just brokers, but our own sales people with strong marketing mentalities. Third, we had to make a commitment to research and development. And finally, we had to develop strong employees through a management training program.

What was transpiring within the corporate cocoon was even more perturbing to most of those involved. In addition to the steady shift to centralization with the accompanying dampening of entrepreneurialism and the addition of a fourth echelon of management, the General Office was substantially expanded. From a total of 161 people, almost half of whom were accountants and auditors in 1976, the staff had swelled to more than 750 in 1985. Such growth required more space in the high-rent headquarters and violated the long-held policy of keeping the General Office small and in close touch with the plant managers. For example, the Tax and Law departments were continually expanded, and the Tax and Law expenses were soaring.

The Public Relations Department in 1978 was comprised of five people, two of them secretaries. A new vice president of public affairs was hired in 1978. One of his qualifications was that he had line experience. Eventually, the staff grew to twenty-six persons. The annual report turned into a book. Costs for photography alone exceeded $60,000 one year. Other expensive intracompany publications were produced. Most of the interviews with the media turned out to be negative. One in *Fortune* in 1985, resulted in the resignation of the head of the Public Affairs Department, and a succession of replacements followed. A new public relations firm was hired, and costs escalated materially.

In the course of centralizing management, many consultants were retained to advise how to restructure the company. Karnes always thought consultants were an unneeded extravagance. Beatrice only used them for special studies for inventory, quality control, and product research. The consultants' visits to Beatrice plants usually proved to be disruptive and had a bad effect on morale. The manner in which the plants were being consolidated resulted in the dismissal of certain people with little consideration for their many years of dedicated service to the company.

The policy of promoting from within was not followed. Instead, outsiders were brought in at high levels of management. Morale sagged even further. The program for early retirement with attractive pension payments for employees who had a certain number of years of service at age fifty-five or more cost the company more experienced and able men and women. More than eight hundred took advantage of the offer.

Dutt also reversed the policy of advertising the brands. The major stress now was on their association with Beatrice, and the objective was to create recognition of the company among consumers via the theme "Beatrice. You've known us all along."

Beatrice became the sole sponsor of America's Marathon/Chicago in 1979. By 1986, the last year it sponsored the race, costs were in excess of $2 million. More than $30 million was invested in an advertising campaign aired during the 1984 Winter Olympics and Summer Olympics.

Then came the blockbuster move that turned out to be the beginning of the end of Dutt's career with Beatrice.

CHAPTER EIGHTEEN

The Battle for Esmark

On March 1, 1984, the start of the 1985 fiscal year, Beatrice appeared to be on the road to recovery. Sales and earnings were rebounding. Jim Dutt had his plans well underway for repositioning Beatrice as a unified, market-driven company. The name was changed to Beatrice Companies, Inc., on June 1 to emphasize this change in identity. Long-term debt was a manageable $779 million.

Behind Dutt was a favorable board comprised of twelve outside directors and only four members of management. The insiders were Dutt, John Conners, William Granger, and Richard J. Pigott. The outsiders included long-term directors, G. A. "Al" Costanzo, Bernard A. "Barney" Monaghan, Jayne Spain, and Omer Voss. The others were Angelo R. Arena, president and chief executive officer of Hutzler Bros.; Alexander Brody, president and chief executive officer of DYR; James W. Cozad, vice chairman of Standard Oil of Indiana; Walter J. Leonard, Distinguished Fellow, Institute for Study of Educational Policy at Howard University; Cedric E. Ritchie, chairman and chief executive officer of the Bank of Nova Scotia; Goff Smith, retired chairman and chief executive officer of Amsted Industries; Russell L. Wagner, retired chairman and chief executive officer of NLT Corporation; and Murray L. Weidenbaum, Malinckrodt Distinguished University Professor and director of the Center for the Study of Business at Washington University.

By the end of the previous fiscal year, February 29, 1984, Beatrice had sold thirty-one of the fifty businesses targeted for divestiture. The sale of the thirty-one companies netted a total after-tax gain of $76 million. The largest of these were the candy operations, purchased by the Huhtamaka Group of Helsinki, Finland. These were folded into Huhtamaka's Leaf, Inc. operations based in Bannockburn, Illinois. Other large units sold included John Sexton & Co., purchased by Rycoff of California, and Shedd, which was bought by Lever Brothers.

In implementing his drive to build a market-driven company, Dutt became a driven man. He abruptly departed from his often-stated program for building Beatrice from within rather than primarily through acquisitions. The major exceptions had been the purchase of the Coca-Cola operations and Louver Drape, Inc., the latter for $41 million in 1982.

As early as February 1984, there were rumbles on Wall Street that several major companies were considering making a tender offer for Beatrice. Among those mentioned were Swiss-based Nestlé S.A., the world's largest food company; R. J. Reynolds, which had acquired Nabisco (which previously had acquired Standard Brands); and Unilever N. V., the Anglo-Dutch concern. To counter a possible takeover as well as to strengthen Beatrice's position as a premier consumer products company, Dutt commissioned William E. Reidy, director of internal strategy, to prepare an acquisition plan. Reidy who joined Beatrice in 1983 had proved effective in a similar role for Dart & Kraft when those two companies merged.

Thirty of the largest food and consumer companies were analyzed in depth to determine which would best complement Beatrice product lines and related functions. Ten factors were considered in the following order: marketing strength, national sales organization, national distribution network, research and development, leading national brands, complementary products and product lines, international opportunities, advanced computer systems, good financial performance, and substantial size and management fit.

The list of prospects was pared to five. Of those, three companies survived the analytical process: the decision was to bid for the Chicago-based Esmark, Inc. It was hardened when Dutt learned that Esmark had taken a position in Beatrice stock, as had several well-known raiders including Ivan F. Boesky. One Beatrice executive reported that Dutt became "infuriated" at Esmark's move. By mid-March of 1984, Esmark had accumulated 1.4 million shares of Beatrice, according to a Securities and Exchange Commission filing. On March 14, Esmark sold that interest back to Beatrice for $46.3 million, according to the filing, receiving a slight premium over market value.

Esmark was still digesting the 1983 leveraged buyout of Norton Simon, Inc. for $1.1 billion which increased Esmark's long-term debt to $713 million. Among the companies Esmark acquired with Norton Simon, Inc. were Hunt-Wesson Foods and Avis's car rental and leasing operations.

Esmark had assembled a highly successful conglomerate over the years under the leadership of Donald P. Kelly, chairman, president, and chief executive officer, and Roger T. Briggs, vice chairman. Operations were decentralized as in the previous Beatrice system, with the management of each division granted considerable autonomy. In its annual report for the year ended October 29, 1983, Esmark was defined as "a holding company with major interests in foods, chemicals, personal products, high fidelity and industrial products, vehicles rental and leasing and distilled spirits." Among its best-known food brands were Wesson Oil, Hunt's tomato products, Peter Pan peanut butter, Orville Redenbacher popcorn, Swift specialty meats, Reddi-Wip whipped cream, and Treasure Cave and Pauly cheeses. Non-food brands included Max Factor and Almay cosmetics, STP gas and oil treatment products, Halston/Orlane fashionwear, Playtex intimate apparel, Jhirmack hair-care products, Pennaco hosiery, Jensen audio-visual components, Danskin knitwear, and Discwasher video game accessories. It also owned Estech, Inc., which produced fertilizer (Vigoro) and industrial chemicals and owned phosphate mines; Eschem, Inc., which made industrial adhesives; EESCO, Inc., which distributed electrical products; and Estronics, Inc. (Jensen). It held 35 percent (1.7 million shares) of the Swift Independent Meat Packing Company. Just before it made its initial offer for Norton Simon in 1983, it had acquired Blue Coach Foods, the nation's largest producer of diced cooked poultry for the food service and food processing industries, and Almay. In May of 1984, Esmark sold its liquor business, Somerset Importers, to the Distillers Company of Scotland for $250 million. It also had sold off its McCall Pattern Company to the TLC Group, headed by Reginald Lewis, for $25 million.

For the fiscal year ended October 29, 1983, Esmark's sales had risen to $4.1 billion with net earnings of $117.4 million, equal to $3.66 per share. All were records. This growth was accelerated at a rapid rate following the consolidation of the Norton Simon purchase. For the six months ended April 28, 1984, Esmark's earnings soared 134 percent from the comparable period of the prior year to $98.1 million, and revenues were up 86 percent to $2.59 billion.

Esmark's marketing capability was another magnet for Dutt in achieving his goal of developing Beatrice into the world's premier marketer of food and consumer products. Especially attractive was the Hunt-Wesson marketing team which consisted of a 500-person sales force, 16 distribution centers nationwide, and a sophisticated research center with 150 people in Fullerton, California. This was augmented by Swift's sales force of two hundred and its research and development facilities in Oak Brook, Illinois.

From time to time, Dutt would confer with Karnes and Grantham at breakfast meetings in Indian Wells, California, where both of the former Beatrice executives had winter homes. When he learned of Dutt's intention to acquire Esmark, Karnes strongly advised Dutt not to make the deal. "It is too big, the debt will be too big, the company has too many commodity items, vegetable oil, poultry and tomato products," Karnes warned him.

Dutt was undeterred. However, many analysts offered the opinion that he was waiting for someone else to set a price for Esmark. That "someone" turned out to be Kohlberg Kravis Roberts & Co. heading a group of investors that included Kelly and Briggs. Early in May of 1984, KKR offered $55 per common share and $39.05 for each preferred share, equal to $2.4 billion for Esmark. Its plan was to take Esmark private through a leveraged buyout. In such a venture, a group of investors takes a company private in a transaction funded largely by borrowing money. Then the debt is paid with funds generated by the acquired company's operations or sale of assets. The Esmark deal had been arranged by the investment banking firm of Oppenheimer & Co.

Two weeks later, Dutt made his move. On May 22, the Beatrice board of directors unanimously approved a cash tender offer for all of the 42.3 million outstanding common and 2.6 million preferred shares of Esmark. The offer to purchase all of Esmark's common stock at a cash price of $56 per share and Esmark's $2.80 cumulative convertible series B preferred stock at $39.70 per share equaled $2.5 billion, topping KKR's bid by $1 million. The offer would expire on June 20. Two days later, Dutt trumped his high bid with an offer of $60 per common share and $42.60 for each preferred share tendered, boosting the price to $2.7 billion.

Why did Beatrice raise the ante $4 per share on the common? According to a report in the Chicago *Sun-Times* on May 25, 1984, Dutt, Kelly, and Briggs met in Chicago on the night of May 23 and hammered out the new definitive agreement because "some of those present at the meeting were certain KKR was willing to go to $58 to $59 per share . . . and there were indications of some definite interest in Esmark by at least one other party."

On May 24, the two companies announced that they had executed a definitive merger agreement for the acquisition of Esmark. The announcement also reported that Esmark granted Beatrice the right to purchase 7,820,000 treasury shares, representing approximately 18.5 percent of the presently outstanding Esmark common shares, for $56. Esmark also granted Beatrice the option to purchase Esmark's principal food business, Swift/Hunt-Wesson, for $1.3 billion in cash.

These lockout options would be exercised only if there were a competing tender offer or anyone acquired more than 30 percent of Esmark. Both options expired on May 31, 1985. Beatrice already owned 426,800 common and 1,000 preferred shares of Esmark.

According to the *Wall Street Journal's* report on May 23, Dutt indicated in an interview on May 22 "that he would go to the mat to buy Esmark. 'I don't lose,' he said. 'For us, this puts everything in place. It's the final seal on what we've been trying to do.'" Dutt added that "if successful, he would keep both Esmark's Swift/Hunt-Wesson food business and its international Playtex business and try to keep the top executives of both." The Swift/Hunt-Wesson Foods operations were under the direction of Frederick B. Rentschler, and Joel E. Smilow was in charge of International Playtex with Walter W. Bregman directing Playtex Products. Dutt also noted that he planned to pay off more than $1 billion of the $2.7 billion purchase price within a year by selling off Avis and other Esmark businesses "that don't fit." According to a *Wall Street Journal* article on May 25, "the sweetened offer would yield Esmark directors $160.6 million for their 2.8 million common shares."

Dutt was ecstatic about the purchase. "With this agreement, we will be able to rapidly conclude a transaction that serves the interests of both companies' shareholders, employees and customers," he wrote in a Mailgram to Beatrice personnel on May 24. "We then will quickly proceed to merge the two companies and carry out our goal of making Beatrice the premier, worldwide marketer of food and consumer products. The combined new company truly will be a dynamic force in the marketplace."

On June 25, Beatrice announced that Dutt had been elected chairman and chief executive officer of Esmark. Reidy, Luiso, and Pigott also joined the board, replacing Briggs, Smilow, and Rentschler. Kelly and Briggs agreed to serve Beatrice as consultants for six months. Kelly had achieved his objective of doing what was best for Esmark's shareholders. The purchase price was a 42 percent premium over what Esmark's common stock had been selling for in the prior year. The price range in Esmark's fourth quarter of fiscal 1983 was $33 to $44. Kelly also did well personally on his "golden parachute" and on his Esmark stock.

Beatrice now had Esmark, but it also had more than $4.5 billion in long-term debt on which it was paying interest at between 12 and 14 percent. In an address to New York security analysts on June 24, Dutt outlined his program for molding the "new" Beatrice. Highlights of his speech included announcement of reorganization of the company's entire food broker organization to almost one-eighth of what it was; realignment of U. S. advertising agencies, reducing the number from 140 to about 10; and realignment of organization of management.

Dutt noted that before the Esmark merger, Beatrice began moving toward freestanding business units—from 430 profit centers to 28. After the merger, operations were divided into three major segments: U.S. Foods, Consumer Products, and International. In addition, there were four other segments: Beatrice Chemical, Avis, Estech, and Estronics.

The $8 billion U.S. Food segment comprised three groups: Dry Grocery, headquartered in Fullerton, California, formerly the Swift/Hunt-Wesson operation; Refrigerated Food, headquartered in Oak Brook, Illinois, which included Swift, Eckrich, Tropicana, and the cheese groups; Beverage, headquartered in Los Angeles, which included Coca Cola bottling operations and bottled water companies.

Luiso was named to head the U. S. Food segment. Reporting to him were Thomas P. Kemp, formerly head of the Beverage Group, who was appointed manager of the $3 billion Refrigerated Group; John R. Attwood, formerly president of Coca-Cola of Los Angeles, who was named head of the $2.2 billion Beverage Group; and Smilow, who was named to lead the $3 billion Consumer Goods segment that included International Playtex and Household Products.

Reporting to Smilow were Nolan D. Archibald, former head of the Beatrice Consumer Products Group, as manager of the Household Products Group, and Walter W. Bregman, president of Playtex, who became head of International Playtex. William S. Mowry, Jr., continued as head of International Food. The four other segments—Beatrice Chemical, Avis, Estech, and Estronics—retained their managers, who reported to Dutt. All were targeted for sale, as were the High Fidelity Group, all chemical operations, Beatrice's cookie and bread operations, its food equipment operations, and Buckingham. Luiso, Smilow, and Mowry all were elected to the Beatrice board in August of 1984.

"Overall, we expect to divest businesses representing sales of $3.6 billion and assets of $1.3 billion," Dutt advised the analysts. No decision had been made on Avis, he added. Dutt also said that Beatrice was going to increase its marketing investment substantially. "With the combined strengths of Beatrice and Esmark, we are going to be out front, taking steps to establish truly world-class brands. We are going to back these brands with the marketing dollars that are necessary. We are there among the best. For example, on a combined basis, our advertising and marketing expenditures for the year will be nearly $750 million dollars." Actually, the total for the fiscal year was $680 million, compared to $288 million in fiscal 1984.

Then the pruning program began in earnest. The Beatrice chemical operations, including Fiberite, LNP, Stahl, Paule, and Polyvinyl Chemicals were sold to Imperial Chemical Industries, PLC, for $750 million. Buckingham was bought by Whitbread (US) Holdings for $110 million. Pacific Molasses Co. of San Francisco took the agri-products business; the Robins Group bought Brillion Iron Works; PVL Limited Partnership acquired the leather operations; and a management team bought Techton Graphic Arts. Gibbons, Green van Amerongen of New York, purchased the Food Service Equipment Group for $116 million. Included were

Bloomfield Industries, Taylor Freezer, Wells Manufacturing, Market Forge, and World Dryer. Custom Technologies went to Fansteel, Inc. for $33 million and STP was sold to Union Carbide for $87 million.

Beatrice also was buying. The most notable acquisitions were Dr. Pepper of Southern California; Rusty Jones, an undercoating service for vehicles; and Swissrose International, a cheese importing and distribution company in New York City.

To formalize Dutt's plans, the company issued a bold new mission statement early in 1985. It was featured in the March-April issue of *Beatrice World*, an internal publication circulated to the company's 123,000 employees. It also was included in the 1985 annual report. The mission statement was intended to be a call to action for all members of Beatrice.

The Beatrice Mission
We have a bold mission. It will challenge us.
It will test us. Nothing else is worthy of Beatrice.
Nothing else will reward us more.
Over the next five years, Beatrice will emerge as the world's
premier marketer of food and consumer products . . . . . .
the power in the consumer marketplace,
wherever we choose to compete.
Each of our brands will be a leader in its category.
Our first priority will be total dedication to
anticipating and satisfying consumer needs. We intend to improve the
consumer's life by providing products of superior quality,
value and convenience. We will place the consumer first in every decision
we make and everything we do.
Only this course of action will enable us to satisfy the needs of our
employees for personal growth and meaningful careers.
Only this course will enable our suppliers, distributors, trade partners
and shareholders to prosper along with us.
The common theme that runs through all
the uncommon efforts of the Beatrice family is
our unfailing commitment to quality and value.
In meeting this challenge, we constantly break new ground,
foster new ideas, develop new technologies
and establish new rules in the world marketplace.
Our presence will be felt in a strong and positive way
everywhere that our products are sold.
This dedication extends to a true concern for the well-being
of all the communities in which we operate.
Quality . . . value . . . dedication to the consumer . . .
a commitment to excellence and originality . . . maintaining
our obligation to our employees, our shareholders,

our suppliers, distributors, trading partners and to our communities . . .
These are the solid cornerstones
on which the future of Beatrice will be built.
These are the standards by which all of us will be judged.

A massive promotion program was launched to maximize awareness of this mission around the world. A videotape featuring Dutt commenting on the company's goals was distributed to all plants. Senior managers received a bronze plaque spelling out the mission's credo. Lucite paperweights and Day-Timer calendars carrying the statement were sent to managers. Each employee received an "I'm a Winner" button and a wallet card. Employees outside of the United States were sent Beatrice "winner" caps. The statement was translated into seven languages. In addition, a large plaque showing the mission message was sent to each operation for prominent positioning in each lobby. Four-by-six-foot posters of the statement were made available to all employees for autographing.

In January, Beatrice launched a sales promotion campaign developed by Flair Communications of Chicago. The theme, "The United Tastes of Beatrice," had the objective of identifying Beatrice to consumers as the only company offering product lines for breakfast, lunch, dinner, and snacks. Thirty products, all bearing the red Beatrice signature stripe, were featured. Free-standing inserts with coupons and special offers were distributed at the end of January, supplemented by thirty-second television spots; point-of-purchase materials including shelf talkers, danglers, channel strips, and stacker cards also were employed. A consumers' sweepstakes offering trips, cash, and a $150 shopping spree also were introduced.

Were all of Dutt's strategies working? For the fiscal year ended February 28, 1985, the company reported that net sales rose 35 percent to $12.6 billion, compared to $9.3 billion for the previous year. Net earnings were up 11 percent to $479 million from $433 million. Primary earnings per share increased to $5.06 from $4.23.

However, in its discussion of operations and financial conditions, management explained that net earnings in both years included after-tax income from business realignment activity. It reported that in 1985, business realignment activity included pre-tax gains from the sales of various operations totaling $700 million. These gains were partially offset by a pre-tax charge of $286 million established for the anticipated cost of restructuring Beatrice's business following the acquisition of Esmark.

"Excluding business realignment activity, earnings were $259 million, down 22 percent from $334 million a year ago," the annual report stated. "On a per share basis, such earnings declined at a slower rate because fewer common shares were outstanding during fiscal 1985. Related primary earnings per share of $2.66 were down 18 percent from $3.23 in fiscal 1984. The declines are primarily due to cost associated with the acquisition of Esmark, significantly higher advertising and sales promotion expenses and the absence of earnings from divested operations. These factors more than offset the earnings from Esmark operations acquired in 1985."

Working capital decreased $82 million to $611 million at year-end, and the debt to equity ratio rose from 49 percent at the end of fiscal 1984 to 199 percent at the end of 1985. This had been reduced to 166 percent by March. Long-term debt was $2.6 billion. Receivables and inventories both had gone up substantially from the prior year, and net interest expense was up to $404 million for the year.

Many analysts thought Dutt's grandiose plan was appropriate for the times. However, there was a countercurrent in these tides of change that had an increasingly deleterious impact on the company's operations and employee morale. The philosophy that Beatrice was a "people" company and the policy of promoting from within were eroding rapidly. One reason was that Dutt's management style was becoming more militant as the pressures mounted to turn his dreams into reality.

There was a continued acceleration in the number of departures of Beatrice veterans, many of them in key positions. Fred Schomer, a twenty-year veteran of the company, resigned as vice president and treasurer in November 1983, to join Acco World Corporation of Northbrook, Illinois, as vice president of finance and administration. A major loss was the March 1984 retirement of Granger at sixty-five as vice chairman and a director. Granger, a friendly, outgoing person and fine operating executive who was highly respected throughout the company, often had acted as a buffer between Dutt and operations personnel. In March of 1985, Conners, also a proven operating manager with fine "people sense," ended thirty-seven years of service to the company, retiring both as a vice chairman and director at age sixty. Most of Granger's and Conners's experience had been in the Dairy Division, as had Dutt's. Dutt was urged by several former directors to keep both men on active duty with the company. Their experience and knowledge of the many phases of plant operations could have been extremely helpful to him at that time.

The executive corps was thinned further after the acquisition of Esmark. Both Rentschler, forty-seven, and Smilow were regarded throughout the food and consumer products industry as superb managers with excellent people skills. Rentschler had been head of Norton Simon's food operation when Esmark acquired it. He moved over to Esmark as president and chief executive officer of the Swift/Hunt-Wesson operations which accounted for $1.7 billion of Esmark's sales in fiscal 1983. Smilow, fifty-one, was chairman and chief executive officer of International Playtex, which had sales of $1 billion.

At the end of June 1984, Rentschler resigned, reportedly by mutual agreement. In an article reporting his departure, the Chicago *Tribune* on Thursday, June 28, quoted First Boston Corp. analyst Al Jackson as saying, "They made a crucial mistake. The one person they should not have lost was Rentschler." Luiso then was appointed to head the $8 billion U.S. Food segment.

Dutt had been shopping for marketing talent for some time. "Marketing skills are uppermost in my mind," he told the New York analysts. "And now we have those skills throughout our organization. Where we needed greater marketing talent, we went out and bought that talent. We got the best that money can buy. We hired people like Malcolm Candlish from Pepsico, who heads our Samsonite operations; Wes Thompson from Coca-Cola, who heads our Tropicana operation; and Norm Ross from Dart & Kraft, who heads marketing for Beatrice Cheese," he said. "We have added good, strong people from Consolidated Foods (now Sara Lee), General Foods, Quaker Oats and Ralston." He also told the analysts he planned to cut the corporate office staffs, which consisted of 525 at Beatrice and 250 at Esmark, to between 150 and 200 people within a year after the merger, which was completed in August. All of these statements and actions depressed employee morale.

The resignation of Smilow in October "to pursue other business interests" triggered another chain reaction. Again Dutt reached outside the company to hire Frank E. Grzelecki, forty-seven, as a corporate vice president and president of Consumer Products on October 31, 1984. He had been president and chief executive officer of Lenox, Inc., a marketer of fine china, jewelry, and luggage, since 1981. He also had been a director of Lenox until its acquisition by Brown-Foreman in 1983. Previously, he had held a number of senior marketing positions at Textron and Colgate-Palmolive. On April 22, 1985, Grzelecki was elected to the board of directors, as was David E. Lipson, who had joined the company on that date as an executive vice president and chief financial officer. Lipson, forty-six, had been the managing partner of International Service and a member of the board of partners of the Arthur Anderson & Co. accounting firm, with which he had affiliated in 1960.

To many, Dutt seemed to be a man possessed. For example, at a widely reported conference with food industry analysts in St. Petersburg, Florida, in February, he became irritated at questions about the reality of his goals. He gestured toward Luiso, Mowry, and Grzelecki seated behind him and warned that they would lose their jobs if his goals were not met.

A succession of other actions caused further concern among members of the board of directors. Among them was Dutt's commitment of $70 million over a five-year period to sponsor automobile racing in North America and Europe. The agreement was with the Chicagoan Carl Haas, whose partner was the actor Paul Newman, and the package included entries in both the Indianapolis 500 and Formula One events. The team sponsored drivers—Mario Andretti on the Indy car circuit, and Alan Jones and Patrick Tambay in Formula One. What alarmed directors and others further was a plan to build racing cars in England. These agreements were not submitted for board approval.

Another irritant was Dutt's frequent absences from the office, when he often used the company's Gulfstream III jet to inspect Beatrice facilities. He made several trips to China, where Beatrice launched Guangmei Food Company, a joint venture, in 1981. The three-way agreement among Beatrice, the City of Canton, and the China International Trust Investment Co. (CITIC) called for the construction of a factory opened in 1984 in Canton to can fruits and vegetables under the LaChoy label. Ultimate plans were to expand into soft drinks and citrus juices. Later, a Meadow Gold ice cream store was opened in Canton. In March 1985, Dutt signed a trade agreement in Beijing with CITIC to form a joint venture known as Beatrice-CITIC Development Company to develop Western consumer products and new opportunities for exporting goods from China.

The Public Relations Department had its own revolving door and became another factor in the deteriorating relations with the media. Shortly after James Murphy was hired from Owens-Illinois' operation in Toledo, I was fired in 1978 after a twenty-three-year association with Beatrice. Peter van Dernoot, who had no public relations experience, was imported from Samsonite but returned to Denver after a short term at Beatrice. Neil Devroy, hired from the Burson-Marstellar public relations counsel, was replaced by William Jenkins. Then Murphy resigned late in 1983. Harry Berns was transferred to special events, and Barbara Knuckles was shifted from public affairs and became a vice president and director of marketing research, reporting to McRobbie. Garry Beckner, who had been hired to direct the Marching Bands and Music Bowls Program, became an assistant director in charge of media relations. Charles Long was hired from *Quill Magazine* to direct internal communications in 1983. Then there is the bizarre merry-go-round case of Robert I. Seger, who had joined Beatrice in 1975 as assistant public relations director. Until then, the Public Relations Department consisted of one man and a secretary. Seger was fired in October of 1984, then rehired as assistant director of special events in January of 1985, and released again in February of 1988.

Along the way, Dutt turned to Douglas J. Stanard, then corporate secretary, to do something about media relations in 1983. Stanard had Dutt hold a news conference and later arranged a luncheon meeting with the media. It only stopped the bleeding temporarily. Stanard became president of Beatrice's European food operations in Brussels, Belgium. He succeeded Robert T. Drape. John Hazelton, Jr., former director of European food operations, was transferred to Australia, replacing Peter Brown. Subsequently, Hazelton also left the company, and Arthur T. Mussett retired. Both were key members of the European team.

Jenkins replaced Murphy and added Patricia Brozowski to his team. Both subsequently left at different times to join FMC, and Lizabeth Sode took charge of public relations. Then, Dutt brought in Richard S. Williamson, a former aide to Ronald Reagan, as a senior vice president for corporate and international relations. Williamson in turn hired several other people from Washington, D.C. That didn't help much, either.

An editorial entitled "Jim Dutt's Sorry Record" in the April 1, 1985, issue of *Crain's Chicago Business* said in part, "Mounting evidence over the past months leads us to conclude that Mr. Dutt, driven by a private vision and an unexplainable impatience, is on his way to ruining an important Chicago company. Indeed, the evidence of adversity has become so compelling that one already can question whether outside directors have effectively exercised their oversight responsibilities."

Karnes became so alarmed about the negative publicity the company had been receiving, particularly in the Chicago press, that he asked for ten minutes of Dutt's time. The essence of his message was:

Get in and "saw wood."
Get your earnings up.
The best thing one can do is get the earnings up. When the earnings come up, most of your problems will go away. "Earnings increases are good news and are good public relations."
Watch your money, reduce the debt! With earnings up, you have more cash flow and you get more support from the financial community.

"Handling of people is critical" Karnes further advised. "You have to listen to their ideas and opinions at times, but it pays off. Often there are people you may not care for but, nevertheless, by granting them a fair hearing and working with them, disagreements can be talked out. If there have to be any terminations, they should be done quietly and on a friendly basis." Dutt had become increasingly inaccessible to staffers. They reported that all requests to him for meetings or decisions had to be submitted in writing to his secretary.

The unfavorable results of the first quarter of fiscal 1986 also were of major concern to shareholders, directors, employees, and analysts. For the three months ended May 31, 1985, sales were up 39 percent to $3.07 billion from the comparable quarter of the previous year. But earnings slumped 20 percent to $58 million from $72 million and primary earnings per share were down 22 percent to 59 cents from 73 cents. Net interest expense had climbed to $69 million from $20 million. In addition, interest for the Prime Vehicle Trust for Avis was another $25 million.

An article by Arthur M. Louis in the July 22, 1985, issue of *Fortune* was another strong indictment of Dutt's management style. "His behavior these days suggests monumental impatience bordering on desperation, and it sometimes seems that the border has been crossed," the article stated. "At management meetings, he will deliver tirades that demoralize rather than inspire. Waving his arms and sweating, he reportedly harangues his followers relentlessly, insisting that they don't work hard enough and that only he can muster the drive, intelligence and skill to bring the vision to reality."

There were other signs of trouble. Standard & Poor's downgraded its rating of Beatrice securities farther to A, and many analysts removed Beatrice from their "buy" lists. The stock performance was lackluster, ranging from $28 to $31 in early 1985.

Personnel problems continued to grow. In July 1985, Reidy, one of the key architects in the acquisition of Esmark and Beatrice's plans for the future, left the company. Once a friend and confidant of Dutt, his departure came without warning. Then Nolan Archibald, a fine operating manager, also resigned to become president of Black & Decker. He had been with Beatrice for nine years and was a serious loss to the Consumer Products Group. Thompson already had left Tropicana.

Following the eighty-eighth annual meeting in San Diego on June 4, 1985, the company had eighteen directors divided into three classes of six each having staggered terms of three years. In addition to Dutt, there were five company officers on the board: Luiso, Mowry, Lipson, Pigott, and Grzelecki. The outside directors included Arena, Monaghan, Voss, Weidenbaum, Brody, Costanzo, Leonard, Smith, Ritchie, Spain, Wagner, and James W. Cozad, vice chairman of Standard Oil, who had been named a director in April 1984.

Separately, the declining earnings, low morale, negative press, defections and firings, and Dutt's arrogance in dealing with people probably would not have affected him and Beatrice to any serious degree. But the cumulative effect, what one director termed "a constellation of factors," became impossible for the board to ignore. Finally, the five top operating officers gave the board an ultimatum—Dutt must go.

Led by Omer Voss, a director since 1971, the outside members of the board met in New York City on Thursday, August 1, and made the decision. The inside board members were insistent. When Dutt learned that it was his turn to be fired, he met with five board members in Chicago the following day. At a full meeting of the board at the University Club in Chicago on Saturday, August 3, he resigned as chairman, chief executive officer, and as a director of the company. The resignation was accepted by a unanimous vote of the board, and Dutt's six-year, turmoil-torn regime ended. He was retained as a consultant, and a severance agreement was worked out under which he received $4.5 million. He then started a venture capital business, and friends noted that he again became the friendly, outgoing person of earlier years.

CHAPTER NINETEEN

From Buyout to
Sellout

The board of directors' first consideration after the resignation of James Dutt was to appoint a chairman. Many of the potential candidates such as William Granger, John Conners, Donald Eckrich, James Weiss, Duane Daggett, and Nolan Archibald had retired early or resigned. The conclusion was that someone from outside of the company should be brought in. Several directors suggested that a member of the board be named as temporary chairman until a qualified person from the outside could be chosen. At one point, the directors turned their attention to Granger, who had worked closely with Dutt for the preceding five years. Granger had retired only seventeen months earlier as vice chairman after thirty-nine years with the company, but was still working periodically with Dutt to consolidate the Esmark operation into Beatrice.

Omer Voss asked Karnes if he would consider returning. Karnes was seventy-four, and his wife, Virginia, again was recovering from another major surgery—a concern that had prompted Karnes to resign from management nine years earlier and from the board in 1980. He agreed, however, to return to the board and to the executive committee.

Karnes had been active since his retirement in July of 1976. He became of counsel to the law firm of Kirkland & Ellis in August of 1976, and continued to practice law until January 1982. In addition, he served on a number of boards of directors, including Borg Warner Corporation, Stone Container Corp., 20th Century-Fox Corp., the Chicago-Milwaukee Corporation, the Midwest Stock Exchange, Datapoint Corporation, and Lou Ana Foods. He also had served as president of the University of Illinois Foundation during a successful capital fund drive from 1979 to 1983. He frequently was invited to lecture to professional groups and at such institutions as Columbia University and Washington State University. One lecture was at a University of Illinois seminar in May of 1985 after Beatrice endowed a chair at the university in Karnes's name for mergers and acquisitions. The first distinguished professor named to this honor was Josef Lakonishok.

In May 1982, the board of directors asked Karnes to serve as director and chairman of the Finance Committee for the troubled International Harvester Co. of Chicago, following a change of management in May of 1982. During the three years he was chairman of the Finance Committee, he took part in three different debt restructurings at Harvester, and as a result Harvester, renamed Navistar, avoided bankruptcy.

The Beatrice board's decision was to elect Granger chairman and chief executive officer and Karnes chairman of the executive committee. Both would return to the board. Granger and Karnes waited in another room at the University Club when the board met there on August 3, 1985. Following Dutt's departure, they were ushered into the meeting room and welcomed with a standing ovation. Granger was elected to the board for a three-year term, and Karnes was elected to fill Dutt's unexpired term to June 1987. The board also announced that five members of Beatrice's senior management, Frank Grzelecki, David Lipson, Tony Luiso, William Mowry, and Richard Pigott, would continue to serve as executive vice presidents and directors.

The details of the changes were released in an announcement distributed to the media on that afternoon. A copy of the release together with a covering letter from Granger was sent by Telex to Beatrice personnel around the world on Monday, August 5. Granger's letter was cheerful and sanguine.

> To the employees of Beatrice:
>
> As you are well aware, our company has gone through many changes over the past few years. As a result of the extraordinary efforts of you, the employees, Beatrice is a stronger, more competitive company. In my 39 years with Beatrice, we never had greater opportunities for success.
>
> I want to assure you that I am committed to the strategy and direction of this company. We have made tremendous progress, and we fully intend to make Beatrice a truly great marketing company.
>
> To achieve our goal, we need your continued support and dedication. Beatrice people have traditionally rallied to meet whatever challenges we face. In the coming months, we will keep you informed of our progress.
>
> I'm excited about the future of this company and pleased to have the opportunity to work with all of you.

On Monday, August 5, he also assembled all corporate employees in the company's training room on the 22d floor of the General Office to outline his plans for the future. The attitude in the room became euphoric. Many staff members and outside observers believed that Granger's assignment was to be a caretaker until the company could find a successor either from within or from the outside. However, he assured all that he did not envision himself in the caretaker role. "I'm here for an indefinite period," he declared. "In the coming months, we will keep you informed of our progress. I'm excited about the future of this company and pleased to have the opportunity to work with all of you." He also advised them that the revolving door for firings and resignations was being closed. Conversely, his door would always be open. He then invited questions and comments. Later in the day, Granger visited the offices of U.S. Foods and Consumer Durables at 55 East Monroe, the former Esmark headquarters, to offer the same assurances. In that single day, morale rose from ceiling zero to a point where staffers could see some blue skies.

The market reaction was startling. Wall Street applauded by going on a buying spree. After a short delay at the opening on Monday, August 5, Beatrice's common stock jumped $2 to close at $32.25. More than 2.6 million shares were traded, compared to an average daily volume of 360,000 shares. It was the second most active stock on the New York Stock Exchange that day. Analysts also were encouraged by the return of Karnes, who was respected in financial circles for his conservative fiscal policies and his abhorrence of debt and high inventories and receivables. Investors were confident that he would rebuild Beatrice's financial strengths.

However, the problems Granger, Karnes, and senior staff members faced were enormous. The general office had grown to six hundred people on five floors, compared to fewer than two hundred people on one and one-quarter floors in 1976. The administrative offices for U. S. Foods also were greatly overstaffed with about 180 people. Worldwide, the company had 123,000 people on its payrolls, compared to 84,000 in 1980. Long-term debt had been reduced to less than $1.8 billion, but receivables were up to almost $1.2 billion, and inventories had risen to a little less than $1.4 billion according to the company's report for the quarter ended August 31, 1985.

Although Beatrice remained profitable, earnings were falling. Net earnings for the six months ended August 31, 1985 were down 26 percent to $128 million, and primary earnings per share dipped 38 percent to $1.08 before adjustments for discontinued operations. Half-year primary net earnings before discontinued operations decreased from $165 million, excluding special items, to $111 million, and primary earnings per share were $1.08 compared to $1.73. The differences were accounted for by the exclusion of Avis, International Jensen, Danskin, and Pennaco, which Beatrice had announced in October that it intended to sell. Interest expense for the six months totaled $151 million.

The annualized dividend payoff was equal to 82 percent of per share earnings, compared to 38 percent in 1976. The dividend had been raised to $1.80 per share, and the forecast of earnings per share for fiscal year 1986 was only $2.20. The company's security ratings by Standard &

Poor and Moody's had been lowered from AAA, which it had from 1975 to 1983, to a single A rating.

Granger and Karnes determined that the bottom line was the first priority. Another concern was the total of $800 million projected for fiscal 1986 for marketing, promotion, and advertising programs. In terms of dollars, Beatrice was now the leading advertiser among U.S. food companies, including such giants as Procter & Gamble, General Foods, and Kraft. Although the company's basic marketing strategies would not be changed, its approach must be, and was, altered to place more emphasis on brands instead of the controversial "We're Beatrice, you've known us all along" campaign created to identify the company with its consumer products.

Granger and Karnes found consultants everywhere, many of whom had no concept of how Beatrice had been run and been built, and who only added to the confusion and duplication. Steps were taken immediately to eliminate consultants in the General Office and also at the office of U.S. Foods. It was estimated that $150 million in operating expenses could be taken out of the company without affecting its sales. This would have amounted to about $1 a share in increased profits; it also would improve the company's stability.

People were another major concern. To stem the loss of more key people, one of the first actions of the board's compensation committee was to work out a program for contracts for a number of top people to protect their salaries and tenures if there was any future merger. Executive recruiters from across the country called Beatrice people on a daily basis.

An illustration of Karnes's program to return the company to greater financial stability involves the Beatrice "Air Force." He considered private planes an unnecessary luxury, and Beatrice had never had a corporate company plane until after he retired. When he returned, Karnes was startled to see that the fleet numbered eight planes, and several pilots were on the payroll. On one occasion Karnes was scheduled to attend a meeting in New York with other directors and officers when his secretary asked him what time he wanted the limousine at the office to take him to the company's private plane for the flight. He politely but firmly declined the offer. "I'm going downstairs, walk two blocks to the subway train to O'Hare Field which will cost me 45 cents, and fly on a commercial plane," he told her. He was waiting for the Beatrice party when it arrived in New York.

The number of planes and pilots was thus cut back substantially. The commitment to the $70 million auto-racing program was also immediately trimmed, and eventually the company bought out the contract.

Sponsorship of America's Marathon/Chicago was terminated after the 1986 race. Advertising budgets were reviewed and cut in many cases. The oversized staff in the General Office, particularly public relations, analysts, and marketing specialists, was pared by terminations. The 35 percent interest in Swift Independent Corp. was sold to a partnership led by the Texas investor Edwin L. Cox, Jr., for $43.8 miilion. In the first three quarters of 1985, the entire Swift Independent Corp. lost $8.87 million on revenues of $2.2 billion.

After the return of Granger and Karnes to key roles in the company's management, there was considerable speculation that Beatrice was vulnerable to a takeover, either friendly or hostile. Some assessments were that the parts of the company were worth more than the whole. However, some Beatrice officials believed that takeover was unlikely because of the company's size and high debt structure. Several meetings with security analysts were held in New York and Chicago to reintroduce Granger and Karnes, and one of the first questions always was about future management. Typical was the reaction of William Leach, vice president of Donaldson, Lufkin & Jenrette, in a company newsletter dated August 7, 1985.

> Much to everyone's surprise, on August 3, 1985, Beatrice's board of directors ousted its controversial chairman, James Dutt. The company named William Granger, a 66-year-old, former vice-chairman of Beatrice, to succeed Mr. Dutt. In addition, William Karnes, 74, who basically built Beatrice before his retirement in 1976, was brought back to be a director and chairman of the executive committee. Although we believe that Mr. Granger and certainly Mr. Karnes will prove to be caretakers until a new chief executive can be found, we regard this transition as initially positive for Beatrice. Accordingly, we are reversing our long-standing negative opinion on the company. Realistically, however, the future attractiveness of the shares is highly dependent on who ultimately is chosen to succeed Mr. Dutt.
>
> Although it remains to be seen who actually assumes control of Beatrice and what direction the company embarks on, we believe that the ouster of Mr. Dutt is a step in the right direction. In our view, the company had seriously diluted its earnings and financial strength with the June 1984 acquisition of Esmark, which itself had just purchased Norton Simon. In addition, Beatrice's management ranks have been decimated by an endless number of resignations and firings.
>
> We believe that this will present an opportunity to accelerate the divestiture of Beatrice's many diverse nonfood activities, such as Avis. Although Beatrice's operating trends have been respectable, earnings have been depressed because of the company's unusually high interest expense and goodwill amortization associated with the Esmark acquisition.
>
> We believe that this may attract take-over speculation to Beatrice.

Beatrice is a company that appears to be worth more in pieces than as a whole. In addition, the company has much better cash flow than reported earnings. Beatrice now has $2.6 billion of goodwill, most of which came from the Esmark acquisition. That results in an annual non-cash non-tax deductible charge to earnings of about $65 million, or about $.60 per share."

Beatrice consistently maintained that Granger had a three-year contract and intended to stay. Morale was improving; steps to reduce the debt were being implemented; and a number of divestitures were planned and about to be completed to improve performance. But the speculation continued, and the stock continued to move up. It became obvious by mid-September that arbitragers were buying the stock in anticipation of a takeover or a restructuring of the company. Names such as Unilever, R. J. Reynolds-Nabisco, and Philip Morris, Inc. were mentioned as prospective buyers. Then Beatrice management people began receiving calls from their investors indicating that Kohlberg Kravis Roberts & Co. (KKR) was interested in acquiring Beatrice. Other calls advised of the interest of Donald P. Kelly and his management team. It became evident that former executives of Esmark, including Kelly and Roger Briggs, had joined with KKR to try to acquire Beatrice through a leveraged buyout by a newly formed company called BCI Holdings, Inc. (BCI).

Founded in 1976, KKR is considered the pioneer in engineering leveraged buyouts (LBOs). Organized as a general partnership, its general partners in 1985 were Jerome Kohlberg, Jr., sixty-two, Henry R. Kravis, forty-two, George R. Roberts, forty-two, and Robert I. MacDonnell, forty-seven. Among its most notable deals had been a $1.98 billion buyout of Storer Communications, a $1.7 billion purchase of half of Allied Corp's Union Texas Petroleum unit, and a $1.25 billion purchase of three units of City Investing Co. Later, it acquired Safeway Stores for $4.2 billion.

The following is an explanation of KKR taken from the Claremont College *CMC* magazine in Pomona, California.

> Kohlberg Kravis Roberts & Co. is an investment banking firm with offices in New York and San Francisco. It was established in 1976 by three men who were pioneers in a new form of corporate takeover that became known as the leveraged buyout (or LBO). As opposed to the sometimes hostile takeovers of high-flying corporate raiders, KKR's buyouts are friendly transactions, undertaken with the active participation of management and the approval of the board of directors. In an LBO, a publicly traded company is taken private by a small group of investors who buy the company's stock. Most of the money for the transaction is borrowed, and this borrowing is the source of the term, leveraged buyout: the leveraging being the borrowing against future cash flow that makes the deal possible.

To buy out a company, KKR's usual procedure was to add its own funds to a pool of money gathered from outside partners. The rest of the purchase price was raised by borrowing from banks and the issuance of high-interest securities, often called *junk bonds.* KKR's strategy usually is to pay down debt quickly, and then try to make a profit by selling the company or taking it public.

Rumors were rampant on Wall Street, and Beatrice stock jumped to $41 per share early in October of 1985 when reports of a buyout by KKR surfaced. The rumors became reality on Wednesday, October 16, when Kidder, Peabody & Co., representing KKR, advised Beatrice that KKR desired a meeting with Beatrice management in order to propose a leveraged buyout. Beatrice advised KKR to present its proposal in writing. That same day, KKR responded with a written offer to the board of directors to acquire Beatrice for $45 for each share of Beatrice common stock, consisting of $40 in cash and $5 in market value of preferred stock.

At a special meeting on October 20, the board unanimously rejected the offer as inadequate on the advice of its advisors, Salomon Brothers and Lazard Freres & Company. The possibility of a leveraged buyout by members of the current management also was discussed. However, the investment banking firm of Goldman Sachs with which management members had discussed the management buyout advised that obtaining the necessary financing was remote, and pursuit of this action was abandoned. The board decided that the way to achieve the full value of Beatrice was for Beatrice to remain an independent company.

Nine days later, KKR raised the ante with a written offer of $47 per common share, consisting of $40 in cash and $7 in market value of preferred stock. At a special meeting convened on October 31, the board was advised by Lazard and Salomon representatives that, from a financial point of view, it would be difficult to express an opinion that the revised offer was inadequate for the Beatrice common shareholders. The board considered expressions of interest in acquiring parts of Beatrice by other parties up to that time, the absence of interest in acquiring all of Beatrice, and the value to shareholders of a hypothetical break-up of the company.

After extensive discussions the board unanimously determined to open negotiations with KKR and to explore all alternatives. It authorized management to take all appropriate actions to develop a transaction that would maximize the value of Beatrice. The board asked Lazard and Salomon to contact about seventy-five parties to determine if any had an interest in acquiring all or parts of Beatrice. Starting on November 8, Lazard and Salomon provided, on a confidential basis, financial and other information relating to Beatrice to approximately thirty-five parties. Although some expressed interest in acquiring portions of the company, no one was interested in buying all of it.

However, it became common knowledge that Beatrice was for sale—at the right price. On November 11, E. F. Hutton & Company, Inc., and the Dart Group Corporation submitted a written offer to the board proposing to buy all of the issued and outstanding common stock for $48 per share. The letter also stated that the proposal was contingent upon arranging adequate financing and that Hutton and Dart were "encouraged" that such financing was obtainable. The next day, Hutton and Dart informed Beatrice's financial advisors orally that they would increase their proposal to $50 per share. The following day, they withdrew their offer.

Meanwhile, on November 12, KKR again revised its offer, increasing the price to $50 per share, consisting of $43 in cash and preferred stock that would have a market value of $7. Three conditions were attached to the offer. First, if BCI Holdings did not acquire Beatrice or if another party obtained or offered a firm proposal to buy 30 percent of Beatrice's outstanding common stock, then BCI Holdings would be entitled to a cancellation fee of $1 per share on approximately 122.9 million shares outstanding, or issuable on conversion or exercise of all outstanding convertible securities, warrants, and other rights obligating Beatrice to issue additional shares.

The second condition concerned the reimbursement of the expenses of BCI Holdings and its affiliates. The third was a provision granting BCI Holdings either of two options. One was the right to purchase certain of Beatrice's grocery food and Tropicana subsidiaries for an aggregate price of $2.391 billion. The other option was purchase of certain bottled water, processed meats, soft drink, and Tropicana subsidiaries for an aggregate price of $2.412 billion. The offer was conditioned on acceptance by the board no later than November 13.

After a lengthy review of this amended offer and all possible alternatives, the Beatrice board accepted it at another special meeting on November 13. One condition of acceptance was that KKR would honor certain amendments of existing benefit plans, pension programs, contracts, and agreements of employees of Beatrice, including its most senior executives. Reconvening on November 14, the board voted to approve and authorize the execution of the initial merger agreement and the asset options agreement. It also approved the employee compensation and pension plan provisions.

But the negotiations did not end there. On January 8, 1986, KKR proposed another modification—an offer of $40 for each share and

10/25th of a share of preferred stock valued at $10 to be issued by BCI Holdings. The dividends on the preferred stock would be paid semiannually at the rate of 14 percent per year. The dividends would be payable at the option of Holdings in additional shares of this preferred stock. A week later, the Beatrice board authorized its financial and legal advisors to explore all possible options, including attempts to improve the terms of KKR's proposed modification and responding to inquiries of other bidders.

Determined to negotiate the best agreement possible for the benefit of shareholders and employees, the board and its representatives held a series of discussions with KKR as well as representatives of plaintiffs in various lawsuits filed against Beatrice, KKR, and others involved with the merger agreement. As a result, KKR agreed to eliminate the asset option, reduce the cancellation fee from $1 to 15 cents per share of common stock on a fully diluted basis, allow Beatrice to solicit competing bids for a four-week period, and to terminate the agreement if Beatrice received a better bid.

KKR also approved payment of the regular quarterly dividends for the fourth quarter. This was paid on April 1, 1986, and was the two-hundredth consecutive quarterly dividend paid on the common stock—and the last. In addition, KKR further improved its offer by increasing the dividend rate on the preference stock from 14 to 15.25 percent, making dividends payable quarterly, and giving the holders of the Holdings preference stock certain limited voting rights in the event of certain dividend arrearages or mandatory redemption defaults. KKR also promised to help make a market for this stock.

The board met to consider all of these modifications on February 2, 1986. It also studied other alternatives again, among them restructuring action involving the sales of certain businesses, retention of others, and liquidation of still others. One was the sale of the soft drink, bottled water, and personal products operations. Another was the sale of the soft drink, bottled water, and Tropicana businesses. A third was the sale of the soft drink, water, personal products, and consumer durables business. A fourth was the sale of all United States food businesses. In each case, the company would re-purchase about half of its common shares. The range of estimated per share amounts to be obtained from the restructurings was from $33.68 to $48.40.

Ultimately, the board concluded that KKR's modified proposal was in the best interest of Beatrice and its shareholders. It approved the offer, and the agreements were executed. Karnes initially had voted against the merger, but with the modifications in the pension plans that provided additional benefits for employees and a higher return on preferred stock for shareholders, he finally concurred.

In one last gasp, the beleagured board asked Salomon and Lazard to solicit other acquisition proposals. They contacted or recontacted twenty parties, but none expressed interest in buying all of Beatrice. Accordingly, a lengthy proxy statement was sent to all shareholders of Beatrice on March 11, 1986, detailing the negotiations, the directors' rationale for the approval of the buyout, and explaining the terms. A special meeting of shareholders was held in New York's Westin Hotel on Friday, April 11, where the acquisition by KKR was approved by 80 percent of the shares outstanding. It was completed April 17, 1986.

Predictably there was considerable maneuvering among arbitragers on Wall Street while KKR's negotiations with Beatrice were in progress late in 1985 and in early January of 1986. Among those involved were Michael Milken, the head of Drexel Burnham Lambert's junk bond operations; Ivan F. Boesky regarded as Wall Street's largest arbitrager; Martin A. Siegel, Kidder Peabody & Company's merger expert; and Robert M. Freeman, former head of risk arbitrage for Goldman, Sachs & Co. Boesky settled what was the largest insider trading case up to that time with the government. Milken was taken to court. Siegel pleaded guilty to two felony counts in the insider trading scandal, and Freeman pleaded guilty to one criminal count of mail fraud.

Even though Beatrice acquired Esmark, and even though Beatrice incurred a large amount of debt as a result of the merger, if Dutt had kept the Esmark management people and had retained several of the key Beatrice management people who left just before and after the Esmark merger, Beatrice was financially strong enough to assimilate Esmark and continue to grow. The problems caused by the Esmark merger were (1) the lack of competent top management people; (2) the high cost of servicing the large debt; (3) the expensive way the company was structured following the merger, such as the costly U.S. Foods general office and marketing staff; and (4) the elaborate advertising program that featured "Beatrice" rather than the brand names. Further, after Dutt left and Granger and Karnes were called back, it was clear to them what was needed, such as elimination of expensive and unproductive activities in advertising, marketing, the duplication of personnel in the U.S. Foods office and the General Office, the elimination of consultants, and the divestiture of several Esmark and Beatrice units that no longer fit the overall company. The funds from the sale of these units would have substantially reduced the debt.

Even in the relatively short time of seventy-seven days, Granger and Karnes were well on the way to implementing such a program. However, the entrance of KKR and Kelly into the picture prevented further progress along these lines. Dutt left on August 3, and KKR made its first offer on

October 19. By November 15, the board, after eight meetings, had accepted the KKR offer. So the total time to accomplish what could have been done was only 108 days.

The board had to make a choice, accept the good offer to protect the stockholders or reject it, and gamble on the future. The board made the right choice to protect the share holders under the circumstances and short time factor. The leveraged buyout for $6.2 billion was the largest in U.S. corporate history outside of the oil industry up to that time; it also was the largest KKR had arranged. The new owners held a private company with sales of $12.6 billion.

In an article in the *Journal for Corporate Growth* (fall 1987), Kelly stated, "On April 17, 1986, the acquisition of Beatrice by BCI Holdings was concluded. To complete the transaction, the funding was provided as follows: $4.1 billion in bank debt, $2.5 billion in debt securities, $1.2 billion in seller's paper (preferred stock), $497 million in equity from KKR and management. Additionally, some $1.4 million in previous debts was retained. This combination of $9 billion in debt with over $497 million in common equity, was certainly a challenge for management. . . . "

Kelly and his staff and KKR systematically went about to reduce that burden rapidly by selling off assets of BCI Holdings to meet bank requirements to reduce borrowings used to finance the buyout. Avis was purchased by Wesray Capital Corp. for $255 million in April 1986. Wesray, headed by former Secretary of the Treasury William E. Simon, also assumed $1 billion in Avis debts. Subsequently, the eleven thousand employees of Avis bought the company from Wesray.

In June 1986, the Coca-Cola and related soft drink operations were sold to Coca-Cola for $1 billion. A year later, Perrier bought the bottled water units for $400 million. Dutt's strategy of switching from Royal Crown to "Coke" proved to be a wise one in retrospect. However, the beneficiaries were the owners of BCI Holdings.

An investment group led by Smilow purchased 80 percent of International Playtex for $1.25 billion in August 1986, and the Americold Cold Storage operations were purchased for $480 million in a leveraged buyout by Kelso and Company, which included a management group. The management at Webcraft Technologies arranged a leveraged buyout to obtain the company, which specialized among other things in printing lotto tickets, for $225 million.

Then, the "cash cow" upon which Beatrice had begun the building of its empire was milked for the last time. In December 1986, the sale of the Dairy Division was completed for $315 million in cash, approximately 15 times earnings, to one of Meadow Gold's long-time competitors, Borden, Inc. This marked the departure of many valued veterans of

Beatrice, including Jay Johnson, James Hill, Harold Kraus, Richard Walrack, Edward Epstein, Ralph Hallquist, Gary Criner, Eric "Wally" Volkman, Jean Dorsch, and Charles Maraffino. The changes made in the overfunded Beatrice pension plan helped employees who had worked for many years.

In June of 1987, Kelly and a number of associates formed E–II Holdings, Inc. as an umbrella company to manage all of the remaining segments of Beatrice except U.S. Food. The prospectus stated that E–II estimated that it would obtain $937 million in net proceeds from all of these offerings after paying BCI Holdings $800 million to retire debt to the partnerships. In December, BCI Holdings retired $525 million of the 15.25 percent junior subordinated debentures.

Kelly was named chairman and chief executive officer of E–II, but also continued as chairman of BCI Holdings. Other key executives of E–II were Briggs, Pigott, Reidy, and James M. Snodgrass, who was named president of E–II Consumer Products Company, Inc. In its prospectus dated July 2, 1987, E–II explained its management philosophy: "Management believes that a substantially decentralized approach to managing operating companies is the best way to maximize a holding company's returns from such companies. Under the company's decentralized system, management of each individual operating company is responsible for attaining financial and other goals established jointly with and then monitored by the holding company and segment managements."

E–II's portfolio consisted of fifteen companies, nine in consumer products and six in food specialties. The consumer products segment included Samsonite luggage, Culligan, Home Fashions, Waterloo, AristOkraft, Day-Timers, Samsonite Furniture, Twentieth Century, and Stiffel. The food specialties segment was made up of Martha White, Beatreme Food Ingredients, Aunt Nellie's, Lowrey's, Pet Specialties, and Frozen Specialties. Total sales for the two segments for the fiscal year ended February 28, 1987 were $1.472 billion, and operating earnings were $125 million.

Another dramatic sequel to the buyout of Beatrice was a battle between E–II and the tobacco and liquor giant American Brands, Inc. The struggle began in December 1987, when E–II disclosed that it held a 4.6 percent stake in American Brands and subsequently indicated it might try to acquire the company in a hostile transaction valued by some analysts at $6 billion.

American Brands countered with the first successful use of the "Pac Man defense"—in which, as in the video game, the competitors try to eat other competitors before they are eaten themselves. It was first used in the battle between Martin Marietta Corp. and Bendix Corp. in 1982. American Brands offered a hostile bid of $875 million for E–II. Ultimately, the two companies agreed to a friendly merger, and American Brands bought E–II on January 31, 1988 for $1.14 billion, equal to $17 per share.

Then American Brands sold E–II to the closely held Riklis Family Corp., a New York City company headed by investor Meshulam Riklis, on June 20, 1988. Riklis paid American Brands about $950 million in cash and $250 million in preferred stock for most of E–II's operations. Included were Culligan, Samsonite, Samsonite Furniture, Home Fashions, Beatreme Food Ingredients, Frozen Specialties, Martha White Foods, and Pet Specialties.

As part of the deal, American Brands paid $645 million to buy back AristOkraft, Waterloo Industries, and Twentieth Century. It also bought back Day-Timers and Vogel Peterson, previously acquired by E–II from American's Acco World Corp. subsidiary, and Stiffel and Aunt Nellie's. Two former E–II executives, Snodgrass and Steven E. Lindblad, acquired Stiffel in September of 1988 from American Brands in a leveraged buyout from a subsidiary of American Brands.

The dismantling continued with the sale of the international food operations to TLC (The Lewis Company) in conjunction with Drexel Burnham Lambert for $985 million on December 1, 1987. It was the largest offshore buyout through 1989. Beatrice International Foods earned $147 million on sales of $2.5 billion in the fiscal year. The purchase made TLC the largest black-owned business in the United States. TLC promptly sold off the Australian operations to Cadbury Schweppes Australia for about $100 million and the Canadian operations to Onex Corp., Toronto, for $240 million. Campofrio was bought by its management in Spain.

That left U.S. Food, now the Beatrice Co., still in the BCI Holdings fold under the direction of Frederick Rentschler. Its sales for fiscal 1987, ended February 28, were $4.8 billion, and pre-tax profits were $448 million. Its operations included Hunt-Wesson, Tropicana, Swift-Eckrich, LaChoy, Fisher Nuts, Orville Redenbacher popcorn, and Beatrice cheese. It went on the block in September of 1987. BCI retained First Boston Corp. to review offers from prospective bidders. The asking price was about $6 billion, which included assumption of $2.2 billion in debt.

The value of the fractional remainder of Beatrice had been reduced further by the purchase of Tropicana by Montreal-based Seagram Co. for $1.2 billion through its American subsidiary, Joseph E. Seagrams & Sons, Inc., in April of 1988. Tropicana's annual sales had reached $750 million by then.

This continued shaking of the Beatrice "money tree," which many thought to be one of the most lucrative leveraged buyouts in history, apparently ran into problems late in the summer of 1988. The so-called

U.S. Foods Division including Hunt-Wesson, Swift-Eckrich meats, and Beatrice cheese products, had been put up for sale at a high price. But the stock market crash of October 19, 1987 plus the high price asked for this remaining division resulted in no buyers for the whole division. Reportedly, more than a hundred prospective buyers turned away from the remaining Beatrice assets, and in July 1988, Beatrice officials announced that the company was no longer for sale.

According to the *Wall Street Journal* article of August 31, 1988, by Robert Johnson and Jeff Bailey.

> The value of Beatrice assets sold so far, about $8 billion, still does not equal the amount the investors paid for the company. Donald P. Kelly, Beatrice's chairman, has auctioned off 10 major businesses, including the Coca-Cola bottlers and Tropicana juice lines, in an effort to break even.
>
> Most prospective buyers wanted only part of the company. But Beatrice officials calculate that the tax liabilities on further piece-meal sales would roughly double, possibly to more than $800 million over the amount that would be paid if assets could be sold together. Beatrice said last week that Mr. Kelly will resign as chairman, October 1. He had long wanted to acquire part of the company as an acquisition vehicle to build a new conglomerate, but Beatrice tax problems may doom such a transaction. As previously reported, Mr. Kelly's auction has apparently fizzled because of the $1.9 billion of intangible assets on the company's books. That so-called goodwill has accumulated from premium prices paid for certain Beatrice assets that had been acquired three times by various owners in under 10 years. U.S. tax laws make depreciation of such assets (goodwill) difficult for domestic companies.

Goodwill must be written off over a period of years as a non-cash and non-deductible tax item. This would amount to a substantial annual penalty for any domestic buyer. So KKR still had part of Beatrice and found it difficult to move.

On October 1, 1988 Rentschler became chairman and chief executive officer of Beatrice Company. It was announced at that time that the Beatrice Company was not for sale and would continue to be operated into the future and might even acquire some small companies. However, Beatrice did divest the Fisher Nut Co. in 1989. This divestiture was required by the government because R. J. Reynolds-Nabisco, also controlled by KKR, owned Planter's Nut Company. Planter's Nut is the largest in volume and Fisher Nut is second in size in the industry.

In September 1989, a new development occurred. Beatrice was considering a large borrowing to pay a dividend to the investors of the original leveraged buyout of Beatrice in April 1986. According to an article by Robert Johnson in the *Wall Street Journal* of September 13, 1989:

Beatrice Co. which went private in an $8.2 billion leverage buyout, one of the largest ever, may borrow again to help pay investors a dividend of as much as $983 million in preferred stock and debt securities.

Such a transaction, which had been used by other investors to wring more profit out of smaller leveraged buyout targets, would be the largest of its sort, Wall Street observers estimated. A big dividend at Beatrice could heat up the leveraged buyout market by attracting more investors. Typically, it takes investors five years to recoup their stake in a leveraged buyout, in which they finance an acquisition largely with debt and repay it mainly by selling assets. In April 1986 Kohlberg Kravis Roberts and Co., a New York investment concern that led the investor group, took Beatrice private. A dividend of $983 million would enable Beatrice investors to more than double their original investment. In return, the investors' original stake of about $417 million has fallen far short of expectations.

For Beatrice, borrowing about $328 million—the rest of the payout would be achieved by issuing preferred stock—would increase its current debt level to about $1.8 billion. When Kohlberg Kravis acquired Beatrice, it took on debts totalling $7.8 billion.

The article also reported, "Beatrice officials said the proposed payout to investors may not occur until 1990, if at all. The size of the issue was scaled back to $251 million in a two-part issue due November 1, 1997 on November 1, 1989."

Thus, as of 1990, the dismantling of the company was continuing, and the final outcome still uncertain. The risks that KKR and its investors took will not pay off in the profits warranted by the huge debt assumed until the remainder of the Beatrice assets are sold. Many analysts on Wall Street believed at the time that KKR and its partners paid too much for Beatrice and that they would have a difficult time servicing the debt. Surely, if interest rates had gone up or if the stock market had gone down earlier, as it did in late 1987, or if the supply of money from banks and investment firms had dried up so they could not have sold the pieces of Beatrice for premium prices, KKR and its BCI Holding investors would have had serious financial problems.

But the interest rates slid down steeply and resulted in large annual savings of interest. The market moved up strongly at the right time, and the supply of money through junk bonds and other forms of leveraged financing remained readily available to many of the buyers as well as to KKR and BCI Holdings. BCI benefited from the elimination of $170 million of annual dividends on Beatrice stock. It took the steps that Granger and Karnes started in 1985 to prune the operations, advertising, and office staffs and thus accomplish an annual savings of about $100 million.

The return to Beatrice and the period that followed were difficult for

Karnes. It was a disappointment to see how many loyal people had left — officers, plant managers, salespeople, supervisors, office managers, and secretaries. The "family spirit" and the happy relationships had vanished; the pride and high morale of being with a winner had disappeared. Many of the fine, growing, profitable companies were gone, as were the excellent people who ran them. The closeness between the chief executive officer and other management people, the open door policy, and the willingness to listen to others were also gone. The General Office was large, sprawling, and impersonal. People on the 26th floor did not have much contact with those on the 25th and hardly knew those on the 24th and 23rd floors. High expenses and duplication were everywhere.

However, Granger and Karnes believed that all of this could be changed. Beatrice was still a strong company with good products and many good people, but it needed leadership and new direction. It also needed to be freed of the burden of high debt and unnecessary and unproductive expenses. They set about to do this and much was accomplished in a short time, but then KKR and Kelly appeared. It was clear that choices had to be made and unfortunately had to be made quickly.

What was best for the stockholders? The owners of the company? Naturally, it would be best for the stockholders if the company remained independent and let the value of the common stock increase to its true value. This could be done with the changes that were being made and could be made given the time. The stock value had increased by 15 to 20 percent within the first few days after August 3, 1985 when Granger and Karnes returned.

KKR's first offer of $40 per share was clearly much too low, and the board dismissed it in a short meeting. However, when KKR made three more offers and reached $50 per share, $43 in cash and $7 in a 14.5 percent preferred stock, the situation was different, particularly since no one else was interested after the extensive search made by two investment banking firms. It was clear that a decision would have to be made to protect the stockholders.

What was best for the employees? Obviously, an independent continuing company with an overfunded pension plan and adequate medical benefits plus incentive compensation for management people was the best. But the KKR offer of $50 a share was the highest price for Beatrice stock in its long history. It really was a cash offer of $50 because it was obvious that the preferred stock with a dividend of 15.25 percent had a ready cash market, and KKR had agreed to provide that market.

Karnes voted against the merger on the first two votes, wanting to get better protection for the employees through the overfunded pension plan. Several changes that helped all employees were made in the pension plan, for example, vesting the pension after seven years instead of ten years of service and a full pension for employees when they reached age sixty after required years of service. The last provision was particularly helpful to many loyal Beatrice employees with longer service.

After the employees were better protected by the overfunded pension plan, a provision placed in the merger agreement that provided that BCI Holdings maintain all employee pension and benefit plans in as good a condition as they were at that time, and the dividend was increased to 15.25 percent on the preferred stock, Karnes voted for the merger to protect the stockholders. It was a fair offer, in fact, the only offer—none other existed after an extensive search. It was, however, a truly sad day for all Beatrice people who had loyally worked so hard to build the fine company. It was also a sad day for Karnes and other officers who had spent fifty years working to help build Beatrice into the premier food company in America.

However, Karnes points out that the Beatrice shareholders were major beneficiaries of the KKR buyout. In accepting the offer of $50 per share, the Beatrice board of directors rightly recognized that its first obligation was to Beatrice shareholders. The offer was an all-time high for Beatrice common stock, equal to 19 times earnings, two and one-half times book value, and 20 times the tangible book value. In the period from August 3, 1985, when Dutt left, to April 17, 1986, when the KKR deal was completed, the market value of Beatrice common stock moved up 20 points, or 67 percent from $30 per share, an increase of more than $2 billion on 102 million common shares outstanding.

"No shareholder who had held Beatrice stock until April 1986 was hurt because the stock had never sold for as high as $50," Karnes noted. "Actually, stockholders who had held stock for many years, or even a few years, made a tremendous profit from the sales of their stock and were able to pay the capital gains tax for 1986 at the low rate of 20 percent."

Hindsight raises several significant questions. If the board had not accepted the KKR offer, it would have had to restructure the company drastically to prevent the price of common stock from drifting back to the lower $40 range or even into the $30 range. The company then would have become a target for unfriendly raiders at a much lower price.

At least 40 percent of the shares, about forty million, would have to have been called at a cash price of about $50. This would have required additional borrowing of at least $2 billion. Since the interest rate at that time was at least 11 percent or higher, this would have saddled the company with an additional interest charge of $220 million a year or more. It was also doubtful if the company could have raised this much debt.

"These additional borrowings plus the long-term debt of more than $1.8 billion already on the books plus high receivables and inventories would have required the sale of several of the company's most profitable consumer product units and food products," Karnes said. "In turn, this would have substantially lowered the cash flow. Beatrice would not have been the same company as we knew it in the early '80s. It would not have been as diversified; it would not have had the growth potential; it would not have been as profitable, and its debt ratio would probably still have been extremely high."

KKR and its investors gambled with their own money and with bank borrowings and borrowings from junk bond buyers who were willing to assume the risk to obtain a high rate of return. If the Beatrice board had restructured the company, it would have been gambling with the shareholders' money. "That would have been fiscally irresponsible," Karnes asserted. The board could not know in the spring of 1986 that interest rates would continue to decline, that the bull market would continue for another eighteen months, or that money would have been available to buy back a substantial amount of stock to restructure the company.

If the board had taken the risky step of restructuring the company, what would have happened to the stock of the company, which would have been burdened by heavy debt, high interest obligations, and lower cash flow after Black Tuesday, October 19, 1987? Undoubtedly, the market price of Beatrice common stock would have slipped substantially after the October 19, 1987 crash. A comparison with the performances of the common stocks of the six leading food companies listed in Table 4 offers one measurement of the probable decline.

Table 4.
NYSE Food Company Market Prices

	Oct. 9, 1987	Oct. 23, 1987	Dec. 31, 1987	June 3, 1988
Borden	55⅞	43½	49½	51⅛
General Mills	53⅝	46	49⅝	48⅛
Kraft	55	49	47⅛	53⅞
Pillsbury	43¾	34½	35⅛	39
Quaker Oats	50¼	43⅝	41⅝	46
Sara Lee	43	38⅝	35¼	38
Average	50½	42½	43	46⅛

In the period from Friday, October 9 through Friday, October 23, 1987, the average decline for the six companies was 15 percent. Reducing the price of Beatrice common by 15 percent from $50 would have lowered it to $43.50 per share. Assuming a recovery in the price of common stock at the average for the same six companies by June of 1988, Beatrice could still be down more than 8.6 percent, to between $45 and $46 per share. At best, the loss to shareholders in the period from October 9, 1987 to June 3, 1988 would have been almost $250 million, based on sixty-two million common shares outstanding after the assumed restructuring. Further, the amount of the dividend the company would have been paying on its common stock is an unknown; but the capital gains tax rate would now be 28 percent, not 20 percent. "Thus, it seems quite conclusive that the Beatrice board made the right decision for the Beatrice shareholders, the owners of the company, to whom it was primarily responsible in April of 1986," Karnes concluded. "In other words, the board fortunately didn't leave the money on the table."

The leveraged buyout of other major food companies such as Kraft by Philip Morris, RJR–Nabisco by KKR and Associates, and Pillsbury by Grand Metropolitan could not have been predicted in April 1986. All had drastic effects on their market prices. The 190-point drop in the Dow-Jones average on Friday, October 13, 1989 had little effect on the prices of food companies, usually the most stable on the stock exchange.

During the 1980s, nine major food processing companies either ceased to exist or ceased to be independent entities: Carnation, now owned by Nestlé; Standard Brands, now a part of R. J. Reynolds; Nabisco, now a part of R. J. Reynolds; Pillsbury, owned by Grand Metropolitan; General Foods, owned by Philip Morris; Kraft, owned by Philip Morris; Norton Simon, merged with Esmark; Esmark, merged with Beatrice; Beatrice, bought and dismembered by KKR; and RJR–Nabisco also bought by KKR in a leveraged buyout for $25 billion.

Many fine single-food product processors such as Oscar Mayer and Frito Lay also ceased to operate independently. Most beer brewing in the United States is done by five major companies, with three of them holding close to 80 percent of the volume. Many retail food chains disappeared, both nationally and regionally. Thus, the food business in America changed dramatically in just a few years. The result was higher consumer prices, with many food imports becoming competitive in the United States. Other industries have also been affected in the same way.

It is, Karnes's opinion that leveraged buyouts, takeovers, and defensive reorganizations of corporations caused by attempted leveraged buyouts have been and continue to be detrimental to the American economy. American business has thrived, grown, and improved because of competition; leveraged buyouts have tended to eliminate competition in some industries such as the food business. Most completed leveraged buyouts have resulted in getting the stockholders more money for their stock than the current market value. However, if the company had been left alone, in most cases that higher price could be achieved in time. Maybe companies would require a change in management—the responsibility of the board. However, they would be without all of the negatives that result from an unfriendly leveraged buyout or takeover. No additional wealth is created in a typical LBO, but the following events always happen: (1) Many long-time, loyal, capable employees lose their jobs; (2) the community loses jobs and the revenue and taxes flowing from those jobs (some communities have never recovered from leveraged buyouts); (3) many individuals are forced to apply for unemployment insurance or eventually go on the welfare roles, causing additional burden to the community; and (4) heavy debt is created for the remaining company or the acquiring company to fund. If and when a recession occurs, many companies will not be able to service the debt and either will cease to exist or will be forced to cut back further and curtail their operations. The surviving companies that successfully fend off the leveraged buyout in the end become loaded with debt and are forced to sell some of their most profitable units. This debt expense and loss of profits cripples the companies' ability to grow in sales and earnings.

When two companies with similar products are joined as a result of a leveraged buyout, competition tends to be lessened, and the consumer in the long run is the victim of higher prices and possibly poorer products. The surviving company has less incentive to improve or add new products through research, which also is detrimental to the overall economy.

The junk bonds created to finance leveraged buyouts have seriously devalued the legitimate corporate bond market and created false and temporary values in the stock market. In an article headlined "Takeover Debt Is a Costly Intruder," in the Chicago *Tribune*, on November 6, 1988, Pat Widder wrote, "Bond holders can get hurt in a buyout, takeover or defensive recapitalization, because new debt usually is required to finance a transaction. That makes the old, safe investment grade bonds a lot riskier than when they were issued, because the massive new borrowing puts added strain on the companies' financial structure and earning power. And the new often non-investment grade or 'junk' debt issued to finance the deal carries higher interest rates making the old bonds worth a lot less."

In another *Tribune* article of November 6, 1988, William Neikirk reported that

> Martin Lipton, the anti-takeover lawyer who tried unsuccessfully to fend Philip Morris off of Kraft, wrote to his clients only last week:
> Our nation is blindly rushing to the precipice as with tulip bulbs, South Sea Bubbles, pyramid investment trusts, Florida land, REITS, LDC loans, Texas banks and all other financial market frenzies of the past; the denouement will be a crash. We and our children will pay a gigantic price for

allowing abrasive takeover tactics and bootstrap, junk bond takeovers. Lipton said research, new product development and capital investment by companies have become an invitation to a junk bond bustup party. While the rest of the industrialized world is investing for the future, we are squandering our assets in a speculative binge of junk bonds, financial futures, program trading, put and call options and other games of today's financial market casinos.

The result is that no wealth is created; no new jobs are created but old ones are destroyed; and great debt is created that becomes a serious future burden to the company. If there is an economic decline, these high-risk securities probably drop in value with a serious effect on banks, insurance companies, savings and loans, pension plans, and other investors who buy them.

In late summer of 1989 some leveraged buyouts financed by large amounts of junk bond debt were unable to make their interest payments, let alone principal payments, and were forced to start selling some of the companies bought with high-risk debt. For example, Canada's Campeau Corporation was forced to file for reorganization on January 16, 1990, under the protection of the federal bankruptcy law.

Articles in the media indicated that the weakness and resulting turbulence in the junk bond market spurred Securities and Exchange Commission inquiries into high-risk debt securities. On October 9, 1989, the Chicago *Tribune* reported:

> The SEC is looking at the amount of secondary trading by dealer firms; how various indexes by brokerage firms are calculated; the identity of all the defaulting issuers and the characteristics of issuers and purchasers and the breakdown of issues by type of security. Last week's requests differ from those in an investigation of junk bond money managers begun earlier this year, people familiar with this case said. In that investigation, commission members surveyed the mutual fund and pension fund managers who buy junk bonds to determine whether they use adequate procedures to price the thinly traded issues in their portfolios.
>
> The SEC however may continue to look at the pricing strategies in the two markets, one of the sources said. Pricing of the bonds is important in calculating a mutual funds net asset value, which is the total value of a funds holder.

By the fall of 1989, the decline in the value of junk bonds forced takeovers and mergers to be financed with more equity, bank debt, and fewer junk bonds. Some deals were postponed because the junk bonds were not saleable. Future deals would require more equity and less debt, and others would be made with exchange of stock. Leveraged buyouts using large amounts of debt became difficult to finance; unfortunately, many made with high percentage of debt may not survive a recession.

CHAPTER TWENTY

The Beatrice Way
Will Work Today

Through the gentle, hands-off application of only a few simple management philosophies and policies over a span of ninety years, Beatrice was carefully constructed into one of the world's finest and best-managed food companies, the leader in a score of specialized product lines. In the three decades from 1952 to 1982, it compiled an unparalleled record of 120 consecutive quarters in which sales and earnings surpassed those of the comparable quarter of the previous year. Since its founding in 1894, it survived a dozen depressions and recessions to emerge even stronger and sounder financially and to become the most profitable food company in the United States.

Beatrice's returns on investment and shareholders' equity were superior in comparison with those of competitors; it therefore was able to reward its shareholders year after year with increasing dividends and larger capital gains. Then, in the relatively brief period of five years from 1982–87, this seemingly indestructible model for the business world was ripped apart, and the pieces were plundered by opportunistic companies and groups managing these segments.

For nearly fifty years, half of them as its senior officer, William G. Karnes was a guiding force in the building of Beatrice. Even after he left the board of directors in 1980, he was frequently consulted by its management people and directors. Then, when the ill-fated plans to restructure the entire company and centralize the management of all operations led to James Dutt's departure, Karnes responded to a summons from the directors to help William W. Granger, Jr., give new leadership to the company. As a result of being there, he unwillingly assisted in negotiating the sale to KKR & Co. Karnes's conclusions about what happened in the late seventies and eighties to change Beatrice, and what led to its ultimate disappearance in a leveraged buyout in 1986, are insightful.

Beatrice gradually ceased to be a people-oriented company. Many of the experienced persons who had been instrumental in helping to build Beatrice were terminated, resigned, or accepted early retirement. Instead of promoting trained successors from within the management network, outsiders were installed in key positions. Although many of them were competent in their fields, they did not know and did not have the opportunities to learn the "Beatrice Way." The right people are important; high morale was essential. Giving people the freedom to operate their plants was a must at Beatrice.

"This was surely true of a company as complex and unique as Beatrice," Karnes said. "Its operations were scattered around the world at more than four hundred locations and managed on a highly decentralized basis. Therefore, people were much more important than in a one-product or even a multi-product company. The same thing is true in regard to hiring people from outside of the company," he said. "In the years from 1940 to 1980, the only people Beatrice brought in from the outside were skilled people capable of running the specialized businesses that became a part of the company along with a few persons with specialized financial, legal or scientific knowledge.

"Beatrice did not put any persons in positions to manage Beatrice people until they had demonstrated that they were fully knowledgeable about the company's management policies, particularly decentralized management. In later years, particularly in the eighties, many Beatrice units ran into problems because of retirements, dismissals or resignations. Outsiders were put in charge who did not know, and who did not follow the successful policies of the past.

"High morale is all important in a company structured like Beatrice," Karnes said. "High morale had been one of the main foundation stones on which Beatrice had been built over the years. The employees knew that they were with a winner. By 1985, employee morale was lost completely."

Decentralized management, another keystone of the success of the company, gradually was phased out, further contributing to the decline of morale at every echelon. Senior management began to speak harshly and despotically instead of softly and persuasively, as in the past. As B. Robert Kill wrote to Karnes, "After 23 years of working in a highly decentralized mode, I found the new, highly centralized style to be not right for me. I liked your way better!"

J. W. Parkman, general manager of Meadow Gold Supreme Ice Cream in Dothan, Alabama, echoed these feelings in July of 1982. He wrote Karnes, "I would certainly be amiss not to thank you for the consideration you have given all of us who were fortunate enough to join Beatrice. From the very beginning, you have leaned over backwards to make things fair; and certainly I deeply appreciate the opportunities you have given me since we sold the company. In addition, I want to thank you most of all for being so kind to my father for as long as he lived after he retired. Beatrice Foods was a subject he never grew tired of bragging about."

The size of the acquisitions increased substantially, contravening the policy of never making an acquisition that could dilute earnings per share. Several were proved justifiable, specifically the Coca-Cola franchises in California and the Midwest, Culligan, and the Termicold warehouses. Others such as Harman International and Tropicana had the effect of diluting earnings. Another negative result was that to reduce its debt the company sold off proven profit-makers such as Dannon, the Chemical Division, Taylor Freezer, the institutional equipment companies, and others.

The conservative financial policies that had been a bulwark of Beatrice's strength were abandoned. The eventual Beatrice-breaker, of course, was the purchase of Esmark in 1984 for $2.7 billion. One effect was that the debt-to-equity ratio, which had been controlled at a cautious average of 25 percent over the years, soared to 199 percent at the end of fiscal year 1985. The dividend payout ratio had been kept at 33 to 40 percent over many years. But by 1985, the annualized dividend rate of $1.80 per common share was equal to 73 percent of the primary net earnings per common share.

The company began to rely more and more on the advice of costly outside consultants who were not familiar with the Beatrice way of management. The consultants' visits to plants were disruptive.

After the acquisition of Esmark, the sales and marketing functions, including advertising for most of the food profit centers, were taken out of the capable hands of plant managers and brokers and assigned to a centralized sales staff.

Other factors included a tremendous expansion of the general office, the huge increase in advertising expenditures to $800 million per year, and added expenditures for special events. All of this, the creation of large debt, and an 85 percent dividend to earnings per share payout added to the problem. These switches in policy and trends occurred frequently and caused the financial analysts to lose confidence in management and give the company bad reports. The slowness of the board of directors in calling a halt to these changes added to the confusion.

Karnes is firmly convinced that the "old" Beatrice way would still succeed. "If the senior management of Beatrice had not strayed from the philosophies and policies that enabled Beatrice to grow year after year, Beatrice would be alive and well and an independent entity today," he declares. "Those philosophies and policies would have enabled it to become an even more viable force in the market places of the world in the late eighties and nineties. Sure, some modifications and refinements would have to be made—we did this over the years—but not abandonment! Regardless of the opinions of consultants, investment bankers and security analysts, a management that understood, believed, followed and nurtured the policies that built the company could use them to lead Beatrice to continuing growth in the future. It has been a source of deep disappointment to me to realize how few officers and directors really understood why and how Beatrice grew, even though we continually tried to teach these concepts to the younger officers and new directors. This lack of understanding or disbelief in the policies of the past by the new senior officers was the major factor that led to mismanagement and the resultant buyout and dismantling of the company. It's a sad and typical case of 'If it works, don't fix it.' "

Index